WRONGED

WRONGED

THE WEAPONIZATION OF VICTIMHOOD

LILIE CHOULIARAKI

Columbia University Press *New York*

Columbia University Press
Publishers Since 1893
New York   Chichester, West Sussex
cup.columbia.edu

Copyright © 2024 Columbia University Press
All rights reserved

Library of Congress Cataloging-in-Publication Data
Names: Chouliaraki, Lilie, author.
Title: Wronged : victimhood in public discourse / Lilie Chouliaraki.
Description: New York : Columbia University Press, [2024] |
Includes bibliographical references and index.
Identifiers: LCCN 2023049534 (print) | LCCN 2023049535 (ebook) |
ISBN 9780231193283 (hardback) | ISBN 9780231193290 (trade paperback) |
ISBN 9780231550239 (ebook)
Subjects: LCSH: Victims—Social aspects—United States. |
Mass media—Social aspects—United States. | Mass media—
Political aspects—United States. | Social problems in mass media. |
MeToo movement—United States.
Classification: LCC HV6250.3.U5 C46 2024 (print) |
LCC HV6250.3.U5 (ebook) | DDC 362.880973—dc23/eng/20231213
LC record available at https://lccn.loc.gov/2023049534
LC ebook record available at https://lccn.loc.gov/2023049535

Printed and bound by CPI Group (UK) Ltd, Croydon, CR0 4YY

Cover design: Julia Kushnirsky

CONTENTS

Preface and Acknowledgments vii

1 Why Victimhood? 1
2 Who Used to Be a Victim? 41
3 Who Is a Victim Today? 75
4 How Can Victimhood Be Reclaimed? 101

Notes 141
Bibliography 201
Index 233

PREFACE AND ACKNOWLEDGMENTS

On February 20, 2020, a normal working day, I finished my class, advised students during my office hours, locked my office at the London School of Economics (LSE), and, after a late lunch with a colleague discussing coauthored work, went home. A few days later, the LSE and many other workplaces in London and the United Kingdom went into pandemic mode and shifted to online teaching. I have not been in my office since then, let alone entered a classroom to teach in person. In January 2024, I am still shielding. I was one of those who, because of a solid-organ transplant, had to shield during the 2020–2021 lockdowns, but a series of further health blows—including a lymphoma diagnosis, a severe episode of acute hemolysis with successive treatments and hospitalizations, and a profoundly dysfunctional immune system—have forced me to live a largely isolated existence to this day. My hope to break free in the coming year includes that we see a further weakening of COVID-19 and that a special COVID antibody serum is made available to the half-million people in the United Kingdom whose immune systems are too fragile for vaccines. Things have never been easy for me healthwise, but the physical and mental struggles of the past few years have been particularly challenging. Physical demise, existential dread, and medical trauma are only part of these struggles.

This is a lot for one person to go through, but ours have been times of extraordinary suffering for many more people than me. Around the world, 6.71 million people had officially been lost to COVID-19 up to December 2022, but the World Health Organization (WHO) has spoken of an estimated 14.9 million excess deaths from COVID-19 in 2020 and 2021 alone. At the same time, as of January 2022, about 1.1 million Americans were out of work at any given time because of long COVID, with the global long COVID figure, according to *Nature*, reaching officially at least 65 million—the majority between the ages of thirty-five and sixty. That millions may suffer does not of course mean that one person's pain should be diminished. It means, however, that a single person's pain is always part of and relative to a sea of suffering that occurs among us on a daily basis and should be viewed in this context. Is this a moralizing call to not indulge in self-pity? No. It is an invitation to reflect on the relational dynamics of vulnerability and privilege. I may have had it hard in the past few years, but I was able to resort to a national health system that is still free for all—part of my despair being the fact of witnessing this system disintegrate and collapse as it tried so hard with so little to care for so many. At the same time, as a white, middle-class, tenured professor living in London, I have also been able to go through all this in relative comfort and some life-saving lifestyle options, such as frequent family countryside escapes that are out of reach for millions of others.

If the relationship between vulnerability and privilege is at the heart of this book, then this is because it has been intensely at the forefront of my mind. Even though much of my past work engaged with similar questions, with *The Spectatorship of Suffering*

(2006) and *The Ironic Spectator* (2013), among other publications, being about Eurocentric media's representing the distant sufferers of the global South as a cause for action for the privileged citizens of the global North, both of these studies relied on suffering as a spectacle and on the privileged as a category of spectatorship shaped by Western narratives and images. Here, my focus shifts to the West as both the sufferer and the narrator of its own suffering. In a way that is different from before, this focus casts old relationships of vulnerability and privilege in new ways. Written in the course of three crucial years, 2019–2022, it throws into relief urgent challenges of inequality and power in the global North, in particular the alarming rise and continuing popularity of far-right populism and its culture wars as the far Right systematically weaponizes narratives of victimhood at the service of a politics of cruelty. It also highlights continuities and discontinuities between past and present systems of power as contemporary controversies over voice, rights, freedoms, and justice in movements such as Me Too and Black Lives Matter challenge historical hierarchies of race, gender, and class both in the West and between the West and the global South.

These are some of the issues that I grapple with in this book. Even though my own experience of suffering has been the personal lens through which I consider privilege and vulnerability together in one go, so to speak, my main concern here is to think through the language we use to talk about these concepts in public and to draw attention to a key distinction that often slips off the radar of public discourse. This is the distinction between pain as a *systemic condition*, or vulnerability, on the one hand, which defines our relative openness to violence in its various structural forms (embodied and social), whether poverty, racism, misogyny, homophobia, or physical disability and illness, and pain as a *linguistic claim*, or victimhood, on the other hand, an act of communication that may be spoken from different positions of openness to violence in a continuum between vulnerability and privilege—a continuum, that is, from radical openness to relative sheltering from most forms of violence. The two, condition and claim, obviously intersect but by no means coincide. And how they come together is one of the key political questions of our times. Pain can indeed be felt and claimed by everyone, but in societies historically unequal and thoroughly digitized, like ours in the West, those who are most vulnerable do not get to be heard. It is instead the pain of the powerful, largely the pain of white men, that ends up mattering the most, and the communication of victimhood becomes, in this sense, not about vulnerability but about privilege. I suggest that only by learning how to navigate the pitfalls of the public communication of victimhood, which means listening to the voices of people's pain while at the same time attending to the broader intersection of contexts within which these voices occur, will we be able to care for those who need it the most—but also to understand and change the structural circumstances of social suffering.

In building this argument, I draw on recent examples from the Anglo-American world, including major political struggles—like those, for instance, around the *Roe v. Wade* overturning or powerful movements such as Me Too and Black Lives Matter—as well as historical examples from the major wars of the twentieth century and the Civil Rights Movement. My analysis of these examples focuses on the dominant cultural texts that seek to shape how we see the world and how we are supposed to act in it, from newspaper headlines and interview soundbites to Twitter threads and from war monuments to historical narratives and court decisions. Trained in discourse analysis and social semiotics, I approach these various texts, linguistic and visual, as discourses—that is, as meanings produced in and through power struggles over who owns the languages of pain, who deserves to be protected as a victim, and who should be punished as perpetrator—that more often than not use victimhood to protect privilege, silence the structurally vulnerable, and legitimize the existing social order.

My theoretical companions in this journey have been many. As always, I take inspiration from Hannah Arendt's normative warning against the uses of pity in the public realm and from Luc Boltanski's unique analysis of how pity organizes political communication around the passions of Western public life—namely, empathy and denunciation but also a distanced reflexivity upon the suffering of distant others.[1] Whereas for Boltanski all three of these affective "tropes" of communication are constitutive of modernity at large, Eva Illouz's argument on emotional capitalism helpfully historicizes the political work that empathetic feeling performed in twentieth-century capitalism when she describes how this feeling gave rise to a dominant "culture of therapy," where personal identities of pain are put to the service of profit.[2] But Illouz's approach, I feel, treats this culture as an overall negative feature of public culture, whereas my own position remains more optimistic. Despite my criticism, which resonates not only with Illouz but also with Wendy Brown's critique of the "logics of pain" as a negative force that blocks positive visions of social change,[3] I nonetheless believe that the languages of pain still hold a radical potential, and my argument seeks to recuperate this potential in a politics of justice. In this respect, Judith Butler, Zeynep Gambetti, and Leticia Sabsay's generative collection of essays on vulnerability as a social force that can be reinscribed into new social struggles for solidarity and justice has been inspiring.[4] My study can be seen, from this perspective, as an analytical deep dive into the discursive potential of vulnerability—a potential that depends on who can best appropriate the languages of pain in the public realm—and, in this analysis, Alyson Cole's work on the far Right as a "cult of true victimhood" has been foundational.[5] Like her, I both acknowledge the value of pain as an important political force and warn against the pitfalls of victimhood as a vocabulary that has no a priori ideological allegiance and can thus easily be weaponized by the powerful.

Even if my own experience of pain informs every twist and turn of my theoretical argument, at no point does it enter the narrative of this book—in part because it is difficult to write analytically about my own circumstances and in part because of my belief that embodied suffering is always traversed by societal forces and needs to link up to structural explanation in order to turn into critical argument. But before I move on from the personal to the deep theoretical waters of victimhood, politics, and power, let me here express my appreciation not only to those who helped me get better and continue living but also to those who made it possible for me, in the midst of everything, to continue living a life of action, as Arendt would put it, full of the joys of thinking, reading, arguing, and writing. To Helle Lehrmann Madsen, I owe a debt of life in both these senses that no amount of gratitude can ever pay back. I am immensely thankful to her not only for donating her kidney to me a decade ago but also for our thirty-plus-year-long friendship and our continuing love and care for each other. I am in awe of her fierce strength and rare generosity and consider myself vastly fortunate to have her in my life. I thank my dedicated medical teams at Hammersmith Hospital in London for their attention and care and Professor Mandeep Mehra at the Brigham and Women's Hospital, whose medical wisdom and personal kindness have been priceless in dark moments. My LSE colleagues Myria Georgiou and Sonia Livingstone provided valuable feedback at different stages of the writing, as did Giota Alevizou, Sarah Banet-Weiser, Kate Nash, Zizi Papacharissi, Sine Plambech, and Robin Wagner-Pacifici. I thank them all for it. Together with Myria, Sonia, Kate, and Zizi, Maryam Abbas, Judith Barrett, Lee Edwards, Carey Jewitt, Mirca Madianou, Shani Orgad, and Yiannis Thavoris also sustained me throughout with their phone chats, Zoom calls, messages, gifts, flowers, and distanced walks. In their various ways, these colleagues and friends gave me strength and optimism when I needed them the most, and I hope they know how much their presence meant and still means to me. My classes in the PhD program of the Media and Communications Department at LSE have always been a unique source not only of intellectual stimulation but also of excitement and fun, reminding me that the best part of being an academic teacher is the opportunity to learn together with one's students. My past students, now colleagues and mind companions, Kathryn Higgins, Angelos Kissas, and Richard Stupart have been particularly inspirational interlocutors in the writing of this manuscript, and I thank them for their generosity. My own PhD supervisor, coauthor, and lifelong friend Norman Fairclough, professor emeritus at Lancaster University, has been a foundational influence on my thinking, and his voice is echoed throughout my work but perhaps most of all in this one. Special thanks also go to my department head, Bart Cammaerts, for his understanding and support; my trusted editor Judith Barret for her faultless professionalism; as well as Afroditi Koulaxi for her work on the bibliography. My editor at Columbia University Press, Philip Leventhal, has been phenomenal. His patience and understanding have allowed me to take the time that I needed to complete this book in peace amid personal turmoil, and his intellectual astuteness has made its argument infinitely better than it would have been without him—though, needless to say, all mistakes and omissions remain my own. Last but not least, my close family, Giorgos, Daphne, Marcel, and Elias, have been there for me every single day in the past three years, and there are no words for the appreciation and love I feel for them. In particular, to Elias, my partner, I dedicate this book with love, gratitude, and admiration; not a page of it would have been written without him by my side.

WRONGED

1

WHY VICTIMHOOD?

Each social group is speaking [the same] native language, but its uses are significantly different, and especially when strong feelings or important ideas are in question. No single group is "wrong" by any linguistic criterion, though a temporarily dominant group may try to enforce its own uses as "correct."
—Raymond Williams, *Keywords*

WRONGED!

On September 27, 2018, Christine Blasey Ford, professor at Palo Alto University, appeared in front of the U.S. Senate Judiciary Committee. She testified against Brett Kavanaugh, then nominee for the U.S. Supreme Court, for sexually assaulting her when they were attending a high school party thirty-six years earlier: "I am here today not because I want to be. I am terrified," she started, confessing that out of shame she had kept the assault a secret for almost thirty years. Visibly shaken, she went on to describe how Kavanaugh pinned her to a bed, groped her, and removed her clothes, covering her mouth as she tried to scream: "I believed he was going to rape me. It was hard for me to breathe, and I thought that Brett was going to accidentally kill me." By the time her testimony ended, the hashtags #IBelieveHer, #WhyIDidntReport, and #BelieveWomen had already gone viral on Twitter and Instagram, garnering support from hundreds of thousands of women around the world, including rape survivors.[1] In a letter sent to the committee by her lawyers, Blasey Ford subsequently described the experience of reliving the incident as "traumatic and harrowing." Following her testimony, "she was subjected to vicious harassment and even death threats."[2]

Brett Kavanaugh fought back. In response to Blasey Ford, he submitted a letter to the committee calling her testimony nothing but "smears, pure and simple," aiming at his "grotesque and obvious character assassination." "I will not be intimidated into withdrawing from the process," he asserted with tears in his eyes, and social media came to his rescue with a deluge of #BackBrett tweets. Despite initial reluctance on the part of the Republican Party, senior conservative senator John Cornyn of Texas eventually called for sympathy for Kavanaugh's victimization. "Every female's got a father, some have a husband, some have a son," he said. "I would think they would want those people treated fairly just like we want Dr. Ford treated fairly." President Trump, too, offered Kavanaugh his sympathy: "It is a very scary time for young men in America, where you can be guilty of something you may not be guilty of," the president said. "This is a very, very—this is a very difficult time."[3]

The media described the battle over Kavanaugh's nomination as a "turning point" in America's history of female witnessing (*Time*), as a "tale of two internets" (*Wired*), and as a "duel with tears and fury" (*New York Times*).[4] Each of these headlines highlighted a significant aspect of what the court battle revealed about American culture: the triumph of women's voices in the age of #MeToo; anxieties around echo chambers that divide political communication into insulated spheres; and the hyperemotional nature of politics in the era of far-right populism. None, however, captured the deepest and perhaps most insidious character of this event as a battle over who is a victim. Christine Blasey Ford said that she decided to testify, initially in confidence, in order to share a truth that matters to all: the trauma of abuse that violated her body and psyche in the past and rendered her vulnerable once again in the present. Her claim to victimhood was anchored on her right to speak out as a survivor who shares her suffering in the name of public interest "so that," as her lawyer's letter put it, "lawmakers would have a fuller understanding of Brett Kavanaugh's character and history."[5] Brett Kavanaugh spoke out against "smears" to defend his "good name." He suffered an unexpected attack at a moment when his thirty-year illustrious career in the nation's judicial system was reaching its pinnacle: "My family and my name have been totally and permanently destroyed by vicious and false additional allegations," he told the committee. "You may defeat me in the final vote, but will never get me to quit. Never," he added.[6]

This stand-off of victimhood had a complex ending. On the one hand, Brett Kavanaugh was eventually voted onto the U.S. Supreme Court as an associate justice,[7] despite Blasey Ford's compelling testimony followed by those of three more women.[8] On the other hand, her statement reverberated with experiences of sexual abuse felt by thousands of women the world over, galvanizing new networks of solidarity and consolidating the legacy of the Me Too movement. Despite its ambiguous outcome, this story offers us two key insights about the cultural status of victimhood today.

The first one is that, as the global virality and international headlines of the story suggest,[9] claims to victimhood are not a particularly American phenomenon but a broader one that concerns Western cultures at large.[10] This is not a new observation. Almost twenty-five years ago, the art critic Robert Hughes said that we live in a "democracy of pain" in which "everyone may not be rich and famous but everyone has suffered."[11] Ten years later, Didier Fassin and Richard Rechtman's seminal study on " the empire of trauma" regarded victimhood as a key moral and political condition of contemporary life: "Trauma," they said, "is not confined to the psychiatric vocabulary; it is embedded in everyday usage. It has in fact created a new language of the event."[12] Carolyn Dean echoed this claim more recently, confirming that "the traumatized victim is central to contemporary Western culture."[13] Although these accounts describe or explain victimhood as a dominant discourse of Western cultures at large, they do not address crucial questions raised by the Blasey Ford–Kavanaugh story: What kind of world is a world of proliferating victims where each of two sides competes to establish its suffering as more legitimate than that of the other? How did this world come to be as it is today? What are the benefits of living in it? And, more important, what are the costs? It is these questions that this book grapples with.

The second insight of the story suggests the reason we urgently need to turn our attention to such questions. Claims to victimhood are claims to power. Blasey Ford, a female voice of suffering who, like thousands of others before her, was shamed into silence for more than three decades before speaking in public,[14] confronts Kavanaugh, a male voice of institutional authority who, like the vast majority of men like him, has been not only historically shielded from accusation (thrice repeated in his case) but also rewarded for his public performances of righteous outrage against his "enemies";[15] he was indeed supported by thousands on social media and eventually installed to the highest of U.S. courts. What I earlier called a stand-off of victimhood is, from the perspective of power, an unequal struggle between claims to pain, where harm inflicted upon a woman systemically open to patriarchal violence (as a sixteen-year-old girl at a party and as a female academic and adult witness at the Senate stand) is conflated with the personal grievance (for having to face an accusation) of a man with superior social and political power and male entitlement (to sex as a young man and to Supreme Court candidacy, now membership, as a middle-aged man). Living in a "democracy of pain," to echo Hughes's term, looks, from this perspective, like living in a world where systemic vulnerability and personal grievance are collapsed into one vocabulary, that of victimhood: *I am wronged!*

While pain is an important part of all politics of justice, against patriarchy but also against other forms of inequality, my argument is that the privileging of pain in the fight for justice personalizes politics, depoliticizes justice, and ultimately favors the powerful—an argument indebted to insights from Hannah Arendt, Wendy Brown, and Alyson Cole.[16] And whereas debates on the uses of victimhood today often begin and end with the question of truth, of how we know whether a claim to pain is true or false, my own interest lies instead in the question of how we can disentangle systemic vulnerability from privileged grievance and how we can reclaim the uses of pain at the service of the vulnerable.[17] Truth and justice are of course always intertwined, and there is no justice without truth. Yet there is also a difference between the two. The question of truth belongs to the epistemological domain of institutional verification—that is, the court and its rules of veridiction or journalism and its rituals of fact checking. The question of justice belongs to the political domain of social contestation around who has the privilege of voice, who can establish their suffering as dominant and so as "true," and ultimately who can benefit from speaking out on their pain over the pain of others—whether in public discourse, in collective memory, or in political rhetoric. Our focus on truth alone, I argue, tends to ignore power and its entanglements with privilege, and this has dire consequences for those who live in contexts of structural openness to violence as their claims to pain hardly ever have the chance to be heard, recognized, or believed in public.

Within this deeply unequal terrain, the proliferation of claims to victimhood produces its own victims by obfuscating truth—that is, by populating public discourse with too many voices of pain while selectively amplifying the voices of the already powerful over those of the underprivileged. And just like the spread of fake news, which blurs the boundary between fact and rumor, so competing claims to pain blur the line between systemic and tactical suffering: between suffering as a *condition*, let me repeat, that ties the self to broader circumstances that perpetuate physical or symbolic violence and suffering as a *claim* selectively adopted by individuals or groups for their gain. Pointing out this distinction helps us better navigate the difference "between fighting for victimized people," which demands an account of the conditions of their suffering, and "promoting a victimhood culture,"[18] which simply encourages the proliferation of claims to pain in public discourse. Fighting for the victimized is the moral drive of my argument, while promoting a victimhood culture is the object of my analysis.

TWENTY-FIRST-CENTURY VICTIMHOOD

My interest in victimhood is an interest in the role that human vulnerability plays in our culture: a Western culture of relative affluence and safety compared to the rest of the world yet deeply divided by its own inequalities of class, gender, race, sexuality, and ability. It is an interest in the political work that vulnerability does to shape the self as a public actor with moral value in the twenty-first century. Grounded in the acknowledgment that vulnerability is an existential dimension of the human condition in the sense that we all can feel pain, my inquiry is about the circumstances (historical and present) under which vulnerability, an embodied and social condition of openness to harm, turns into victimhood, a communicative act that attaches the particular moral value accrued to the vulnerable to everyone who claims it.

The Blasey Ford–Kavanaugh case is one illustration of the political work performed by the communication of victimhood in that each party's claims to pain, assault for her and humiliation for him, conjures up a different narrative of vulnerability and mobilizes a distinct dynamics of solidarity: feminist alliances versus conservative and misogynist alliances. This slipperiness suggests that we might best understand *victimhood* not as a single linguistic term, a word with a specific meaning attached to it, but, as I later argue in detail, as a whole politics of communication, where competing claims to pain and their communities of recognition struggle for domination and where, consequently, the truth of suffering does not come to reflect the systemic conditions of violence behind the claims but rather the balance of power within these struggles. The omnipresence of such claims to pain today defines our moment *both* as a continuation of past iterations when the suffering self also figured prominently in our collective conversations *and* as a new, distinct moment shaped by the present juncture.

What is distinct about twenty-first-century victimhood is that vulnerability is situated within a succession of recessions, first the post-2008 economic crisis and more recently the postpandemic one, which have not only impoverished the already poor but also had significant impact on the middle classes around the world, especially those in low- and middle-income countries.[19] Despite initiatives taken in the 2020–2022 period to mitigate the catastrophic impact of the pandemic and the subsequent energy crisis on Western national economies, the outcome has been "a worsening of inequality, both within the U.S. and between developed and developing countries," where, as Joseph Stiglitz says, "global billionaire wealth grew by $4.4 trillion between 2020 and 2021, and at the same time more than 100 million people fell below the poverty line."[20]

The paradox of this moment of compounded crises is that despite how these crises have highlighted the catastrophic weaknesses of a long-term neoliberal hegemony—namely, the thin governance of its global financial institutions, the relentless privatization of welfare infrastructures, and the growing gap between rich and poor—not only did this order not collapse, but it also further enforced itself, deepening old and accentuating new dimensions of social inequality. "A phase of revelation and intensification of social strains," Paolo Gerbaudo says of the pandemic period, this moment "has seen both new grievances emerging—for example, anger at restriction of movements, or outrage at the underfunding of emergency services—and old grievances being felt more acutely, including racism, social inequality, and cuts to public services."[21] This stubborn commitment to the market-driven logic of profit at the expense not only of the vulnerable but also of the hitherto relatively safe in Western societies has in the past decade precipitated popular distrust toward all forms of institutional authority and technocratic expertise—from banks to politicians to the media.[22] As Lawrence Grossberg writes, citizens now "experience themselves as victims of people or forces outside of their immediate lives and communities, in circumstances of economic and racial anxiety, which result in expressions of resentment, rage and even a reactionary desire for revenge."[23] I return to this point in chapter 3 as I discuss the weaponization of pain by the far-right populisms of Boris Johnson and Donald Trump.

Grossberg's broader point is, however, that neoliberalism not only materially sustains the divide between rich and poor, between the privileged and the disadvantaged, but also inflicts serious emotional harms on the latter in ways that affirm their self-perception as victims. This is what Nicolas Demertzis, among others, calls the people's "lived experience of injustice" as a sense of being deprived of something that people feel rightfully used to belong to them.[24] Operating as "a site of revenge to displace the hurt (a place to inflict hurt as the sufferer has been hurt)," as Wendy Brown describes it,[25] this sense of resentment can emerge and has emerged across the political spectrum, from the right to the left.[26] My interest, however, is only in the resentment felt by the far Right: a political space that has in the past decade capitalized on these crises and managed to win elections, trump liberties, and threaten long-standing democracies in the name of the people as victims. What is worse is that beyond and above its electoral power, the far Right has by today evolved into a formidable cultural force with "hypodermic" effects on the social body as a whole, nurturing identities of "us" versus "them" and normalizing hate against minority groups, whose vulnerability is often systemic on the grounds of race, gender, sexuality, or ability. Warning of the affinities between far-right populism and fascism, a link I discuss in chapter 4, Jason Stanley defines the latter precisely as a politics of division that "distinguishes 'us' and 'them,' appealing to ethnic, religious and racial distinctions" and that works through "resentment that flows from unmet expectations . . . [and is directed] against minority groups."[27]

One way in which neoliberal harms contribute to this normalization of the far Right is by creating global market conditions in which the shrinking of national industrial workforces (and their pay and welfare) together with the privileging of high-end migration for profit establish conditions for low-skilled migrants, largely from the global South, to be cast as an "illegal" threat that victimizes "native" workers. In this way, neoliberalism, as Richard Saull argues, has long legitimized a "racialized moral economy" of migration that the far Right has since further amplified in promoting its own narratives of hate—narratives where "immigrants, the symbol of cosmopolitan globalization, become the scapegoats for the losses and fears of 'natives.'"[28] A constitutive feature of global neoliberalism (pace its postracial claims), this racialized economy of migration resonates differently on the two sides of the Atlantic, with the United States predominantly scapegoating "falsely entitled insiders" such as Black and Latinx people and the United Kingdom scapegoating "national or cultural outsiders—immigrants and Muslims" as unfairly privileged minorities responsible for the suffering of the ("native" British) people.[29] From the victories of Brexit and Trump in 2016 to the continuing dominance of authoritarian populism the world over and its lethal border politics, far-right rhetoric still capitalizes on and benefits from this vocabulary of victimhood and its sensibility of resentment.[30]

Another way in which neoliberalism produces resentful victimhood is reflected in the vicious male chauvinist attacks against women's testimonies of patriarchal violence. Trump's statement "This is a very . . . difficult time" for "young boys" in response to Blasey Ford's testimony is an example. His reversal of empathy from the female victim to her alleged perpetrator is what Sarah Banet-Weiser describes as an "insidious flip" in the structure of "neoliberal patriarchy"—a system that tends to individualize the subordination of women to patriarchal oppression by turning the structural violence of patriarchy into a story of a few "bad apples" yet presents the individual man's claim to suffering (say, Kavanaugh's tears for being disgraced) as an attack against all men: "This rerouted victimhood," Banet-Weiser writes, "works to retrench patriarchal gender relations by redefining what it means to be disempowered, vulnerable, and violated."[31] These two examples suggest that situating victimhood in the postrecession neoliberal context and all that this entails culturally and politically helps us understand both how claims to pain have become central to Western discourse and how this centrality relies on preexisting structures of power and inequality that shape collective conversations, such as racism, xenophobia, and popular misogyny.

To understand contemporary victimhood, however, we also need to turn to the past. I next take such a step back in time, zooming into the historical legacy of the languages of pain in the twentieth century (in the section "Twentieth-Century Victimhood") to show how victimhood has come to operate as a communicative backbone of emotional capitalism (in the section "Victimhood as a Politics of Pain"), before returning to the present to discuss how social media platforms affect the circulation of claims to pain and the spread of victimhood narratives in our times (in the section "The Platformization of Pain").

TWENTIETH-CENTURY VICTIMHOOD

The term *victimhood* has a long history. Whereas until the seventeenth century it appeared primarily within a religious context to refer to sacrificial offerings,[32] the Anglo-Roman uses of the term gradually moved outside the religious context and took on the more secular meaning of the state of being inflicted by harm or of being killed.[33] It was, however, only in the nineteenth and early twentieth centuries that the term *victim* slowly came to adopt the more general meaning of "oppressed person," someone who suffers injury or misfortune or simply someone who is taken advantage of.[34] Around the same time, the noun also turned into a process, "to victimize," signaling the act of harming someone, and into a subject, "victimizer," denoting the actor of the harmful process.[35]

This historical transformation registers a parallel shift from a ritual meaning, where sacrificial victimhood involved bodily harm for a common cause, toward an individualized meaning, where victimhood became tied to the corporeal and emotional harm of particular persons—a process reflected in, among other contexts, the twentieth-century transformation of soldierly suffering, as I show in chapter 2. Although this shift in the meaning of victimhood is indicative of a broader orientation in Western modernity from religious collectivism (forms of life centered on communities of faith) toward secular individualism (forms of life privileging the affiliations of private interests), contemporary victimhood is nonetheless present in both dominant individualist discourses of "my pain" and collectivist discourses that speak in the name of whole communities of grievance. Indeed, as the prevalence of the word *das Opfer* across Germanic languages suggests, these two meanings, "offering" and "sufferer," coexist today, selectively animating different claims to suffering and so configuring different political affiliations in different moments in time,[36] a point I revisit in chapter 3 as I discuss the emotional attachments of far-right populism. For now, I zoom into the formation of victimhood as the vocabulary of the harmed self in late modernity. To this end, I trace the birth of the twentieth century's core languages of pain—namely, the languages of trauma and rights—under the subjects "the Holocaust as a resource for the languages of pain" and "the languages of pain"—the latter shaped in part by but not fully originating in the former.

The Holocaust as a Resource for the Languages of Pain

Perhaps no other name better encapsulates the duality of victimhood as a catalyst of both individual and collective identity than "the Holocaust."[37] I approach the Holocaust, a paradigmatic event of mass atrocity against Jewish, Roma, and other marginalized populations, as a major symbolic resource that shaped the use of the languages of pain in the post–Second World War order—a period that Annette Wieviorka calls "the era of the witness."[38] Although these languages are undeniably entangled with much longer histories of colonial violence, the Holocaust still remains foundational to the formation of twentieth-century victimhood by means of *trauma testimonials* by the survivors of the camps as much as by means of the legal status of survivors as *rightful citizens.*

As *trauma,* victimhood after the Holocaust has come to refer both to the linguistic problem of unspeakability in the face of extreme pain and to an existential condition of the modern self as a self in crisis: "The Holocaust," Anna Hunter writes, "constitutes a traumatic narrative not only as historical trauma in narrative form" but also "as a trauma to narrative itself enacted as a crisis of signification and representation"—something we also observe in the parallel trajectory of soldierly trauma at war in chapter 2.[39] It was first in the Adolf Eichmann trial in 1961, a seminal moment in the mediation of the Jewish trauma through daily radio broadcasts and news reports,[40] that the surviving victims' pain broke through their private conversations and was communicated in the public sphere: "The trial," as Sandra Ristovska puts it, "translated the private and suppressed trauma into public cognizance" and so acknowledged the suffering of the victims, "who were initially deprived from the means to express their vast sufferings."[41]

Beyond the public legitimization of trauma, however, the Eichmann trial was simultaneously the first act to position Holocaust victimhood within *legal discourse*. Even though the right to be protected from genocidal violence had already been introduced in 1948,[42] it was this trial that endowed the victims of Nazi atrocity with "legal subjecthood"—that is, with the authority not only to tell stories of Holocaust suffering but also to have such stories taken seriously as admissible evidence in court.[43] Insofar as it opened up a "public scene of the recovery of language" for those victims whose experience was hitherto defined "by the language of the oppressor," Shoshana Felman argues, "in effect" the trial "did not simply repeat the victim's story, but historically created it for the first time."[44] I, like Felman, take the Eichmann trial to be a catalyst in authorizing the languages of trauma and rights as the public languages of pain in our times.

It is instructive nonetheless to approach the Holocaust in the context of a more layered process of the voicing of victimhood in twentieth-century modernity—a context that also incorporates other histories of suffering, violence, and conflict, which, together with the Holocaust, also contributed to "the changing status of victimhood . . . from something to be ashamed of to a sign of grace and moral righteousness."[45] Postcolonial witnessing similarly involves harrowing testimonies of mass suffering that caused immense pain to the millions of Black and Brown people subjected to the long-lasting dispossession, oppression, and atrocity committed by their European rulers—an experience that, as Aimé Césaire recognizes, bears strong historical affinities to the totalitarianisms of twentieth-century Europe (fascism, Nazism, and Stalinism), where "the white man . . . applied to Europe colonialist procedures which until then had been reserved exclusively for the Arabs of Algeria, the coolies of India and the 'niggers' of Africa."[46]

Granted this historical affinity between colonialism and the Holocaust, where both share, as Dominic LaCapra also notes, "problems of traumatization, severe oppression, a divided heritage, the question of the founding trauma . . . and so forth,"[47] their experiences of pain were nonetheless not entirely similar to one another—with the multiple forms of colonial violence extending beyond a singular event across space and time and with colonial suffering expressed in diverse voices and genres across different cultures.[48] In addition, as critics have observed, the colonial experience of victimhood remained long invisible in Western public discourse because the Western world largely followed the narrative templates of the Holocaust as "a generalized symbol of human suffering and moral evil,"[49] and so it modeled the distinct and specific experiences of atrocity from postcolonial contexts along the lines of the more familiar Holocaust imagery, including, for example, emaciated bodies and barbed wire, or by using Holocaust language, such as fragmented, discontinuous narratives and the paucity of unrepresentable pain.[50] In so doing, as Stef Craps says, Western discourses on colonial trauma "failed to live up to a cross-cultural ethical engagement" in that they "marginalize or ignore traumatic experiences of non-Western modernity . . . and generally disregard the connection between metropolitan and non-Western or metropolitan and non-Western or minority traumas."[51]

Although my own history centers on Western trajectories of victimhood, it does so with the purpose of locating the silences of postcolonial pain within such trajectories precisely to highlight how the formation of the Western victim always takes place in "a punctual dialogue" with the simultaneous erasure of non-Western and nonwhite victims.[52] Just as testimonials of colonial suffering were long molded into Western templates of representation, so the collective memory of modern wars, as I show in chapter 2, also employed narratives and rituals of commemoration that misrecognized the pain of Black and Brown soldiers and later non-Western civilians in the wars of the West, thereby creating uneven narratives of victimhood in line with colonial hierarchies of place and human life.

The Languages of Pain

Where do the languages of pain employed in the Holocaust come from? What are the broader histories of this vocabulary of victimhood? And what are the present contexts of its use?

Two "grand languages" of pain, after Lyotard's "grand narratives" of modernity,[53] shaped our current definition of victimhood as individual vulnerability that accrues moral status to the claimant and can bring political communities together: trauma and human rights. Both languages are part of a dazzling panorama of ideas (psychoanalysis, Marxism, liberalism, postcolonialism) that emerged out of the twentieth century's momentous events, including, beyond the Holocaust, the world wars, decolonization, and the end of the Cold War.

Eva Illouz's description of twentieth-century modernity as "emotional capitalism" frames my own understanding of these languages of pain. In her classic study entitled *Cold Intimacies* (2007), Illouz argues that the socioeconomic organization of liberal capitalism, with its emphasis on the self-expressive individual, brought with it a new culture of emotionality, where claiming one's personal pain is never simply an act of self-description but is primarily about affirming one's presence as a worthy self among others in the public sphere: "Modern identity is increasingly performed," Illouz says, "through a narrative which combines the aspiration to self-realization with the claim to emotional suffering."[54] Illouz's argument on emotional capitalism draws attention to the tight embrace of the capitalist economy with personal feeling in two ways: first, by analyzing how the media industry taps into the profit-making potential of emotions, as in the popularity of sentimental genres of self-confession, such as the *Oprah Winfrey Show*, or in the recent rise of dating platforms that datafy and commodify romantic love; and, second, by dissecting the ways in which the synergy between economic and technological efficiency taps into the feelings of employees or consumers to increase profit for the workplace, as in Illouz's work on affective organizational cultures and online consumption and desire.[55]

My use of her term *emotional capitalism* relies on these important insights but extends beyond them because my own aim is different: to explore how the distinct configuration of emotion, economy, and technology in our times has rendered victimhood hegemonic in Western politics and culture. In other words, I focus on how emotional capitalism mobilizes the universal force of "feeling pain" to turn public discourse into a marketplace of victims where claimants ultimately compete for dominance—a marketplace where both a feminist politics of civil duty and a reactionary affirmation of male identity rely alike on the tears of their respective victims to animate communities of empathy. The success of emotional capitalism in aligning the "losers" of neoliberal capitalism with the perpetrators of their victimhood, as in the discourse of far-right populist governments, I suggest, lies precisely in this capacity of pain to disavow any a priori political attachment and, by claiming the "truth" of the human condition, to attach itself to different positions of privilege and vulnerability across the spectrum.

How did this configuration come to be? How did the emotionality of pain manage to speak the language of political universality? To address this question, we need to go beyond the common assumption that pain speaks to "our" common humanity and so transcends politics and instead to see that pain entails its own political struggles over status and power—a "politics of pain," as I later explain. It is this politics that, grounded as it is on the languages of pain, shapes the self as a victim while producing its own exclusions in the process. Illouz's own interest lies in the language of psychotherapy, where the self is described as a vulnerable individual socialized in dialogic relationships of empathetic listening: "the traumatized self." My inquiry, however, demands that we broaden this focus to engage with yet another key language of modernity, that of human rights, which presupposes a similar, albeit not identical, dialogic sociality but treats the self as a vulnerable subject entitled to legal protection—what we may call "the injured self."

THE TRAUMATIZED SELF

The *traumatized self* emerges within the psychoanalytical tradition, which aspires to heal the hidden vulnerabilities of the psyche through conversational therapy. Drawing on the Greek term *trauma*, meaning "wound," the concept of the traumatized self concerns a self that has been shattered following an overwhelming experience of violence or loss, an experience that cannot be rationalized yet recursively returns as a haunting feeling to disrupt the coherence of our existence. At the heart of this disrupted sense of self lies the impossibility of putting words to it. Trauma is that which harms the self without the self being able to grasp it in language, and it is this double wound, the original shattering and its relentless return upon us, that places suffering at the center of the psychoanalytical tradition.[56]

Violent events are regarded as central to the wound of the self, with the Holocaust being viewed as Western modernity's founding trauma. However, dominant strands of psychoanalysis think of trauma as something that is not primarily historical, occurring in the course of human timelines, but profoundly existential, beginning with life itself. Lacanian psychoanalysis, for instance, speaks of trauma as the primal violence of separation that occurs at birth and in early infancy as human beings leave the womb and are "born into language."[57] We are, in other words, victims from birth as life pushes us out of a state of prelinguistic being, where our needs are merged with and provided by the mother, toward a state of symbolic being, where we depend on language both to express and to repress our experience. And it is language that keeps hurting us. As a means of self-expression, language leads to miscommunication, misunderstandings, and ultimately silence, while as a mechanism of repression it never fully succeeds in protecting us from our deepest wounds—life always manages to trigger the primary event and threaten anew our inner self.[58]

The rise of what Illouz calls the "therapeutic culture" of emotional capitalism is driven precisely by this premise of psychoanalysis, where we all are victims of the very processes of socialization that enable us to grow into adulthood. In this culture, we are never "fully grown up," as Jeffrey Alexander puts it, "but remain childlike in an adult world hoping as much for dependence as for autonomy."[59] Here, it is not only our relationship to the mother but also our involvement in other intimate and institutionalized relationships—with teachers, partners, friends, and colleagues—that can victimize us, so that, in the words of Frank Furedi, "from birth, marriage and parenting, through to bereavement, people's experience is always interpreted through the therapeutic ethos."[60]

Within this daily minefield of potentially harmful encounters, therapy culture promises to empower the traumatized self by returning to language itself—this time as a tool of healing rather than a means of harm. Psychotherapeutic interaction, the speaking out on one's vulnerabilities in safe environments that seek to "tame" the unconscious, here breaks away from the analyst's couch and into the public realm. Therapy talk, as Illouz notes, is today fully entrenched in Western ways of speaking, urging us to attend to the trauma in all of us and routinely orienting our interactions toward the imperatives of self-confession and empathetic listening: "The transformation of the public sphere into an arena for the exposition of private life, of emotions, and intimacies," she says, "cannot be understood without acknowledging the role of psychology in converting private experiences into public discussion."[61]

Although therapy culture is a distinctly twentieth-century phenomenon, connascent with the Freudian/Lacanian paradigm of psychoanalysis, therapeutic communication, organized around the sharing of pain and its empathetic recognition, has deeper roots than psychoanalysis. It began in the eighteenth-century "culture of sympathy," the dominant sensibility of the French and Scottish Enlightenments, when the norms of political community relied no longer on punitive regimes of autocratic rule but on pastoral governance that cared for the people.[62] The modern self, accordingly, broke from the obligations of feudal loyalty and was now attached to the rise of capitalism and its civil imperative to recognize and respond to the suffering of other humans, with benevolence and compassion being part of the moral universe of market-oriented societies.⁶³ In *Theory of Moral Sentiments* (1759), a foundational text on the moral experience in modernity, Adam Smith's account of society places the spectacle of the sufferer at the heart of public life and elevates civil imagination into a catalyst of fellow feeling, or feeling for the pain of others: "By the imagination," he writes, "we place ourselves in his [*sic*, the sufferer's] situation, we conceive ourselves enduring all the same torments, we enter into his body, and become in some measure the same person like him, and thence form some idea of his sensations, and even feel something which, though weaker in degree, is not altogether unlike them."⁶⁴

Therapy talk can be seen from this historical perspective as a twentieth-century mutation of Smith's sympathy, where suffering takes the specific form of psychic trauma, yet shares with that earlier culture a similar focus on the public displays of pain as a practice of civil education. Fully embedded in media formats, celebrity culture, and platform activism, citizenship still remains now, as it was then, "a genuine pedagogy of feelings and introspection" that aims as much at healing the self as at shaping the liberal polity.⁶⁵ This pedagogy, however, has been a thoroughly Western conception of political pedagogy that did not apply to European colonies, subjected as they were to "a systematic negation of the other person,"⁶⁶ and it is still today, as we shall see, only very selectively and instrumentally applied to the global South.⁶⁷

The hashtags #MeToo and #IBelieveHer can, from this perspective, be seen as contemporary practices of civil education that use their collective iterations of pain to amplify women's personal experiences of sexual harm.⁶⁸ Earlier television talk shows such as Oprah Winfrey's similarly constituted popular sites for the performance of a "*suffering* and *victimized* self" that seeks to "empower itself by *talking* about its predicaments."⁶⁹ Even though both of these instances of therapy talk are potentially empowering practices that can encourage bonds of feminist solidarity, the commercial nature of their platforms introduces a foundational ambivalence to their communication. Driven by profit, mediated therapy, Illouz continues, is reduced to a hyperemotive genre that turns stories of pain into entertaining drama and neglects to explore the social reasons of the suffering; David Krasner adds that it also has turned Black families' dramas and "their strategies for overcoming oppression" into "models for the white women's self-satisfaction."[70] Echoing a similar concern, Rosalind Gill and Shani Orgad ask today whether the Me Too moment is about women's self-expression or consumer attention: "Is it sexism," they wonder, "or sex that 'sells'?"[71] Catherine Rottenberg extends this by posing the following race and class question: If "it is only powerful, wealthy and mostly white women" who come forward to speak out, then "when and where [are] claims of sexual harassment and assault . . . heard and whose voices count?"[72]

The traumatized self, in summary, emerges within psychoanalysis to treat the sufferer as a public figure deserving of an empathetic response. Drawing on the Enlightenment legacy of fellow feeling, this language of pain is today pervasive across Western contexts in the form of therapy culture—ways of thinking and speaking that may rightly speak of mental health and well-being yet perform victimhood within racialized and commodified contexts that depoliticize the structural conditions of suffering and spectacularize pain for the benefit of the media.

THE INJURED SELF

The *injured self* emerges in the language of human rights, which, in contrast to psychoanalytic trauma, speaks of injustice-related injury and considers the self to be in need of legal protection rather than only of therapy.[73] This means that even though the self of human rights is still vulnerable, this vulnerability is no longer associated with narratives of the psyche but with narratives of social inequality as a harmful condition of the self. These are the narratives of revolution that cast injury as the driving force for collective struggle and social change and the narratives of reformation that regard injury as the motivation for institutional reform to protect the individual person.

Narratives of revolution treat social injury as the effect of dominant economic and political structures that subordinate, impoverish, and disenfranchize the dominated self and the communities to which the self belongs—whether the working class under capitalism, women under patriarchy, or Black populations under colonialism. Marxian narratives, for instance, may be critical of the language of rights, yet, as Samuel Moyn notes, they did articulate the nineteenth-century struggles of the workers firmly within the discourse of the "rights of man"—in particular the "right to work" as a "minimum core" of "human dignity."[74] Informed by a left-wing vision, early feminism similarly mobilized the language of rights to redress the masculinist, class-centered rhetoric of socialist movements and to demand an enhanced understanding of injury that critiques patriarchy's division of labor and its confinement of women to the domestic sphere.[75] Finally, the antislavery movement framed the postbellum struggle over what legal status the newly freed Black population would claim as a struggle for civil rights.[76] To protect this population from turning into second-rate citizens, the movement fought for rights that were meant to guarantee Black people's equal membership in the political community of the American nation, so that, as W. E. B. Du Bois put it, the world would understand "that Black Africans are men [*sic*] in the same sense as White European and yellow [*sic*] Asiatics."[77]

Whereas the narratives of revolution raise the question of rights as part of a collectivist vision of social transformation that aspires to change the current social order in the name of social justice, the *narratives of reformation* use rights not to transform the social order but to protect the vulnerable within it from its most injurious effects. Reformation reflects, in this sense, a specific historical moment of post–Second World War politics that insists on treating injury as a harm to be addressed but, instead of revolting against the structures of harm, works to protect people from them. In this postwar order, Kate Nash claims, "the human rights movement has grown to address state violence and persecution, not the structural injustices of global capitalism."[78]

The postwar expansion of human rights from the national to the international level is at the heart of this agenda of social protection, having managed to "deliver a larger egalitarian package" across nations than any prewar arrangement had done before.[79] This globalization of rights was accomplished in part because of the universal vision of the "human person" inherent in the reformative version. Combining conservative, Christian, and liberal democratic visions of the injured self, the "human person" is no longer a class-, race- or gender-specific individual but an all-encompassing figure of vulnerability that continues to this day to act as the most evocative and efficacious signifier in global politics: "Human rights," as Moyn puts it, "have become the core language of a new politics of humanity that has sapped the energy from old ideological contests of left and right."[80]

Even though the language of rights does appear to be significantly distinct from therapy talk, I argue that the two share a historical origin in the culture of sympathy. Both constitute, in the words of Michael Meranze, a crucial communicative resource of modernity "through which individuals could articulate their openness to suffering others,"[81] and, in this sense, both posit the vulnerable self as the source of public emotion and action. Unlike therapy with its reliance on fellow feeling, however, the language of rights draws on the narratives of indignation in its two versions, the denunciatory and the reconciliatory. Just like fellow feeling, indignation is a political emotion par excellence yet inserts suffering not into the psychological structure of trauma but, as Boltanski puts it, "within a structure of exploitation and domination."[82] Recognition of the suffering other is still a key stake in the communication of indignation, but this time such recognition is about validating anger as a fair response to the structural causes that led to the suffering in the first place; in Mervi Pantti and Karin Wahl-Joergensen's words, "anger and moral outrage on behalf of the suffering victims can be a powerful motivation for dissent and opposition when there is someone to blame for the injustice."[83]

Whereas anger is clearly evident in the narrative of revolution, typically associated with the antisystemic activism of both left- and right-wing social movements, reformation is informed by a "quieter" affective register. Grounded on "a universal memory" of suffering and its postwar imperative of "never again," this register is "self-consciously framed in the language of rationality, reasonableness, pragmatism, and modesty."[84] Important advances in, say, the digital rights of citizens in the European Union owe their institutionalization precisely to these reformative efforts by activists, policy makers, and other stakeholders who worked together to protect social media users from the extractive and exploitative practices of big tech.[85] Within the terrain of international politics, however, it is this pragmatism of the reformative narrative, where the aim is to shape institutional policy in line with hegemonic geopolitical agendas, that has been criticized for reproducing neocolonial relations of power and for leaving unprotected those who need human rights the most:

migrants, refugees, civilians in conflict zones, racialized minorities.[86] Like therapy, moreover, the language of reformation is further problematized for its attachment to the neoliberal marketization of global governance, where, for instance, major humanitarian and human rights nongovernmental organizations utilize branding strategies that turn rights from instruments of social change into self-gratifying tools of doing good: "By increasingly relying on the marketing logic of the corporate world as well as the digital technologies of media culture," as I have put it elsewhere, human rights claims "have come to respond to the political collapse of revolutionary narratives with the celebration of a neoliberal lifestyle of 'feel good' altruism."[87]

The injured self, in summary, is associated with human rights, the second grand language of pain in emotional capitalism. Like psychoanalysis, rights discourse draws on the Enlightenment culture of sympathy but, unlike it, mobilizes instead either righteous indignation and protest against injustice in its revolutionary register or pragmatic intervention at the service of the vulnerable in its reformative one. In both its registers, however, this language is also criticized for perpetuating neocolonial relations of global power and for situating pain within commodified regimes of online activism that strip off the pain of its political force.

VICTIMHOOD AS A POLITICS OF PAIN

The aim of the historical review in the previous section was to understand how the vocabulary of victimhood we use today came to be. To do this, I located its languages of pain—trauma and rights—in the context of emotional capitalism and showed how their legacies are defined both by colonial histories of power that selectively attach the value of the victim to certain selves rather than to others *and* by neoliberal marketization that commodifies therapy into sensational stories or reduces human rights activism to consumerist choices. In both versions, our vocabulary of victimhood tends to individualize suffering and to leave outside public discourse the structural causes that lie behind it.

In light of this history, I argue that we need to approach victimhood not as a universal quality of all humanity (we all can feel pain) but rather as a communicative act participating in a certain kind of politics—what I call a "politics of pain." Inspired by Hannah Arendt's critique of pity, the politics of pain refers to the arousal of urgent emotions when we are confronted with the spectacle of suffering and its demand for an immediate response without consideration of why the suffering occurs in the first place. In her discussion of the French Revolution, Arendt similarly reflects on Robespierre's encounter with the sans-culottes of Paris, arguing that it was the sheer force of this spectacle of miserable destitution that led Robespierre to react with the indiscriminate violence of the Terror but without regard to its human and political consequences: "The ocean of suffering around him and the turbulent sea of emotion within him," Arendt explains, "drowned all specific considerations ... the considerations of friendship no less than considerations of statecraft and principle."[88]

Arendt's observation on pity confirms what is already implied in my discussion—namely, that the communication of pain is not an inconsequential add-on to public discourse. Insofar as it presents citizens with the urgent imperative to acknowledge the suffering of others, the speaking out on pain is constitutive of our political cultures and the struggles for domination that take place within them. It is, in particular, the pressure for an *immediate* response to pain, effectively foreclosing questions of what context these claims are made in, that lies at the heart of such struggles. Boltanski eloquently expresses the taboo of publicly questioning claims to pain when he asks, "Who, for example, would dream of saying that the inhabitants of a country ravaged by famine have what they deserve?," concluding that " the urgency of action needing to be taken to bring an end to the suffering invoked always prevails over considerations of justification."[89] It is this urgent attention to the claim to suffering, the visible or audible act of communicating injury or trauma, at the expense of an inquiry into the condition of the self, the invisible positions of openness to harm one occupies in social space, that *both* links victimhood to its earlier modern legacy of the Enlightenment and colonialism *and* endows the term with its present political efficacy as simultaneously a promise of benevolence and a weapon for cruelty.

Within the framework of a politics of pain, we can now better grasp why victimhood is not a signifier that can be objectively attached to the self as an essential identity but rather, to repeat, a communicative act that employs the languages of pain developed in liberal modernity so as to enable us to speak about and feel for the vulnerable self: "I feel wounded" or "I am wronged." Put otherwise, the victim is not a person per se but an iterative act of speech through which the self is produced as vulnerable at the very moment it claims to suffer. It is this performative capacity to summon the self anew around different claims to trauma or injury and so to call up different communities of recognition around them that, I argue, renders victimhood a site of struggle in public discourse. Contemporary politics is, in turn, largely a politics of pain insofar as it heavily relies on this mutable practice of linguistic "articulations," to use Stuart Hall's words, where pain and the self come together in ways that are "not necessary, determined, absolute and essential for all time" but provisionally settle the identity of the victim at different moments in time.[90] Who is produced as a victim, around which claim to suffering, and within which community of belonging are thus questions of political communication that cannot be taken for granted but are precisely the stake in the critical analysis of public discourse.

As a consequence of this performativity of victimhood, the emotions of suffering also blur and mix, so that the response to another person's pain does not always appear in the form of pure empathy or pure indignation but is articulated in hybrid claims, where the two emotions coexist. To go back to my opening example, both Blasey Ford's anguished testimony and Kavanaugh's aggressive self-defense are instances of affective hybridity in that both actors claimed trauma (of sexual abuse and of character assassination, respectively) as much as injury (speaking out to inform and protect others from damage and speaking out to defend and protect oneself from reputation loss, respectively). Their performances, in turn, mobilized distinct suffering selves. Blasey Ford's "powerful vulnerability" strengthened her identity as a good citizen, and she was subsequently praised for being "pretty credible, pretty likable, pretty believable,"[91] while Brett Kavanaugh's tearful face downplayed his political identity and presented him as a mere vulnerable man—"every female's" "father," "husband," "son," as Senator Cornyn put it. Affective hybridity shows here not only how pain is attached to different emotions—inviting empathy (Blasey Ford) or provoking outrage (Kavanaugh)—but also how, in so doing, it can summon the self in simultaneously various relationships to vulnerability. Both protagonists appear thus as sufferers in that both are wounded and wronged; as perpetrators, wherein they have inflicted pain upon one another; and as survivors, with Blasey Ford's vulnerability being praised as "actually a superpower"[92] and Kavanaugh's tears being combined with the defiant posture of "I will not give up." And it is, in turn, precisely by relying on this nonnecessary articulation of the self with pain, to recall Hall's words, that in my example victimhood severs pain from its conditions of existence, blurring the distinction between victim and perpetrator. Kavanaugh's tearful accusation of Blasey Ford can in this sense be described as an act of tactical or reverse victimhood, where his white male tears aim at casting himself as a sufferer and projecting suspicion on the female victim's motives with a view to discrediting her testimony.[93]

Victimhood, to summarize, emerges out of a long legacy of liberal capitalism—"emotional" from its early days—and its languages of pain. This legacy has situated vulnerability within a durable politics of communication consisting of iterative and hence mutable claims to suffering that are today in the grip of neoliberal marketization and commodity activism. Located at the heart of this iterative process, the victim does not constitute an essential identity but rather exists as a semantic category that is open to multiple articulations of meaning—"something that," as Grossberg puts it, "belongs to anyone who cares to embrace it"[94]—and thus that can blend the emotions of injury and trauma and flip the roles of victim and perpetrator in ways that produce political effects.

THE PLATFORMIZATION OF PAIN

Although our languages of pain are deeply grounded in the past, there is nonetheless something irreducibly new about the uses of victimhood today. The platformization of pain—that is, the performance of vulnerability on and through the commercial logic of social media platforms—has transformed the premises upon which victimhood is now claimed. It has done so in two ways: by reorganizing the communicative politics of pain and by expanding the realms of suffering in which victimhood can be claimed.

To begin with, platformization has enabled everyone with a mobile phone and a social media account to broadcast their pain to the 4.48 billion users across social media platforms.[95] Such openness on internet platforms had earlier been greeted as a democratizing move, where marginalized groups found a way to voice their suffering and mobilize social forces for political change. Merlyna Lim, for example, had early on argued that to understand the massive Arab Spring protests of 2011 against the Hosni Mubarak regime, we need to explore the online habits of Egypt's oppositional youth. Their engagement with Facebook and Twitter, she said, gave them "the means to shape repertoires of contention, frame the issues, propagate unifying symbols, and transform online activism into offline protests."[96]

In the course of the past decade, however, most scholars became ambivalent about this potential. Rather than a matter of benign technological connectivity, they contend, such expansion of voice has been driven by digital platforms' corporate interests, which capitalize on user attention and engagement for profit. This means that even though social media platforms continue to make a difference, for instance in the case of the hashtag #MeToo, where they amplified women's voices about their experiences of violence and abuse,[97] they often do more harm than good. A sinister counterexample that makes the point is the emergence of misogynistic activisms that claim victimhood in order to legitimize violence against women. In this context, Alice Marwick and Robyn Caplan discuss the "manosphere," a male-only community in websites such as incels.com that spreads its "misogynistic ontology by portraying feminism as a man-hating movement which victimizes men and boys" and that uses this portrayal as an excuse for attacking women.[98] Such groups instrumentalize the communication of pain to turn women into wrong-doers who sexually manipulate their "vulnerable and innocent victims."[99] This online amplification of misogyny, critics argue, should be seen not only as a matter of patriarchal ideology but also as a matter of the algorithmic logic of platforms that in the pursuit of profit maximize the visibility of any claim to pain so as to monetize user attention: "The misogynist manosphere," as Molly Dragiewicz and her colleagues' research shows, "is significantly empowered by the ability to exploit the affordances and algorithmic characteristics of the contemporary digital media environment."[100]

The platformization of pain, to summarize, does not simply disseminate content but further reorganizes the communicative politics of pain in terms of how and by whom claims to pain are made, who gets the most visibility, and which online communities get legitimized and empowered or not.[101] At the heart of this process lie the platforms' technosocial architectures, specifically their capacity for anonymous and automated connectivity, which enables competing claims to pain to proliferate online, disconnected from their conditions of emergence—that is, both from the identity of the claimant (through anonymity) and from the context of the claim (through automation)—and so further dismantles the distinction between sufferer and perpetrator.[102] At the same time, the platforms' orientation toward virality—quantifying user engagement by response counts (retweets, likes) and size of communities (followers)—amplifies already popular claims to suffering without asking questions about who makes them or in which contexts of violence those claims are made. As José van Dijck puts it, "There is no quality assessment built into these [app] buttons[, so that] online quantification indiscriminately accumulates acclamation and applause and, by implication, depreciation and disapproval."[103]

Beyond restructuring the communication of victimhood, platformization has also expanded the realms of vulnerability within which claims to pain can be made. Digital violence, particularly in the form of online hate speech, has today extended these realms of suffering in that as hate speech goes online, it transfers already existing claims to trauma or injury onto social media platforms. Just like offline, online hate speech is about attacking persons or groups on the basis of their race, religion, gender and sexual orientation, ability, or looks, but, unlike offline speech, online attacks can now reach previously protected spaces such as the home and persist in time because past abuse can exist indefinitely in digital archives.[104] Focusing on these new ways in which the digital realm both sustains and expands the violence of predigital encounters, Sonia Livingstone notes that research on cyberharms should concentrate on the spaces of connection between the two, where "mobile and online risks are increasingly intertwined with pre-existing (offline) risks in children's lives."[105] Indeed, cyberbullying, as Shari Kessel Schneider and her colleagues have shown, intensifies and worsens the trauma already experienced by children in the schoolyard: "Victims of cyberbullying alone," the authors say, "reported more distress than did victims of school bullying alone," including depression and suicide attempts.[106] At the same time, trolling both raises claims to trauma by causing psychological harm to those subjected to it and potentially leads to social injury in that fear and ridicule can silence vulnerable voices and consolidate existing social hierarchies.[107] As Nicola Henry and Anastasia Powell have demonstrated, the systematic shaming of women's online confessions of abuse is a key method through which "gendered injury and shame are perpetrated, experienced, performed, and defined online."[108]

This proliferation of online acts of violence has accordingly also expanded the domain of digital recognition through which these new vulnerabilities can be heard and validated online, and in this way digital violence has inevitably also forced us to rethink our languages of pain. We can see this in efforts to update psychoanalytic discourse by way of new counseling services and self-empowering tool kits that aim at reskilling the parties involved and in new elaborations of digital rights discourses and interventions for young users, where evidence-based policy making navigates a fine line between recognizing harms and appreciating opportunities for them.[109]

Even though such struggles for online well-being and safety are of paramount importance, the domain of digital recognition has simultaneously been criticized for being co-opted by state and corporate interests as a tool of surveillance and commodification. Behavior-monitoring apps at schools, for example, promise to personalize the regulation of students' conduct to protect the most vulnerable, yet they also operate as pedagogic "dataveillance," storing the students' personal data for commercial purposes.[110] Similarly, mobile apps for mental health, such as #Mindful, encourage people to monitor their daily activities to achieve spiritual balance but also encourage "the migration of everydayness as a commercialization strategy," as Shoshana Zuboff puts it, where individual data are used "to produce new varieties of commodification, monetization, and control."[111]

The platformization of pain, to conclude, marks the current moment of emotional capitalism as one where the self is constituted through a new relationship with the market and technology. As a result, the languages of pain—trauma and rights—become both more specialized and diffuse in the public sphere and more all-encompassing and ambivalent in their social effects.

First, by expanding the sites wherein claims to trauma or injury can be made, platformized pain may, on the one hand, encourage institutional reforms to protect the vulnerable from markets but also may, on the other hand, lead to a further entrenchment of the already commodified languages of victimhood in public discourse. The more vulnerable people become online, simply put, the more these languages are refined to protect them yet also are commercialized and sold back to them as resources to manage their pain. Second, by reorganizing the networks of communication through which claims to suffering circulate, platformized pain amplifies their visibility while at the same time shaping and regulating this visibility in line with the interests of the tech industry. The more people go online to voice their pain, in other words, the more their claims—already decoupled from their contexts—spread through new logics of anonymity, automation, and popularity that render the link between claims to pain and their contexts essentially irrelevant. It is within this nominally open but thoroughly monetized and historically hierarchical landscape of communication that victimhood intersects with post-truth—a landscape that may not always be spreading fake news yet by monetizing and selectively amplifying pain ends up blurring the boundary between systemic suffering and tactical suffering at the service of already dominant and often reactionary agendas. This is the point that I now turn to in the final section of this chapter.

WHO USED TO BE, IS, AND SHOULD BE CALLED A VICTIM?

What is the take-away from my rethinking of our vocabulary of victimhood, past and present? The take-away is that the critical analysis of victimhood cannot grasp the positions of victim and victimizer at face value as they appear "on the surface" of public discourse. Insofar as the communication of suffering has never presupposed an a priori unity of claims to pain with the conditions of the self, it follows that the study of victimhood should start from accepting this radical contingency of the victim.

My recurrent distinction between claim and condition (or context) functions, in this sense, not as a fixed boundary that exists "out there" but as a heuristic device, a useful analytical frame through which to interrogate the relationship between the two in specific spaces and times. Therefore, instead of starting our inquiry with the quest to separate "real" from "fake" victims, it would be better to ask the questions that matter the most in the pursuit of truth: Under which conditions do certain claims to pain constitute certain selves as victims? Which positions of power do these selves speak from? What kinds of benefits do their claims accrue to them and the communities they bring together? And what kinds of exclusions do these claims presuppose and consolidate?

These questions, which I return to in chapter 4, thematize the significance of power in the analysis of victimhood. They keep us alert to the fact that claims to pain do not occur in a vacuum but are always spoken from a position that reflects and reconstitutes the systemic relationships of power that this position occupies in social space.[112] By this token, the claims to pain we encounter in public discourse are not all that exist, for there is suffering around the world that remains unseen and unspoken: "Silence," as Lois McNay says, represents "the ways in which individuals often find it difficult to put into words experiences of deprivation that are lived as feelings of shame, boredom, hopelessness and so on."[113] In this light, even though my choice of the Kavanaugh–Blasey Ford example was instructive in illustrating the power dynamics between a privileged white man whose believability has historically been taken for granted and an accomplished but relatively less privileged woman whose believability remains fragile to this day,[114] my focus on the asymmetry between the two obscures the fact that both actors possess enough symbolic power to name and define their own suffering in public.[115]

Using Sara Ahmed's Marxian metaphor of the capacity to speak as a "form of capital," I argue that claims to pain do not simply attach value to those who appear as victims, as I have argued so far, but already presuppose the existence of such value for those claimants, who in speaking out further enhance their capital for themselves. Kavanaugh's public meltdown, as we remember, occurred from a position of intersecting social and political privileges that both ensured Republican support for his election onto the Supreme Court and guaranteed his formal protection against further scandal despite a number of sexual abuse accusations beyond Blasey Ford's.[116] "The value originally advanced," as Ahmed, referencing Marx, puts it, "not only remains intact while in circulation, but increases its magnitude, adds to itself a surplus-value or is valorized. *And this movement converts it into capital.*"[117] It is this process of "capital accumulation," where some voices but not others are capable of speaking out and so gain ever more recognition, that renders victimhood both an open "market" of communication and a radically unequal one: "Being recognised as a victim," as Tami Amanda Jacoby notes, "is a right and even arguably, a privilege, not equally bestowed on all injured people."[118]

This differential capacity to speak and be heard lies at the heart of my analytical distinction between tactical and systemic suffering. For insofar as the politics of pain privileges the voices of the powerful at the expense of the powerless, the suffering of those who need to be heard the most—those whose suffering is systemic—goes unnoticed. Tressie McMillan Cottom eloquently captures this structural incapacity to be heard as a matter of distance from positions of symbolic power—a distance defined, in her words, as "the farther away you move from our dominant assumptions about who should have expertise." Speaking in particular of Black women's suffering, she says that "for Black women that means we're dealing with racist ideas and stereotypes about whose knowledge is valuable but also we are dealing with gender stereotypes about who should be allowed to speak and to lead, . . . and we are also dealing with class issues because African American women, for all of the reasons I would hope many of us know, are less likely to be represented in high income status groups."[119] In this light, reconstructing the possible connection between claims to pain and their conditions of existence so as to reconstruct the power differentials that regulate the communicative politics of pain turns out to be an important dimension of the critique of victimhood. This style of critique, as Edward Said says, involves "the use [of] one's mind historically and rationally for the purposes of reflective understanding,"[120] and it is precisely this reflective understanding that I also attempt to practice in my analysis of the concept throughout this book.

My narrative is organized around four core questions, each addressing one of the dimensions of victimhood I have discussed in this chapter: "Why Victimhood?," the present chapter, explains the reasons why it is urgent to study the vocabulary of victimhood at this moment in time; the next chapter, "Who Used to Be a Victim?," turns to the past to study the emergence of a hierarchy of victimhood across gender and race lines in emotional capitalism; "Who Is a Victim Today?" subsequently focuses on the present to examine the populist weaponization of victimhood in the recent pandemic; and, finally, "How Can Victimhood Be Reclaimed?" turns to a programmatic proposal of how victimhood can be used to the benefit of the structurally vulnerable.

Chapter 2 retains the historical sensibility of the current chapter, but in posing the question "Who used to be a victim?" it shifts focus from the languages of victimhood to the histories of the victim, specifically of the war victim during "the age of catastrophe."[121] The self is here the male soldier of modern wars, "a central and recurring image of trauma in our century,"[122] whose trajectory bifurcates in a dual fate: on the one hand, a white man who transforms from a silent warrior enduring enormous suffering in the name of national honor to an eloquent, self-reflexive professional encouraged to speak out on his (and his victims') personal pain, and, on the other, a Black combatant and, later, a non-Western (nonwhite) civilian whose suffering remains silenced or marginalized in public memory across time. Emotional capitalism is revealed in this history to be an a priori masculinist and racialized zero-sum game of collective memory that gives birth to white male vulnerability as the only worthy victim of late modernity while systematically excluding nonwhite masculinities from its affective remit.

Chapter 3 turns to the discourse of Anglo-American far-right populism in the first COVID-19 wave (broadly defined between February and September 2020), asking how Boris Johnson and Donald Trump, both elected to protect the people as victims, managed the communication of pandemic suffering at a moment when their countries were topping global mortality rankings. My analysis identifies three populist strategies of communication—*normalization*, *militarization*, and *obfuscation*—that together worked as a form of mass gaslighting to hide the human cost of the pandemic, suppress compassion for its victims, and explicitly call up or implicitly assume new victims: those whose liberties were temporarily curbed by public-health measures. In light of massive asymmetries in the infection and mortality rates of white and nonwhite populations, these strategies reveal how older racialized and gendered hierarchies of life and death are still sustained in the emotional capitalism of the twenty-first century.

Chapter 4 takes issue with this far-right politics and, using the overturning of *Roe v. Wade* in June 2022 as its example, develops a systematic critique of victimhood in two directions: first, it *raises awareness* of the linguistic tropes through which the far Right tactically weaponizes claims to pain at the service of a microfascist politics of cruelty; and, second, it *develops a heuristics of victimhood* that dissects the contexts and actors of situated claims to pain to help us better navigate the distinction between systemic suffering and tactical suffering. Informed by the normative quest of its title, "How Can Victimhood Be Reclaimed?," the chapter concludes with a recommendation for public discourse to go beyond the politics of pain and its affective responses to suffering, empathy, and anger by combining these emotions with collectivist narratives of justice—narratives that, currently marginalized as they are, dominated much of the twentieth century's drive for social change. It is only by employing such narratives in our struggles for change, I conclude, that we may ultimately come to recognize the suffering of the vulnerable precisely for what it is: a matter not of victimhood but of injustice.

2

WHO USED TO BE A VICTIM?

With the [First] World War, a process began to become apparent, which has not halted since then. . . . A generation that had gone to school on a horse-drawn streetcar now stood under the open sky in a countryside in which nothing remained unchanged but the clouds, and beneath these clouds, in a field of force of destructive torrents and explosions, was the tiny, fragile human body.

—Walter Benjamin, *The Storyteller*

MASS SUFFERING IN THE TWENTIETH CENTURY: INDUSTRIAL AND POSTINDUSTRIAL WARS

Peter Jackson's acclaimed First World War documentary *They Shall Not Grow Old* (2018) begins with the voices of British veterans at the Western Front, speaking of the horrors of trench warfare in understatement: "a job to be done," in the words of one soldier; "I'm afraid there was a little bit of slaughter," in those of another.[1] In contrast, participants in twenty-first-century Western conflicts speak openly about the emotional suffering of soldiers, not only in terms of post-traumatic stress disorder (PTSD), the psychological effects that exposure to war violence bears upon combatants, but also in terms of moral injury, the inner scars left on soldiers by the sense of doing wrong to others. "Unlike post-traumatic stress, which is a result of a fear-conditioned response, moral injury is a feeling of existential disorientation that manifests as intense guilt," Thomas Gibbons-Neff explains in reference to the U.S. veterans fighting in Afghanistan and Iraq.[2] The Iraq War veteran Tyler Boudreau contrasts the U.S. Army's skirmishes in occupied Iraq with the First World War's massacres on no-man's land: "In an occupation," he says, "there aren't going to be blood-speckled bodies stacked up around fighting holes or littered in the trenches . . . moral injury just isn't going to look like that. It's going to be dull. It's going to be a man with a shovel or a farmhouse search. It's going to be a hug."[3]

This shift in the communication of the suffering self from the understatement of "a bit of slaughter" to the paradox of a hug as injury tells the story of how the modern experience of war came to be invested onto the languages of pain, turning such experience from a soldier's unflinching dedication to a bigger cause into a psychosocial event forever scarring their personal life. But it also tells the story of whom this shift to personalized pain came to privilege as the rightful claimant of pain and whom it excludes. Peter Jackson's reliance on soldier voices in *They Shall Not Grow Old* is indicative of this implicit act of privileging. Relying on archival material from the Imperial War Museum in London, the documentary is restricted to white British veterans, thereby rendering voiceless "the vast worlds of colonial war experience and the lives of non-White soldiers," who, as Santanu Das reminds us, fought alongside white, Western troops: "Four million non-White men would be recruited into the European armies as soldiers or laborers."[4] Fast-forward to our century, "nonwhite soldiers" are now included in Western war memorials, but Jackson's choice still "reveals," as Das says, "an ingrained hierarchy" of place and human life at play not only in the memory of past wars but also, as we shall see, in the "humanitarian" wars fought by Western armies in the name of protecting non-Western civilians from violence or oppression—wars that ironically register the largest numbers of non-Western civilian casualties in the history of warfare.[5]

What this double move captures is how the slipperiness of victimhood, the open linkage between vulnerability and the self inherent in the communicative politics of pain, behaves in the long term. It reveals that the emotional capitalism of the twentieth century cannot simply be told as a story of the rise of the languages of pain: trauma and rights. Emotional capitalism should also be told as a story of voicing and silencing—a dynamic process of power that attaches those languages unequally across Western and non-Western selves. It is this dynamic of power that historically renders Western, white sufferers more visible than non-Western, nonwhite "others" in Euro-American public spheres and, in so doing, helps sustain hierarchies of humanity in global geopolitics.

Unlike in the previous chapter, then, in this chapter the vulnerable self is no longer presented as an ideal type associated with each of the two languages of pain. Rather, the self is now an embodied figure always bound up with the changing experiences of twentieth-century mass violence. The injured or the traumatized, it follows, emerge precisely at the intersection of these embodied experiences of suffering and the languages of pain available at their time as the two came together to shape how we speak and think about the victim across time. In other words, the unprecedented experience of industrialized killing and, later on, of insurgency wars helped define who is a victim, and, in turn, the languages of psychoanalysis and rights put this experience into discourse, rendering soldierly suffering meaningful to us as "shell shock" in the First World War, "post-traumatic stress disorder" in Vietnam, and "moral injury" in Iraq and Afghanistan.

This means that when in this chapter I speak about the emergence of the Western self as a suffering individual, traumatized or injured, I am not writing about a self whose corporeal suffering exists outside the narratives that describe it.[6] My interest lies, rather, in tracing how the formation of this self took place through a historical politics of pain: the uneven attachments of trauma and injury onto certain bodies rather than others and how these attachments gradually enabled some bodies to speak about their victimhood while silencing others. Far from adopting a technodeterminist approach that places technologies of killing at the heart of social change, then, my approach emphasizes instead the role that the languages of pain, embedded as they were in the power relations of twentieth-century emotional capitalism, played in shaping our memories of past wars as much as our conceptions of victimhood.

WAR SOLDIERING AND MALE SUFFERING

The suffering soldier at war has predominantly been a masculine self. In the most catastrophic events of the past century, it was male bodies as frontline army recruits who were turned into mass gun fodder—more than 99 percent battlefield casualties in the American Civil War and 97 percent in the First World War, my first case study, were indeed men. And it was those male bodies that first became the object of scientific study and institutionalized intervention. But even after the Vietnam War, when a drastic fall in combat mortality was combined with a greater recognition of psychosocial victimhood, it was still largely male suffering, as my second case study shows, that remained central in debates on war suffering. At the same time, women's participation in Anglo-American armies remains relatively low to this day,[7] while civilian women and children in the conflict zones of the global South still suffer the highest mortality ratios.

Even though, therefore, this chapter traces down the racialized politics of pain through which hierarchies of male suffering at war came to consolidate Western conceptions of the victim in public memory and discourse, gender is central to this politics, too. This focus on masculine pain does not ignore the well-established fact that women have always been constructed as more emotionally fragile, if not altogether irrational, compared to men within the masculinist rationality of modernity and its binary hierarchy of genders. It highlights, however, the fact that because such rationality was predominantly embodied by male selves,[8] men's mental breakdown in industrialized war was treated as an alarming development, which required their urgent "remasculinization."[9] In contrast, from the suffragettes of the early 1900s to the feminists of the 1960s, the public voicing of women's pain developed largely through collective social struggles, often by strategically appropriating the sociomedical discourses already established to diagnose and voice the pain of wounded men.

Early psychiatry, including nineteenth-century Freudian psychoanalysis, for instance, was originally theorized as a disciplinary technology for "unruly" female bodies.[10] Linking symptoms of mental malady with women's respectability, these early paradigms focused on treating female "hysteria" through, among other therapies, hypnosis or the "rest cure" but failed to connect hysteric behavior with the repressive environment within which women lived: "Many mental illnesses in the 19th century," Suzie Grogan argues, "were a form of protest by women against exploitation by men and the restrictions society imposed upon them in terms of behavior, ambition and independent thought."[11] However, it was only when soldiers of the First World War began exhibiting similar symptoms of reaction against the restrictions of trench life, as we will see later in this chapter, that a review took place of how the human psyche responds in repressive environments and how psychic wounds can be treated—a review concerned primarily to avoid the "feminization" of men by war. It was, indeed, "the demand for the revirilization of the demoralized soldier," as Ruth Leys put it, that "limited the deployment of the hypnotic suggestion," a treatment that was applied to soldiers suffering under shell shock early on in that war.[12]

At the same time, during that war and subsequent wars, women undertook the role of nurses and carers on the frontline, with the figure of the volunteer nurse being "understood as an extension of womanhood itself in the public imagination."[13] Even though early feminist protests, catalyzed largely through the experience of the First World War, succeeded in safeguarding women's partial participation in the political process,[14] their primary role as carers was also sustained after the war, when not only were women asked to withdraw from the economy they had kept going during the war to make room for the reentry of returning veterans, but, importantly, they also had to assume "the greatest responsibility for pulling themselves together to ensure a happy family life" in the midst of a male mental-health crisis.[15]

With female pain still publicly muffled even after the Second World War, women's struggle for voice was subsequently informed by the public recognition of the Holocaust, so that, as Diane Enns argues, "the feminist movement in the 1960s and 1970s in North America benefited from the victim discourses that arose from growing interest in Holocaust survivors," with feminists "attempt[ing] to raise awareness of sexual abuse against women by comparing it to what went on in the Nazi death camps."[16] In this effort, second-wave feminists appropriated the narrative template of disclosing trauma for their own purposes, sharing their pain in public as a radical act of turning the personal into political and so becoming at that time one of "the primary carriers of th[e] emergent therapeutic politics of identity."[17] After Vietnam, when the terminology of PTSD for war veterans was publicly established, feminists used Judith Herman's pioneering work to campaign for the recognition of domestic violence as a source of forms of suffering similar to battlefield trauma: "The symptoms of trauma which war veterans experienced," explain Cathy Humphreys and Stephen Joseph, "had much in common with the reactions by women (and a minority of men) within the domestic sphere both as survivors of childhood sexual abuse and domestic violence."[18] More recently, and as the protection of civilians, largely women and children, has purportedly become the main priority in twenty-first-century war zones, conceptions of war pain as "moral injury" are still oriented toward the care of Western armies and their practices of "killing to protect" rather than on healing the moral injuries inflicted on those supposedly under protection: "One of the glaring oversights" of this "humanitarian" conception of war, Rosemary Kellison argues, "is the near-total absence in scholarship on ethics of war of the voices of non-combatants who live through war," ignoring how war inflicts "grave damage to their most important personal and social relationships, as well as to their senses of moral self and personhood."[19]

If this chapter is a history of the victim from the perspective of soldiering masculinities, then, it is because such a perspective offers unique insights into how the historical figure of the victim emerged within emotional capitalism through long-term multi-institutional engagements with male suffering at war. Although, as I take care to demonstrate, there is no doubt that male war victimhood is a heartbreaking experience of loss and mourning for generations of young men, their families, and their communities—who can read soldiers' memoirs of the First World War without tearing up?—this chapter focuses on how this emotion and this memory of devastation and grief are unequally distributed not only in terms of gender but, importantly, also in terms of race.[20]

WAR WOUNDS AND THE POLITICS OF PAIN

Karen Halttunen draws attention to the hierarchies of race in relation to the voice and visibility of victims when she discusses the role of nineteenth-century literature in consolidating the culture of sympathy among Euro-American publics. The presence of victims, she argues, was crucial to these publics' sentimental education so that in the new literary genre of the abolitionist novel, among others, "a wide range of victims . . . [was] endlessly flogged: bound or chained, stripped to the waist, and whipped until the blood poured down and pieces of flesh flew, and the victims writhed with pain, cried out for relief, and sometimes fainted or died."[21] This graphic visibility, though, was also treated as a problem in that it was thought to misrepresent the victims' pain as fiction and therefore to numb feelings of compassion. Reflecting on the threat of compassion fatigue of "civilized societies," John Stuart Mill wrote at the time: "One of the effects of civilization (not to say one of the ingredients in it), is that the spectacle, and even the very idea of pain, is kept more and more *out of sight* of those classes who enjoy in their fullness the benefits of civilization."[22] This chapter relies on Mill's observation that the portrayal of human pain is essentially a political question of hierarchical visibility and voice—a politics of pain, in other words—in order to update Halttunen's account of historical struggles over the representation of racialized suffering in the West up to the current moment.

In this spirit, I follow the major wars of the past hundred years to reconstruct an arc of transformation of the white male self from a silent stoic to a self-expressive sufferer who speaks out on their trauma or injury. Although this shift toward voicing trauma has been celebrated for leading to a "softer," more empathetic version of masculinity,[23] and rightly so, my analysis of it also charts a parallel process of silencing of Black and Brown soldiers and later of nonwhite civilians from the global South—of all those people living outside Western zones of prosperity and safety, whether in the global South or within racially stratified Euro-American societies. Manifested in, among other ways, the selective use of combat rules and commemoration rituals, this parallel track demonstrates how emotional capitalism has systematically enabled white actors to present themselves as traumatized or injured but has left racialized "others" outside the remit of the languages of pain. Working in conjunction, the voicing of "our" pain and the silencing of "theirs" constituted victimhood as a zero-sum game that not only treated the suffering of "others" as if it were insignificant but also construed the white male sufferer as the only worthy victim. Building thus on the theoretical argument of chapter 1—namely, that victimhood is a politics of communication that separates claims to pain from their condition of suffering and so amplifies only the pain of those who already have a voice—the historical argument of this chapter highlights continuities between past and present uses of pain in public discourse.

The notion of the war victim as by default a white male sufferer, I argue next, can be studied through a focus on two chronological turning points: first, the shift from the *American Civil War* to the *First World War*, where the norm of the silent sufferer was challenged by the experience of the shell-shocked soldier as an early figure of combat trauma in industrialized war; and, second, the shift from the *Vietnam War* to the *millennial conflicts of Iraq and Afghanistan*, which illustrates how claims to white male pain fused psychoanalytic with rights-based languages of pain that define the suffering self still today—a move that also signals a departure from collectivist narratives of patriotic sacrifice toward increasingly individualistic ones of healing and self-reflection. Throughout this history, the voicing of soldierly suffering emerges not so much as a straightforward move from flesh wound to emotional suffering but rather entails subtle rearticulations in the relationship between language and pain.[24]

To chart these articulations, my account draws on Elaine Scarry's definition of war precisely as a relationship "between the war's obsessive act of injuring, and the issue on behalf of which that act is performed."[25] This definition helps me highlight how the activity of killing one another involves the attachment of soldiers' wounded bodies to broader narratives (of, say, nationhood, freedom, responsibility to protect) and how, as each war differs from previous ones, these attachments give rise to ever-changing models of the soldierly self—models of chivalric bravery or patriotic duty or humanitarian goodness. For instance, the stoic silence of wounded warriors in the seventeenth-century culture of chivalry did not mean that soldiers felt no or little pain but rather that their pain was not supposed to be communicated because it was not regarded as one of the ways they performed their masculinity: "What one felt inwardly while fighting bravely or running away was not probed too deeply," Yuval Harari says, because soldiers were then judged by their deeds, and so their "inner feelings were irrelevant."[26] A change occurred in the eighteenth-century culture of sympathy and nineteenth-century literary tradition of romanticism, which first allowed the self to express emotion in language: no longer attached to the norms of religion and "freed from the tyranny of kings," as Harari again puts it, "the inner voice of feeling" was now believed to "always favor what was good and right."[27]

This modern view of emotion as the true expression of the inner self lies at the heart of emotional capitalism still today, with the industrialized conflicts in late nineteenth century and the twentieth century being major catalysts in the gradual process of self-expression. As events of unprecedented violence and profound grief, these wars not only contributed to inaugurating the twentieth century as one of emotional introspection but also led to dramatic changes in the philosophy of warfare, in particular to the recent rise of "humanitarian" wars.[28] It is to these wars that I now turn as exemplary case studies of our changing politics of pain and their vocabulary of victimhood.

WARS OF THE NINETEENTH AND EARLY TWENTIETH CENTURY

The American Civil War

The arrival of industrial warfare in the mid–nineteenth century, in particular the American Civil War (1861–1865), had a major impact on the experience of human pain in that it exposed the body to novel techniques of wounding.[29] The replacement of slow, single-shot canons with repeating-magazine rifles, according to Christon Archer, marked "perhaps the greatest revolution" in the conduct of combat: "Range, accuracy and volume of fire increased dramatically," he notes, so that "frontal attack by cavalry and infantry became almost suicidal."[30] The emotional shock of this hitherto unknown way of war is reflected in the testimony of one Civil War eyewitness, who, startled by the violence, recounted how soldiers "marched steadily on to the mouth of a hundred canon pouring out fire and smoke, shot and shell, mowing down the advancing hosts like grass; men, horses and colors going down in confusion, disappearing in clouds of smoke."[31] The automation of killing, as this quote vividly illustrates, made a big difference not only in the war's scale—with at least 620,000 deaths, the Civil War was the bloodiest war in U.S. history[32]—but also in its manner of killing, bringing about a new awareness of bodily fragility that put under pressure the traditional narrative of the self as a stoic sufferer.

Part of the chivalric military code,[33] as I already suggested, stoicism refers to the masculine norm of defiance under duress, according to which the self who can bear physical pain without flinching is regarded as "a real man"; according to this norm, Jessica Meyer notes, "the most manly was the veteran who had suffered without complaint."[34] Even though stoic manliness came under pressure in the industrialized battles of the Civil War, nonetheless the chivalric norm not only survived but also reasserted itself in postwar national discourse. This was accomplished largely through what Drew Gilpin Faust calls "the work of death" that Americans engaged in during and after the war. New rituals of mourning and acts of remembrance, such as the institution of military cemeteries and memorials, played a key role in domesticating the shock of mass death and in bringing Americans together in a political community of grief: "Southerners and Northerners alike elaborated narratives of patriotic sacrifice that imbued war deaths with transcendental meaning," Faust explains. "Soldiers suffered and died so that a Nation—be it the Union or the Confederacy—might live."[35]

The romanticized idea of "the Nation" as a homogenous entity that encompassed all Americans, however, was challenged by the erasures that the postbellum memory project imposed upon Black Americans.[36] First of all, there was inequality on the battlefield. Unlike white soldiers, whose killing in combat followed the war's rules of engagement, for instance, Black combatants were killed indiscriminately "even when such action demanded suspension of fundamental rules of war and humanity."[37] Moreover, the massive sacrifices they made for the new nation—out of 180,000 Black soldiers in the Union army, 33,000 fell in battle, 4,000 were injured, and many more died from disease—were not recognized in the collective narratives of commemoration.[38] Instead, the national mythology absorbed Black deaths under the reconciliatory narrative of white unity between the Union and the Confederacy and forgot that the emancipation of the enslaved population was at the heart of the conflict. Speaking of the postwar struggle of Black people against this erasure, David Blight notes that Frederick Douglass's efforts to "save the legacy of the Civil War for blacks—freedom, citizenship, suffrage, and dignity[—]came at a time when the nation appeared indifferent or hostile to that legacy."[39] Indeed, in the decades following the war, the postbellum regime of Jim Crow laws in the South and segregation rules across the country produced its own structures of Black exclusion and oppression that perpetuated violence against Black citizens—what Isabel Wilkerson theorizes as a primordial "caste system," "the source of inequalities that becloud and destabilize the country to this day"[40]—even while the country was styled as a democracy of opportunity for all.

It was white supremacy disguised as national reconciliation that sustained the long-term silence over the injuries suffered by Black citizens in the war; as W. E. B. Du Bois put it, reflecting on this white rewriting of the war's history, the reconciliatory rhetoric was an attempt "to forget the history" of Black people, "to distort the story of abolition, and to pretend that slavery in America was a sign of race superiority instead of proof of moral degeneration."[41] By thus weaving what Charles Mills calls a veil of "white ignorance" over public discourse, the postbellum order not only silenced Black pain but further enabled white Americans to claim victimhood for themselves.[42] The Southern white narrative of the Civil War as a lost cause, a heroic moment of self-sacrifice, where the Southern ways of life were lost in the name of the united nation, was central to those claims.[43] Mobilizing popular art and public rituals, the postbellum period consolidated this nostalgic myth of the United States as an innocent nation "instead of looking at the war as a tragic failure," where, as Gaines Foster puts it, "the nation had failed to . . . eliminate the contradictions between its egalitarian ideals and the institution of slavery."[44]

In summary, despite the new ferocity of industrialized conflict, the American Civil War did not manage to break down the chivalric relationship between pain and language because of its ritualized pact of silence around soldierly suffering. Instead, by commemorating the white dead combatant as a noble embodiment of the nation, this war managed to replace chivalric honor with a national mythology: "In the nineteenth century, as warfare became more industrial and less a matter of hand-to-hand fighting," as Robert Nye explains, "the personal honor that now resided in the individual soldier was shared with the nation in a kind of reciprocal embodiment."[45] This sanctifying attachment, however, was not a privilege accrued to all. Not only were the deaths of Black soldiers neither recognized nor commemorated, but in the postbellum era Black citizens were also excluded, subordinated, lynched, and persecuted; and even though alternative, emancipatory narratives of collective memory around Black freedom persisted among African Americans, what has until recently remained dominant is the myth of the Civil War as white victimhood.

The First World War

A shift in the chivalric norm, already emerging in the nineteenth century,[46] was more clearly registered during the First World War (1914–1918). The first global conflict of the twentieth century, this war extended from France to Turkey (then still the Ottoman Empire) and from the Middle East to Africa, yet its public memory predominantly focuses on the Western Front, its main European battleground, with its large civilian armies locked in trenches and killing each other with lethal mechanized weapons: "It was violent even by comparison with the Second World War, in which the overall death toll was higher," argues the historian Michael Roper, as "an average of 457 British men were lost each day in the First World War, compared with 147 in the Second."[47] It was not only the First World War's scale of death, claiming approximately 10 million lives on all sides and fronts,[48] however, that challenged the norm of stoicism but also the soldiers' experience of inaction that amplified their suffering. It was a war in standstill fought out in ditches dug in muddy earth; "men," as the psychiatrist John T. MacCurdy wrote at the time, "remain for days, weeks, even months, in a narrow trench or stuffy dugout, exposed to constant danger of the most fearful kind . . . which comes from some unseen source, and against which no personal agility or wit is of any avail."[49] It was a war, in other words, that reduced martial agency to the passive anticipation of random enemy hits.

This combination of wanton violence and loss of control lies at the heart of a prototheory of trauma in the form of "war neurosis" or "shell shock" that at the time came to dominate the scientific discourse of the suffering self: "Neurosis," as Eric Leed puts it, "was a psychic event not of war in general but of industrialized war in particular" owing to "the increasingly alienated relationship of the combatant to the modes of destruction."[50] The experience of witnessing horrific scenes of suffering among one's fellow combatants without being able to help them or to protect oneself from a similar fate was a catalyst for this early theory of trauma; as Captain F. G. Chandler, a British frontline medical officer, put it, "There is the horror of seeing men and animals wounded and maimed and mutilated, or torn to pieces or lying dead in some grotesque attitude. . . . One has to inhibit nausea and disgust, and the feeling that one may oneself be like that in a few minutes' time, and I believe that it is these inhibitions that constitute the chief strain of this kind of warfare."[51]

Manifested as disturbed disconnection from one's surroundings, shell shock was a form of unarticulated horror felt by "bodies" that "were sound but they had no minds," as the memoirist Leon Standifer later put it, describing shell-shocked soldiers of the Second World War convalescing in a U.S. hospital.[52] Suspended between the psychological, where the soldiers' constant awareness of imminent death was seen to turn "'rational' fear" into "ceaseless, total dread," and the physiological, wherein such dread was evident in corporeal symptoms, including "trembling hands, startled reactions, hyper-awareness, insomnia, nightmares,"[53] this inability to communicate was early on misdiagnosed as a form of physical damage (a kind of concussion), with those failing to recover following conventional treatment executed as cowards.[54]

It was psychoanalysis, among other psychiatric approaches, that connected the two, the psychological and the physiological, in that it explained shell shock's symptoms as the somatic display of psychic wounds: "Trapped in a closed and intolerable situation beyond their control," Mark Micale writes, "men had few psychological skills for expressing directly the unbearable levels of anxiety to which they were subjected." As a result of this lack, he concludes, "they too [like women before them] were driven to the primitive language of somatic symptom formation."[55] Within this new diagnostic framework, a framework that had earlier failed to recognize a similar causality of suffering in mental illness among women, the wounded soldier broke through the ideal of the unflinching "real man" and emerged for the first time as an exhausted, traumatized fighter.[56] Although obviously not all First World War combatants suffered from neurosis,[57] this early appearance of the soldier as an emotionally fragile figure marked a paradigmatic shift in the relationship between pain and language that challenged the national mythology of the stoic warrior.[58]

Bursting through the tight confines of the chivalric self,[59] the extreme pain of trench warfare came to fully engulf this self in its own grim reality: "Injury" in this context, Scarry writes, "is here and there and there and there and everywhere he [sic] can turn his eyes, so that all the shelves and all the rooms and all the streets up and down the city are covered with blood, slaughter, battle and war."[60] Just as language broke down and combatants were swallowed up by the intensity of their psychic pain, however, language also contained the promise of recovery.

By offering soldiers the space to begin their self-narration anew,[61] psychoanalysis played a key role in the recognition of the self as a victim in two ways. It offered the Freudian vocabulary of trauma to describe war neurosis as the site of an inner conflict within the combatant, "a conflict between the instinct to preserve life and the social and military necessity for duty,"[62] and it placed dialogue at the heart of its therapeutic method—what the renowned First World War psychotherapist W. H. Rivers called the "talking cure": "a therapeutic treatment based on the principle of catharsis," as Robert Hemmings explains, "whereby the patient was encouraged to eschew repressive tendencies and give voice to the traumatic memories . . . without dwelling excessively on them."[63]

Even though the narrative of heroic sacrifice eventually survived the First World War, with the "work of death" helping, as before, in collective processes of national healing,[64] shell shock nonetheless highlighted the value of the language of trauma within and beyond the military. "In 1914," as Roger Luckhurst says, "trauma enters a new ecology of industrially and bureaucratically organized war," with "shell shock" developing "as a dynamic construction between psychology, neurology, military bureaucracy, technology, the political imperatives of warring nations and public opinion."[65] This new acknowledgment of soldierly pain with its emphasis on "talking though" inaugurated, indeed, the voicing of pain as a legitimate method of repairing the human psyche, yet, pace Luckhurst's reference to "public opinion," such a method still remained strictly confidential, confined as it was within medical and military institutions—a fact "implying," as Fiona Reid writes, "that there was something embarrassing about nervous debility despite the fact that all were vulnerable to it."[66]

This reappraisal of the vocabulary of victimhood in the First World War was not only a tentative and reluctant event but also a selective one. Just like the American Civil War, this conflict, too, recognized the psychic suffering of its white soldiers only. Informed by the imperial politics of the warring European nations, the suffering of Black and Brown soldiers recruited in the wars of their colonizers was marginalized in both psychoanalytic discourse and the commemorative rituals of the war.[67] In the British Empire, for instance, medical officers, both British and Indian, declared that Indian troops suffered "very little insanity" during the war and that "'shell shock' was practically non-existent" among them—a denial that Hilary Buxton describes as a form of "imperial amnesia."[68] In the United States, shell-shocked Black soldiers who participated in the later stages of the war were blamed for their condition, as white British soldiers had been initially, with the U.S. Army claiming the Black soldiers were racially predisposed to low mental capacity and mental illness and, on top of that, often excluding them from treatment.[69]

A parallel form of amnesia was exercised in relation to the war deaths of the colonial subjects of the British Empire. Whereas in European contexts soldiers' graves across military cemeteries included the full names of white victims to honor their memory,[70] beyond Europe practices of naming reflected the status differentials between white officers and colonial soldiers. Approximately 45,000 to 54,000 military personnel of Indian, Egyptian, Somali, and East and West African origin were commemorated unequally because the Imperial War Graves Commission decided to archive the names of local troops only in its death registers and to reserve gravestone inscriptions for British officers only.[71] A further 116,000 casualties, but likely as many as 350,000, mostly East African and Egyptian army personnel, were not commemorated by name or possibly not commemorated at all when the commission went so far as to abandon the idea of individual graves altogether and commemorated "native" troops through a single memorial stone. "Plainly," Michèle Barrett argues in her study on subalterns at war, "the lives and deaths of the 'native troops' in the First World War were not regarded as of the same value as the lives of the British."[72] It is only very recently that the Imperial War Graves Commission, in response to an independent "Non-commemoration Report" castigating its colonial omissions, has addressed this history by saying that "the failure to stand firm and practice the ideals of equality of treatment for all in Africa and elsewhere in the 1920s and the 1930s was wrong then and is wrong now, and we intend to act immediately."[73]

To summarize, informed by racialized hierarchies at the heart of Western armies, practices of silencing in the First World War legitimized a moral hierarchy of humanity that honored white deaths but excluded the Black and Brown fallen from this order of humanity, depriving the latter of the possibility to be properly mourned and remembered alongside their fellow warriors. At the same time, while the mental pain of white sufferers became slowly but surely recognized in the language of trauma and therapy, the pain of the colonized continued to remain unacknowledged, thereby reproducing in this war, too, a regime of "white ignorance" similar to that of the postbellum United States.[74]

LATE TWENTIETH- AND TWENTY-FIRST-CENTURY WARS

Vietnam War

If the First World War was the first war to acknowledge that combat harms not only the body but also the psyche, the Vietnam War (1965–1973) was the first to show that the psyche itself is not only harmed but also inflicts harm on others.[75] In this way, Vietnam became a catalyst in voicing war pain as a matter not only of therapeutic talk for its soldier-victims but also of political protest against its soldier-perpetrators. Unlike the celebrated Second World War, the quintessentially heroic war of the twentieth century, Vietnam, a guerrilla conflict fought by civilian American troops in aid of the South Vietnamese army against the Communist Vietcong, was an unpopular one, "a Bad War after a Good War."[76] The disapproval was due not only to the war's outcome, a U.S. defeat, but also to the ignominy of its strategy and tactics. As opposed to the First and Second World Wars, where dying was honorable as much as pitiful, the suffering in the Vietnam War (broadcast daily on television, for the first time)[77] was met with shame and indignation: the loss of American lives was denounced as futile and cynical at the service of a Cold War anticommunist agenda, while the civilian Vietcong deaths were seen as brutal for the local victims and brutalizing for those doing the killings.[78]

The military logistics of the war played a role in this brutalization of the U.S. soldiers' psyche as Vietnam was fought on expansive grounds where jungle conditions and hostile locals created a terrifying combat zone for the American army.[79] In the absence of territorial boundaries to measure gains and losses, U.S. foreign policy adopted a body-count approach, which encouraged soldiers to kill as many enemies as possible—with fatalities in the U.S. army reaching 58,209 and among the South Vietnamese alone estimated to be from 500,000 to 2,000,000—while simultaneously placing the soldiers themselves in constant jeopardy.[80] Casualties for Americans were indeed massive, with one in eight at risk of dying or being mutilated (as opposed to one in twenty-five in the Second World War), and even though the rotation system was meant to ensure that soldiers avoided long-term exposure to combat, for those who were exposed to it, "being in harm's way was much more constant" nonetheless.[81]

Soldiers returning from the battlefield were consequently caught up in an emotional double bind: "vilified for the very first time for the cruelty they had visited upon the civilian population" but also carrying a "psychological scar tissue," which "ensured that victimhood would become the war's main language."[82] They were, in other words, both victims and perpetrators of a war that lacked popular legitimacy. This kind of trauma was more complex than shell shock in that it combined the pain of soldiers perceived as "baby killers" with the pain of their being subjected to extreme violence. "The men who fought in Vietnam had a different sense of betrayal from the men of the First World War," writes Samuel Hynes; "they had been doubly betrayed—by the politicians and generals, and by the war protesters of their own generation."[83] Unlike in that earlier war, which never redeemed the Germans as victims of the Entente's cruelty, the antiwar protests that swept America in the late 1960s and early 1970s accused the U.S. Army of "waging a murderous oppressive war against a small people struggling to be free."[84] And it was this hybrid status of the Vietnam wound, what Ron Eyerman calls "perpetrator trauma,"[85] that the language of PTSD came to capture.

Whereas the identification of this form of trauma relied primarily on the medical diagnosis of the psychological harms that violence in Vietnam inflicted on individual veterans, the term *post-traumatic stress disorder* also reflected the era's political demands to place the responsibility for those harms away from the individual perpetrator-victim and onto the circumstances that produced the traumatic event in the first place—circumstances that referred primarily to the U.S. imperialist militarism in the Cold War and its infamous killing tactics, notably the use of the napalm bomb.[86] In its novel emphasis on context rather than on the person, Didier Fassin and Richard Rechtman argue, PTSD "introduced a radical shift in the social significance of violence," whereby "while the new concept of trauma eschewed any valuation of the individual act, it revealed the unbearable character of the event, in general." Following on the legal precedent of the Eichmann trial in 1961, when testimonies of Holocaust trauma first became legitimate voices of suffering in the public sphere, Vietnam testimonies of PTSD similarly became instrumental in locating both the civilians caught in the line of fire *and* the soldiers suffering in battle within a new, political-legal framework of human rights—a framework that recast veterans not just as killers but as wounded beings "with a residue of humanity evidenced by the traumatic memory they retained of their actions."[87]

Black veterans' participation in the Civil Rights Movement in the 1960s and early 1970s acted as a catalyst in this politicization of the PTSD experience by linking perpetrator trauma—that is, the soldiers' own victimization in the Vietnam bloodshed—with the Black experience of systemic racism within their own U.S. Army, a form of "home" violence that is in itself a documented cause of trauma and had already been registered among Black leaders in previous conflicts.[88] Black men, for instance, counted for 9.1 percent of all fighting men in Vietnam, yet their death casualties were roughly 30 percent higher than white ones.[89] Moreover, despite the fact that Black soldiers suffered from PTSD in higher rates than white veterans, with more than 70 percent of Black soldiers who saw heavy combat afflicted by the condition, their diagnosis and treatment were far more problematic than that of white soldiers, "complicated," in part, "by the tendency to misdiagnose Black patients."[90]

In the context of the Civil Rights Movement, it was this high frequency of PTSD experience among Black soldiers in particular that led them to criticize the Pentagon's Cold War agenda and identify with the colonial plight of Vietnamese civilians—a sense of affinity that led "African American soldiers," as Daniel Lucks observes, to "concur with Martin Luther King Jr.'s denunciation of the Vietnam war as 'gangrene in the soul of America'" and to show a "profound skepticism about the U.S. invading weaker, non-White nations."[91] Such forms of identification were further responsible for expanding the language of rights beyond Black people's civil, political, and legal rights within the United States and in the case of Martin Luther King Jr. to encompass an "ecumenical" discourse of justice—one that, driven by what he called "an overriding loyalty to mankind as a whole"—was committed to support decolonization struggles across the global South.[92] As Jonathan Rosenberg puts it, "The civil rights leaders identified themselves . . . as part of this 'imagined community' of reformers that wedded their domestic aims with the aspirations of those working to liberate peoples of color around the world."[93]

If these Vietnam-related struggles complicated the languages of pain by expanding war trauma from the psychological to the politico-juridical domain,[94] the post-Vietnam era also saw the radical popularization and depoliticization of the vocabulary of PTSD across societies of the global North in at least two ways. First, as a diagnostic narrative of psychic trauma, PTSD gradually broke through the strictly circumscribed practices of psychotherapy and the law into a range of other institutions, where it is "progressively applied to a wide variety of occurrences, such as rape, terror attacks, accidents, crime, etc."[95] It now forms a core part of the technocratic "technologies of the self" through which organizations manage their "human resources." By the same token, its entry into media discourse and the genres of popular television, such as the talk show and reality entertainment, saw PTSD further fuse with preexisting narrative formats of intimate self-confession—with their roots, let us recall, in Holocaust testimonials, feminist voice, and sentimental literary culture—thereby propelling the rise of therapy culture and its prolific sharing of personal pain in public.[96] Second, the vocabulary of PTSD as a human rights discourse of protection from war injury has since the Vietnam War become fully incorporated into the legal framework of contemporary warfare, leading to the thematization of suffering not only in arguments about the outcome of the conduct of war but also, as we shall see, in arguments about the cause of waging war—what Samuel Moyn calls "the self-humanization of the military under law."[97]

In summary, the articulation of war pain in the vocabulary of PTSD brought trauma and rights together in new ways. On the one hand, this articulation exposed the soldierly self as a perpetrator as much as a victim and, on the other, recognized the universality of war pain not only for the self but also for the adversarial "other." In problematizing the distinction between victimhood and violence or self and "other," the language of PTSD further politicized war suffering, locating the responsibility for war trauma away from individual combatants and onto the social contexts that enabled their violence in the first place. Even though this politicization of war pain was at the time informed by the Civil Rights Movement, the widespread recontextualization of PTSD in organizational bureaucracies and media discourses has had two ambivalent consequences: it rendered this language of pain more popular than any other before or after it and at the same time reduced it to an intensely personalized, technocratic, and instrumentalized vocabulary of victimhood across the contexts where it is used.

Afghanistan and Iraq Wars

Nowhere is the centering of the languages of pain more evident than in the West's twenty-first-century counterinsurgency conflicts in Afghanistan and Iraq—the conflicts of a multilateral world order that replaced the twentieth-century wars of sovereignty with wars of security.[98] Unlike the former, which were mass-casualty events involving primarily Western states fighting over territorial borders, security wars aspire to minimize casualties and purportedly are fought in the name of vulnerable humanity, seeking "to spare others pain or to terminate oppression."[99] The Afghanistan and Iraq Wars were waged precisely on such humanitarian grounds—namely, to protect civilians (within and outside these countries) either from the oppressive regime of the Taliban or from the alleged nuclear weapons of Saddam Hussein.[100]

Much as the humanitarian ethos of these wars puts human life, or "the individual, both the soldier and the civilian," as Christopher Coker puts it, "at the heart of the war equation,"[101] they are nonetheless waged to promote the interests of Western powers for regional influence and global control.[102] Driven by the logic of "securitized nationalism" after September 11, 2001, such wars rely on more racially inclusive army forces than ever before,[103] and they promote a rhetoric of transnational benevolence but still conduct a geopolitics of control over "threats" against the West, in particular the United States and other powers of the North Atlantic Treaty Organization alliance. As Arundhati Roy, speaking of the Iraq invasion of 2003, puts it, "Neoliberal capitalism isn't just about the accumulation of capital (for some). It's also about the accumulation of power (for some) and the accumulation of freedom (for some). Conversely, for the rest of the world, the people who are excluded from neoliberalism's governing body, it's about the *erosion* of capital, the *erosion* of power, the *erosion* of freedom."[104]

Stemming from the paradox inherent in their securitizing logic of killing in the name of saving lives, the "humanitarian" wars of the twenty-first century thus subject the soldiering self to their own distinct form of harm. It is in response to this paradox, where the self now deals with the impact of killing those meant to be cared for, that the vocabulary of moral injury first emerged as a new language of pain in military discourse.[105] Far from suggesting that all soldiers feel compassion for non-Western populations, moral injury highlights instead the normative justification that Western armies use as they fight distant wars in the name of civilians in need. It is the clash between this compassionate justification and the lethal violence of combat—manifested, for instance, in the split second when a skirmish goes wrong—that can trigger moral injury: "a profound sense of betrayal of 'what is right' either by a legitimate authority or by oneself."[106] This sense of betrayal incorporates the language of trauma as PTSD in that morally injured soldiers are seen as emotionally traumatized by their own acts of violence, but it also encompasses human rights in that those soldiers simultaneously suffer from the contradictory expectations placed upon them by the humanitarian logic when in the heat of battle they face the often impossible task of separating whom to protect from whom to attack. The difference from PTSD is that "humanitarian" soldiers' acts of violence occur now not despite their attempts to protect but precisely in the name of protection, and it is this crucial slippage that renders moral injury a distinctly insidious category of victimhood.

This novel quality of soldierly pain also configures anew the relationship between language and pain in that it highlights for the first time that the self can be hurt not only by the violence inflicted *by* others, as in the First World War, or inflicted *to harm* others, as in Vietnam, but also by the violence inflicted *to protect* others. As the journalist David Wood, speaking of a skirmish gone awry, wonders, "How do we begin to accept that Nick Rudolph, a thoughtful, sandy-haired Californian, was sent to war as a 22-year-old Marine and in a desperate gun battle outside Marjah, Afghanistan, found himself killing an Afghan boy?"[107] In recounting this episode of moral injury, Wood's words also reveal just how this language of pain draws attention to the suffering soldier rather than to his victim, for it is the (sandy-haired) American soldier, Nick, who is affectionately portrayed and fully named rather than the Afghan boy, who remains faceless and unnamed in his story. This self-oriented vocabulary of moral injury, by referring to suffering "others," consolidates compassion for "ourselves" and casts Western soldiers "not as perpetrators, but as victims of the devastation" in security wars.[108]

Like PTSD, then, moral injury works to recover a residue of humanity in the perpetrators of security wars. Yet unlike PTSD, which was steeped in collective outrage and demanded responsibility and justice for its victimized perpetrators, moral injury absorbs its own paradox of killing those one protects in an emotional register of personal care and self-reflexivity—a register that occurs, as the therapist Alison O'Connor writes, within "a non-judgmental space that is neither a therapy nor religious setting [and] where ethical and existential questions around forgiveness, reconciliation, atonement . . . can be explored."[109] The centrality of speaking out, previously part of a collectivist culture of protest for social change, is here situated within a spiritual framework of personal introspection and shared storytelling that, in contrast to Vietnam, individualizes the pain of humanitarian wars and depoliticizes its social conditions of emergence. As Rita Brock and Gabriella Litini, founders of the Soul Repair Center in the United States, put it, "To listen to veterans . . . we must be willing to engage their moral and theological questions with openness and to journey with them as we are mutually transformed in the process."[110]

By construing the Western soldier as the primary victim of their own violence to others, however, this psychospiritual discourse further elides the West's own complicity in the violence of the wars it fights. More than this, even though the compassionate soldier may be expressing their pain for the suffering of the "others" they harm, in the process they absorb the pain of the latter into their own injury and effectively silence the voice of local populations in the global South, whose rights Western armies often violate instead of protecting.[111] The journalist's voice that speaks of the death of a young boy in Iraq through the emotions of the U.S. soldier, for instance, performs precisely this task in that by "see[ing] so much of oneself in another's experience . . . one completely obscures the existence of another subject."[112] This erasure is only one way in which civilians on the ground are silenced in security conflicts. Combined with killings by the use of drones, where the death of suspect subjects is either represented as a technical matter of chessboard pieces being "knocked off" the board or euphemized as "collateral damage,"[113] this "hypervisibility" of the compassionate soldier minimizes the moral wrongness of deaths in global South conflicts and renders their loss and grief invisible to the global North.[114]

Thus, although, in summary, the "humanitarian" wars of the twenty-first century have no doubt moved away from the massacres of the previous century and have attempted to minimize the pain and death of the battlefield through a new ethos of caring benevolence, the costs of the wars in Iraq and Afghanistan and other post-9/11 war fronts—entailing more than 387,000 civilian deaths and 38 million displaced up to 2023—reveal the dehumanizing forces at the heart of this military ethos.[115] Routinely hidden from narratives of freedom and democratization, the death toll of such wars on local populations as well as their patterns of selective recognition and commemoration highlight, in fact, their continuity with colonial legacies of global power. As David Kennedy argues, these wars are fought on the assumption of "a clash of civilizations or modes of life" between "us" and "them" and so harbor an affinity to the Cold War and its "postcolonial and anticolonial conflicts from Algeria to Vietnam."[116] Instead of generating protests, however, these contemporary wars seem to keep alive an old myth: Western armies and their soldiers, white again this time, are the only victims worth honoring.[117]

THE RACIAL HIERARCHIES OF WAR VICTIMHOOD

Taking as its starting point the warring soldier as an exemplary figure of twentieth-century suffering, this chapter has focused on the work that the vocabulary of victimhood has historically performed to establish racialized hierarchies of humanity in late modernity. The chapter constitutes, in this sense, an attempt to contextualize the politics of pain and its power relations, as I put them forward in chapter 1, in the longer-term process of social change that occurred during and after "the age of catastrophe."[118] Guided by a conception of war as a structure of reciprocal injury, where wounded bodies acquire meaning through culturally specific narratives of justification (the nation, freedom, or humanity),[119] my analysis of soldierly suffering traced how the languages of pain (trauma and rights) organized these narratives in ways that cast the wounded white man as the quintessential victim of modern times.

As these narratives fused and shifted alongside changing war technologies and geopolitical orders, from industrialized conflicts to the Cold War to humanitarian conflicts, they simultaneously transformed victimhood from a condition of bodily suffering due to violence to the soldier's flesh to a condition of psycholegal suffering that affects the soldier's emotional interiority as much as their moral sense of being. Simultaneously, the shift from the materiality of the flesh to the intangibility of morality also signals a parallel mutation in war victimhood from collectivism, or war as carnage inflicted on mass armies in the name of the nation, to individualism, or war as injury that occurs within the person in the name of vulnerable humanity—a mutation that is a matter of emphasis because the two still coexist in practice.

The language of shell shock was the first to locate pain in the psyche as trauma, albeit retaining some somatic manifestation, while the language of PTSD expanded this psychological focus to include the law, where injury is further connected to civil rights violations and, more recently, to the "humanization of international law."[120] In all three cases, pain turned from something to be endured by suppressing emotion to a matter of managing emotion. Whether such management occurs though therapeutic self-confession or through rights-driven practices of protest and regimes of individual protection, this transformation suggests that the human psyche is no longer seen exclusively as the object of medical intervention but has also become an affective technology of the self—a technology of protest or introspection.

This morphing of soldierly pain into an increasingly intangible condition, where, unlike a physical wound, PTSD or moral injury leaves no visible scars, in turn contributes to the broader trajectory of emotional capitalism I examined earlier, where the communication of victimhood has now become a matter of the performativity of emotion as a marker of the true self. If pain can't be seen on the skin, it has to be felt and claimed in public. Even though I have already problematized the politics of pain for disconnecting the self from its conditions of vulnerability and for rendering the victim a radically contingent category, nonetheless it is here important to draw specific attention to a further ambivalence inherent in this turn to self-expression. By challenging the restrictions of chivalric stoicism and its suppression of feelings, the shift has indeed encouraged the emergence of a more positive, self-reflexive, and emotionally articulate masculinity of the "new man."[121] Yet as my analysis of the toxic masculinity of far-right populism in chapter 3 shows, this mutation should not be seen as a clear-cut shift from one model of masculinity to another but as a more complex shift wherein the two models coexist and the ideal of the tough man in contempt of those who are in pain can still shape public discourse—with dire consequences for the most vulnerable.

This trajectory of transformations in the soldierly self, however, is one not only of ambivalence but also of exclusion. It has highlighted the exclusion of women's pain, a foundational erasure in the twentieth century's institutional voicing of pain, and of nonwhite persons' pain—that of Black and Brown soldiers and, more recently, of civilians in the conflict zones of the global South. Whether the victims are the Black fallen of the American Civil War, the colonial soldiers of the British Empire in the First World War, the Black Americans in Vietnam, or the women, children, and men under protection in Afghanistan and Iraq, their pain, as this chapter demonstrated, has hardly been honored in history and is only selectively remembered, if at all. The case of the Afghan translators left behind in Afghanistan, powerless and in mortal danger, as Western militaries withdrew and the Taliban grabbed control in August 2021 is one recent example of this history of imposed erasures.

Our current vocabulary of victimhood relies on this history of exclusions—another reminder that vulnerability is not defined as a "universal" property of humanity but as a particular entitlement of white men as the quintessential victims of twentieth-century modernity. White men suffer as they fight, suffer as they kill, kill as they protect, and suffer for protecting. Although all these forms of pain are no doubt intrinsic to the core purpose of war as a practice of reciprocal injury, at the same time they perpetuate a conception of the Western male self as the only actor who is fundamentally good and only accidentally bad and who, for all the violence he inflicts, is deserving of medical expertise and compassion. Caught up in cycles of devastating violence but also of healing, this privileging of white male pain has at least in part endowed men with the legacy of "testimonial entitlement," of being believed when they make complaints of pain and suffering, as opposed to women, whose claims to pain have historically gone underrecognized.[122] Similarly, non-Western selves live, fight, and die without the power to speak and without recognition or memory of their own sacrifice, pain, and loss.

Emotional capitalism consequently also emerges here as a masculinist and Eurocentric project that by leaving racialized others outside the remit of emotion and memory reproduces neocolonial hierarchies of suffering and human life. The selective use of combat rules and the white narrative of reconciliation in the Civil War; the lack of personalized graves or even cemeteries for the fallen in the British colonies during the First World War; the increased recruitment numbers, the greater length of combat time, and the misdiagnoses of PTSD among Black Americans in Vietnam; as well as the disregard for "collateral damage" in both Iraq and Afghanistan are all testimonies to this active work of racial forgetting in its diverse forms and across time.

As I now move on to chapter 3, examining how struggles around the voicing of pain have played out in Western contexts in the twenty-first century, my historical account of racial forgetting is here to remind us that the communication of victimhood is already grounded on preexisting and sedimented relations of power between the global North and the global South—relations that, while fixating on the pain of the powerful, mobilize strategies of erasure to perpetuate the neglect of vulnerable "others."

3

WHO IS A VICTIM TODAY?

The result of a consistent and total substitution of lies for factual truth is not that the lie will now be accepted as truth and truth be defamed as a lie, but that the sense by which we take our bearings in the real world—and the category of truth versus falsehood is among the mental means to this end—is being destroyed.

—Hannah Arendt, "Truth and Politics"

MASS SUFFERING IN THE TWENTY-FIRST CENTURY: THE FIRST PANDEMIC WAVE

"This is the worst public health crisis for a generation," Boris Johnson, then prime minister of Great Britain, announced on March 12, 2020. "I must level with you, level with the British public, many more families are going to lose loved ones before their time."[1] This was a whole two months after COVID-19 had been identified in China as a virus of concern, five weeks after the WHO had declared it a global emergency, and a month after the prime minister's speech at the Royal Naval College, where he referred to the virus as a "nuisance" that could damage his Brexit economy: "When there is a risk that new diseases such as coronavirus will trigger a panic and a desire for market segregation . . . then at that moment humanity needs some government . . . willing at least to make the case powerfully for freedom of exchange."[2] On March 8, in a similar spirit President Donald Trump announced that the U.S. economy would not be threatened by the new disease because COVID-19 had killed fewer people than the flu: "So last year 37,000 Americans died from the common flu. It averages between 27,000 and 70,000 per year. Nothing is shut down, life and the economy go on. At this moment there are 546 confirmed cases of coronavirus, with 22 deaths. Think about that!"[3] Both Johnson and Trump were late taking public-health measures as cases soared in their respective countries, and when Johnson eventually announced the United Kingdom's first lockdown on March 26, Trump was still bargaining deaths with money: "You're going to lose a number of people to the flu. But you're going to lose more people by putting a country into a massive recession or depression."[4]

After more than 230,000 deaths in the United Kingdom and more than a million deaths in the United States,[5] these leaders' failure to act promptly to protect their populations has since come under critical scrutiny. The U.K. House of Commons Science and Technology Committee report of 2021 spoke of "major deficiencies" in the first phase of the pandemic, where the government "made a serious early error in adopting this fatalistic approach [the impossibility of suppressing transmission] and not considering a more emphatic and rigorous approach to stopping the spread of the virus." A U.S. congressional investigation was equally critical of the Trump government: "Trump Administration officials engaged in a persistent pattern of political interference in the nation's public health response to the coronavirus pandemic[,] . . . making harmful decisions that allowed the virus to spread more rapidly."[6] As a result, during the first wave, both leaders inflicted more COVID-19-related death and suffering upon their nations than almost any other nation in the world—with the United States first and the United Kingdom third in the global rankings for excess deaths in 2020.[7]

In the context of this public-health crisis, the most serious in a century, in this chapter I ask how the two governments—both elected on the promise to protect their people from external harm (inflicted by the "corrupt elites," the "European Union bureaucrats," or the "migrants")—managed the challenge of communicating the suffering and death of the pandemic, largely caused by their own policies, to their national communities. One answer is that they did so through lies, and, indeed, these lies have already been thoroughly scrutinized by both journalists and academics.[8] My argument, however, is that we need to go beyond the singular focus on deception. We need to approach the two leaders' discourse as a broader set of communicative strategies that are reflective of authoritarian or far-right populism discourse, its Anglo-American versions in particular,[9] because this discourse has something important to tell us not so much about these populist leaders' pandemic failures but, importantly, about the politics of pain and its *performance of victimhood* in our times.

If chapter 2, then, was a history of the victim as a white male figure that emerged in "the age of catastrophe" through the investment of wounded bodies in Western languages of pain, this chapter focuses on the present to examine how the figure of the victim was performed by two white male leaders in two of the world's wealthiest democracies, the United Kingdom and the United States. Each with important legacies of political liberalism, these democracies were nonetheless ruled by authoritarian populists who came in power via the liberal system and from within the ranks of their respective conservative parties:

the Conservative Party (or the Tories) and the Republican Party. It is this intersection of the pandemic as a key moment of twenty-first-century mass suffering with authoritarian populism as a politics of cruelty intrinsic to liberalism that renders the United Kingdom and the United States an instructive case study on the perils of contemporary victimhood.[10]

AUTHORITARIAN POPULISM AND VICTIMHOOD

A rich and diverse body of work, accounts of authoritarian populism converge around the diagnosis that liberal democracy is today threatened by a mix of far-right, ethnonationalist, and white-supremacist forces that seek to undermine democratic institutions and civil society "from within" and to impose tyrannical political structures based on the one-man power of self-interested strongmen.[11] In authoritarian populism, Aurelien Mondon and Aaron Winter say, democracy is redefined as "power being held by the people (demos) for reactionary ends"—a power that, despite Trump's subsequent electoral defeat and Johnson's ousting from Downing Street, is just as real a global threat right now as it was back then.[12] This corrosive process occurs, theorists argue, through the division of the political community into categories of "Us" and "Them," where populist leaders emphasize "the need to defend 'Us' (our tribe) through restrictions on 'Them' (the 'other')."[13] In so doing, authoritarian populists install a primary antagonism within the community between a vulnerable "people," populism's primary political subject in need of defense, and a threatening "other," someone "deemed to oppress or exploit the people and therefore to impede its full presence."[14]

In its reliance on "the people" as a figure of suffering, I propose, populism can be seen as a historically specific manifestation of the communicative politics of pain that mobilizes the languages of trauma and injury as symbolic catalysts for the formation of political community.[15] Although all democratic discourse shares a common origin in the politics of pain, as I mentioned in chapter 1, routinely drawing on these two languages to promise to alleviate the suffering of citizens through narratives of redemption,[16] populism differs from other democratic discourse in that it uses such narratives to place the people as victim in relations of *enmity*, rather than antagonism, to their opponents and to mobilize emotions of resentment and outrage toward those opponents: "Pain, discomfort, suffering and deeply held grievances are as much a driver for populist mobilization as they require appeasement and healing," Filipe Carreira da Silva and Mónica Brito Vieira explain, so that "the more people feel wronged by the system, the more likely it is for them to listen to populist claims of redemption."[17]

Along these lines, Nadia Urbinati has developed a definition of populism that centers precisely on the relational dynamics of victimhood and enmity. Populism, she argues, consists of "a triangular symbolic space around three actors and their relationships: the people, representing the innocent victim, the political class, as the malicious rogue and ... populist leaders as 'the redeeming hero.'"[18] Indeed, whether in the language of emotional trauma, as when Trump described the people as "forgotten," "ignored," or "American carnage," or of social injury, as in Johnson's description of Brexit politics as an attempt to "take back control" and restore Britain's long-lost self-determination, the communication of pain lies at the heart of the populist justification to rule.[19]

My own focus on the relationship between populism and victimhood stems from a particular interest in identifying the symbolic strategies through which populist leaders appropriated (consciously or otherwise) the languages of pain in their attempt to communicate the tremendous suffering they inflicted upon their own people during the first pandemic wave.[20] Rogers Brubaker has already theorized this tension between promising to protect people and letting people die as populism's "paradox of protection," raising the question "Why has populism turned anti-protectionist during the pandemic?" Even though, Brubaker explains, "we think of populism as protectionist," in the sense of "claiming to protect 'the people'—economically, demographically, culturally, and physically—from threats," nonetheless, "faced with the Coronavirus [sic], populism has been anti-protectionist"; it has taken the side of "openness against closure" and challenged "what they ['the people'] see as the overprotective nanny state."[21] This stance is exemplified in my opening quote from Johnson, when his stern forewarning to the nation—"I must level with the British public, many more families are going to lose loved ones"—cast the people no longer as victims but as inevitable casualties of the virus and himself as a "pragmatic" leader facing reality head-on.[22]

However, whereas Brubaker offers neoliberalism as his explanation for this paradox of protectionism, my own approach provisionally suspends the question of "why" and starts with the question of "how": How did populist discourse mobilize the languages of pain in its communication of pandemic suffering? How did this discourse rework the redeeming hero/innocent victim binary that is so central to populist politics? And what does this pandemic politics of pain tell us about victimhood in the emotional capitalism of the twenty-first century? Informed by a performative understanding of populism as an open-ended process of the articulation of pain with various narratives of redemption from such pain, these questions aim to identify the symbolic strategies through which Trump and Johnson conjured up particular emotional attachments and communities of grievance to serve their own political agenda.[23] Despite their differences, the two leaders shared a similar cruel indifference to their people and a similar will to weaponize pain to their own benefit: "Johnson's political approach has always been a muted and cosier version of Trumpism, adapted to British political conditions," Patrick Cockburn commented in the *Independent*. "Both men are political campaigners of proven effectiveness plugging into nativist fears and ambitions. In contrast to Trump's divisiveness, Johnson specialises in appeals to national unity and support for the NHS [National Health Service], yet the consequence of having these two leaders in office during the pandemic has in both cases been a great number of people dying."[24]

The two leaders' authoritarian populism, I explain, employed three strategies of communicating pain—*normalization* (the virus is just the flu), *militarization* (the pandemic is a war), and *obfuscation* (hydroxychloroquine cures the virus)—that together sought to ignore the suffering of the people and to attach victimhood to a privileged few. In so doing, on the one hand they turned the lives of racialized minorities, Black and Brown women in particular, and of essential workers, mostly belonging to such minorities,[25] into ungrievable lives, and on the other hand they reinvented the victim in the figure of those few who claimed to suffer from the trauma of lockdowns or from the civil rights violations of compulsory masking—in a kind of "reverse victimhood" that, instead of protecting, exposed their communities to further risk (see the subsequent section "Strategies of Populist Victimhood").

It is this erasure of pain combined with appeals to reverse victimhood (explicit or implicit), I conclude, that shows authoritarian populism to be a key mechanism in the reproduction of societal hierarchies of human life in emotional capitalism today.[26] In line with the politics of pain, discussed in chapter 1, this perpetuation of hierarchies worked by dislocating the link between *systemic suffering*, experienced by the classed, racialized, and gendered groups most likely to be exposed to the virus, and *tactical suffering*, claimed largely by antilockdown and, later, antivaxxer activists—a minoritarian community of far-right libertarians that was nonetheless legitimized and in the United States openly encouraged in public discourse.[27] While, as we shall see, the systemically vulnerable suffered the highest number of deaths, the voice of the tactically vulnerable was amplified on social media as they protested for a life without restrictions. The erasure of the vulnerable in authoritarian populism should, from this perspective, be seen as part of the practice of forgetting that we encountered in my history of the victim in the previous chapter—one that reveals the ambivalence of platformized pain as both a resource of compassion and a catalyst of cruelty (see the subsequent section "The Suppression of Compassion: Pain and Cruelty").

STRATEGIES OF POPULIST VICTIMHOOD

Of the three communicative strategies of populist discourse, the first one, *normalization*, was used in February–March 2020 to deny the severity of the pandemic threat and delay the imposition of measures; the second, *militarization*, was abruptly introduced in mid-March as the mood shifted from life as usual to emergency lockdowns and was employed largely to downplay the emotional impact of mass deaths and to stir up anger against the "enemies" of the people; and the third, *obfuscation*, ensured the circulation of false or misleading information that covered up the government's infliction of pain onto the people while allowing/enabling new tactical appeals to victimhood to gain visibility within the nation's political community.

Normalization

"This is a flu. This is like a flu," President Trump said in an official government briefing on February 26, 2020, one of the multiple times that he repeated this assertion in the early days of the pandemic: "It's a little like a regular flu that we have flu shots for. And we'll essentially have a flu shot for this in a fairly quick manner." The same discourse was still dominant in the United Kingdom as late as March 5, when the prime minister said, "Don't forget, even if you get this illness, for the overwhelming majority of people, even in the elderly groups, it will be mild to moderate," while in the same interview he described how he continued to interact with people without taking precautions: "I've been going round hospitals as you can imagine and always shake hands. People make their own decisions. Washing them is the key rather than barring all forms of human [contact]."[28] Trump followed this practice, too, as he was often seen to shake hands and take selfies with people well into March 2020.[29]

By "normalization," I refer to the strategy of ignoring or downplaying the increasing threat of the virus so as to construe a "business-as-usual" version of reality that maintained a sense of uninterrupted continuity in people's everyday life. Whether in the form of euphemisms (flu), behavioral modeling (shaking hands), or institutional classifications (U.K. governmental advisers, for instance, keeping the risk level of the virus as "low" and then "moderate" until mid-March 2020), this strategy set the scene for a comforting sense of normality in the first six weeks of the pandemic, when, despite rapidly rising infection numbers, the U.S. and U.K. governments had little to no engagement with COVID-19.[30] As late as March 11, 2020, when Italy reached 827 deaths and other European countries (Spain and France) were about to shut down, Trump was still comparing COVID-19 with the "regular flu," and the U.K. Scientific Advisory Group for Emergencies rejected the possibility of a lockdown.[31]

The two countries differed in some ways, of course; for instance, the United Kingdom more explicitly considered a "herd immunity" approach that Johnson described as allowing "the disease to make it through the population" while protecting the most vulnerable, and this approach was widely criticized by experts for "lead[ing] to a catastrophic loss of human lives without necessarily speeding up society's return to normal."[32] Both the United States and the United Kingdom, however, ended up topping international metrics in terms of COVID-19-related excess deaths, or the number of deaths over and above what would be expected in noncrisis conditions, with 122,300 excess deaths in the United States and 65,700 excess deaths in the United Kingdom.[33] Further estimates indicate that earlier lockdowns would have saved 36,000 and 20,000 lives, respectively, in each of the two countries.[34] Employed at the same time as the world was witnessing the COVID devastation in Wuhan, China, and Bergamo, Italy, normalization thus worked as a strategy of denial that lulled people into unprotected encounters with the virus and led them to mass contagion and death—what the U.K. Health and Science Parliamentary Committee report called a "self-inflicted" "veil of ignorance through which the UK viewed the initial weeks of the pandemic."[35]

One of the key implications of normalization was that it rendered irrelevant any narrative of redemption that might have enabled the mitigation of this tragic loss of life. For, insofar as the world remained "normal," according to this approach, any attempt to encourage people to take protective measures and save lives would be, to echo Johnson's words, "unnecessary" or "panic-triggering." Within the scope of normalization, it was protective measures, not the virus, that were cast as a "threat." In his study of elite discourse in the U.S. media, Austin Hubner establishes that such discourse consistently "grounded COVID-19 as a threat to one's way of life *rather* than a serious threat to one's health."[36] Brigitte Nerlich and Rusi Jaspal similarly observed that early government communication on COVID-19 in the United Kingdom "construct[ed] social distancing as a threat to people's sense of continuity."[37]

Trump's and Johnson's desire for social life to continue uninterrupted despite the warnings situate normalization squarely within a neoliberal discourse of government, a discourse that regards individual and market freedom as matters of self-regulation rather than state control.[38] Evident in Johnson's commitment to avoid "market segregation" driven by coronavirus "panic" and in Trump's insistence that "nothing is shut down, life and the economy will go on," not only did this logic delay public-health measures but also, as we shall see, produced a vocabulary of victimhood that led to an alternative set of claims to pain: lockdown as injury, an infringement of people's rights that undermined their livelihoods, or as trauma, for instance in Trump's (false) claims that isolation would lead to rising suicides: "People get tremendous anxiety and depression, and you have suicides. . . . Probably and—I mean, definitely—would be in far greater numbers than the numbers that we're talking about with regard to the virus."[39]

Concerns around the potential traumas and injuries of lockdown measures were inevitably also present among liberal democratic governments, of course, and rightly so. Conditions of continuous unemployment and/or prolonged isolation, particularly in unsafe contexts, can lead to serious forms of violence, such as increased poverty, mental-health decline, and domestic abuse, especially toward the most vulnerable, such as women and racialized minorities.[40] Whereas many of those other governments took measures to mitigate the implications of such measures, the far-right weaponization of trauma and injury at the service of a libertarian discourse of freedom, in which the personal choice to mingle and consume weighed more heavily than the collective responsibility to protect lives, was a distinctly populist feature. Driven by the two leaders' specific interests—namely, boosting the Brexit economy for Johnson and being reelected for Trump—this libertarian discourse rendered the United Kingdom the last but one European country to implement a lockdown and the United States an uneven patchwork of state lockdowns.[41]

Normalization, in summary, was a strategy of denial that prolonged a false sense of normalcy and safety in both countries at the cost of thousands of lives. Informed by a libertarian logic of freedom as individual choice, this denial of the COVID-19 threat construed pleas to protection as constituting a threat to everyday life and rendered irrelevant a redemptive narrative that would have properly prepared people for the risks of the virus.

Militarization

"We must act like any wartime government and do whatever it takes to protect our economy. Yes, this enemy can be deadly, but it is also beatable—and we know how to beat it[;] . . . however tough the months ahead, we have the resolve and the resources to win the fight."[42] Boris Johnson's words on March 17, 2020, signaled the end of normalization by declaring war against the virus. Like Johnson, who used the third-highest number of military references in his discourse on the pandemic compared to twenty other world leaders at the time, Trump also employed martial language routinely.[43] For instance, in a COVID-19 press conference on March 18, he said, "It's a war, I view it as a, in a sense, a wartime president. . . . It's the invisible enemy. That's always the toughest enemy. But we are going to defeat the invisible enemy. . . . It'll be a total victory."[44]

The notion of "militarization" captures this metaphorical way of speaking about the pandemic as war, which works to bring the invisible threat of viral contagion onto the concrete terrain of a face-off between enemies and, in so doing, establishes a set of "structural correspondences . . . between the virus and an enemy, health professionals and an army, sick or dead people and casualties, and eliminating the virus and victory."[45] Even though this metaphor was commonly used in many countries,[46] I argue that authoritarian populism employed militarization not only to construe the COVID-19 infection risk as a battlefield, as other political approaches did, but also uniquely to model people's feelings about the pandemic along the lines of a warlike masculinist hardiness. It did this, on the one hand, by *de-emotionalizing* people's suffering—that is, by suppressing the expression of grief—in its discourse and so rendering narratives of consolation and redemption unnecessary in public communication and, on the other, by *re-emotionalizing* the pandemic experience through a new antagonism between "Us," or the nation, and "Them," or other nations, migrants, racialized minorities, and, in the United States in particular, public-health experts and measures as sources of popular oppression.

The absence of empathetic language in Johnson's and Trump's communications was a key factor (though not the only one)[47] contributing to the de-emotionalization of pandemic pain. Going back to Johnson's cynical forewarning, "I must level with the British public, many more families are going to lose loved ones before their time," we can now see how it contributes to the militarization of the pandemic by naturalizing COVID-19 deaths as inevitable sacrifices in the battle against the virus rather than by grieving them as preventable and unnecessary tragedies of thousands of lives cut short. Resonating with broader references to Britain's wartime experience (for instance, in the health minister's statement about the pandemic as a "generational test analogous to our forefathers' Second World War" and in the multiple comparisons to the Blitz),[48] this militarization of the pandemic sought to bring the national community together around a spirit of "resilience, stoicism and camaraderie" reminiscent of that "Good War," when "the British public . . . showcased their famous stiff upper lip" to the rest of the world;[49] similar militarized references to Pearl Harbor were made in the United States.[50]

Such references signal what in chapter 2 I examined as the chivalric spirit of war—an affective orientation of soldierly endurance under duress characteristic of "real" manhood. In tension with the languages of pain and their civil pedagogies of compassion, this militaristic language was appropriated by the two white male leaders to downplay the widespread sorrow that marked the pandemic experience in both countries. When, for instance, Trump was confronted with the rising number of deaths among his own rally attendees, which he did nothing to avert, he replied: "They are dying. That's true. And you—it is what it is but that doesn't mean we aren't doing everything we can."[51] And when called to acknowledge the bereaved relatives of COVID-19 victims in the first wave of the pandemic, Johnson made scant acknowledgment of their grief and instead attacked the leader of the opposition, jokingly mentioning his "Calvin Klein briefs"—a response that was widely condemned for its inappropriateness: "That's hardly the response of the party of compassionate Conservatism," Labour protested at the time.[52]

Manifested not only in language but also in public gestures of insubordination against measures of public protection, such as the refusal to wear a mask or keep social distancing (remember Trump's and Johnson's handshakes and selfies in crowds), this macho performance, what Jayson Harsin calls an "aggressive masculine performance of trustworthiness," regards empathy as an "admission of personal vulnerability," in Christina Cauterucci's words, and seeks to avoid it.[53] Johnson's biographer, Sonia Purnell, shed light on this stance of toxic masculinity when she wrote about his hospitalization for COVID-19 in April 2020: "He has a very weird attitude to illness. He was intolerant of anybody who was ill. Until now, he has had a very robust constitution . . . and this will be a huge shock to him. His outlook on the world is that illness is for weak people."[54] This attitude may in part, at least, explain how his government allowed for COVID-19's devastating impact on care homes and hospices, which accounted for 44 percent of the total of excess deaths in England and Wales in March–June 2020.[55] Trump echoed this sentiment when he similarly gestured toward a hierarchy of lives, hailing the resilience of "the young," while "othering" the elderly as dispensable: "It affects elderly people. Elderly people with heart problems and other problems. . . . That's it. You know, in some states, thousands of people, nobody young. Below the age of 18, like, nobody. . . . You look—take your hat off to the young because they have a hell of an immune system. But it affects virtually nobody."[56] Even though there are differences between the two, with Johnson as an early victim of the virus appearing more cautious than Trump,[57] both nonetheless relied on a hypermasculinized discourse, which by privileging unflinching resilience muted grief and turned up the anger against the "enemies" of the people.

Re-emotionalization, then, involved the construction of threat through blame. This is the case when Trump named COVID-19 "the Chinese virus," fueling anger toward the East Asian population of the United States and leading to a significant rise in racist attacks against Asian residents across the country, and when he blamed the Black Lives Matter protests for the rise of COVID-19 cases as part of his effort to discredit the movement and amplify white-supremacist fury against it.[58] In the United Kingdom, Johnson's attack on the care homes staff for the homes' staggering number of deaths (the highest in Europe) sought to shift responsibility from the government's failure to protect the elderly onto the health-care workers, many of whom were dying in serving those homes—the very "heroes" he simultaneously called U.K. citizens to celebrate.[59]

The construction of heroes, indeed, took place through appreciative references to medical staff, such as in the "clap for our carers" campaign in the United Kingdom, which stirred up a sense of national togetherness around the valiant work of "our" care workers.[60] Such idealizations of the nation's doctors and nurses as self-sacrificial soldiers at the frontline of the war have been criticized for creating unrealistic expectations of individual workers when the institutional contexts in which they were employed failed to protect them.[61] The 119 deaths of NHS staff in the first month of the first U.K. lockdown were all a result of the lack of COVID-19 protective equipment across hospitals and care homes—a consequence of governmental negligence and its drive for private profit during the pandemic as much as of longer-term austerity cuts in the NHS.[62]

The combination of this building up of "our" heroes and the vilification of "our" enemies helped thus establish a narrative of redemption that centered on national victory against the virus; recall here Johnson's "we have the resolve and the resources to win the fight" and Trump's "we are going to defeat the invisible enemy.... It'll be a total victory." Militarization aimed, in this sense, to construe "the nation" as a homogenous and united community of hardened citizens bound together by their gratitude toward their valiant compatriots and by their enmity toward their dangerous "enemies."[63]

What this construction of unity concealed, however, were the deep structural inequalities that divided each nation along race, gender, and class lines in ways that led to disproportionate losses among its most vulnerable communities in comparison to the losses from (largely white) middle-class communities.[64] From March to July 2020, for instance, mortality rates in the most-deprived areas of the United Kingdom were double those in the least-deprived areas, with the highest excess mortality rates observed in poorer regions such as Northwest and Northeast England; at the same time, mortality rates among Black and Brown groups were "up to three times higher than those of the White population," while the mortality rates of people in frontline and lower-waged occupations were double the rates of middle-class people.[65] The picture was similar in the United States, where a Johns Hopkins study reported that "to date, of 131 predominantly black counties in the U.S., the infection rate is 137.5/100,000 and the death rate is 6.3/100,000.... This infection rate is more than 3-fold higher than that in predominantly White counties." Moreover, an MIT report suggested that "black women as a group are four times more likely to die of COVID-19 than White men."[66] And even though mortality rates among Black men was the highest of all social groups, Black women were indeed the most vulnerable of the vulnerable. As Denise Obinna argued in January 2021, they "[are] disproportionately represented as 'essential' or frontline workers" and so more at risk of contagion, yet at the same time they "often lack job security," while "they are also at risk of having their symptoms minimized or dismissed by medical practitioners even when they show visible symptoms of COVID-19."[67]

The strategy of militarization was launched in mid-March 2020 to swiftly replace the earlier, misleading sense of normalcy with a new bellicose extraordinariness that worked in two ways. It de-emotionalized the mass death toll in the United Kingdom and the United States, downplaying grief and ignoring people's feelings of loss, and at the same time it re-emotionalized pandemic suffering through a redemptive narrative of national victory with its own set of heroes and villains that glossed over governmental failures and structural inequalities within the national community.

Obfuscation

"Our country remains extremely well prepared," Johnson assured the British people in March 2020 as deaths from COVID-19 in Italy reached 79. "We already have a fantastic NHS, fantastic testing systems and fantastic surveillance of the spread of disease."[68] In reality, however, not only was the NHS already depleted of infrastructural and human resources, but at the start of the pandemic the U.K. government also quickly channeled "eyewatering sums of money" to private partners and left the public-health system struggling to care for its sick.[69] At the same time, while the rest of the continent was preparing for the months to come, the U.K. government was doing very little to catch up.

As a Reuters COVID-19 report noted, "Between February 13 and March 30, Britain missed a total of eight conference calls or meetings about the coronavirus between EU heads of state or health ministers—meetings that Britain was still entitled to join"—thereby also missing the opportunity to participate in the union's purchase scheme for ventilators, to which Britain was invited.[70] Around the same time, Trump echoed the line wherein U.S. preparedness was so robust that it did not even need to be tested because, he claimed, the virus was transient and would "go away": "We're prepared, and we're doing a great job with it. And it will go away. Just stay calm. It will go away," he said on March 6, a line he repeated seventeen times in the February–June 2020 timeline as daily cases soared from zero to 40,000 daily and "U.S. deaths increased by 20% during March–July 2020."[71]

These are just two examples of obfuscation, a strategy consisting of the dissemination of false or misleading information with the intention of concealing facts and confusing people's understanding of how the pandemic was governed. Part of what the WHO called an "infodemic,"[72] pandemic obfuscation was made up not only of fake assurances but also of the manipulation of science and scientists, conspiracy theories about the origins of the virus, and the encouragement of bogus treatments. An example of the latter is Trump's recommendations for the use of the antimalaria drug hydroxychloroquine and later of the horse antiparasitic ivermectin as COVID-19 "cures"—both part of his broader weaponization of presidential authority to undermine the U.S. Centers for Disease Control and its scientists.[73] In the United Kingdom, Johnson confidently promised that the U.K. test-and-trace system would be "world-beating," yet, as the journal *Nature* notes, he "abandoned [it] with no explanation," then "scrambled to ramp up testing in April [2020], but

[it] repeatedly failed to meet its . . . targets, lagging weeks behind the rest of the world."[74] Johnson also sought to cover up government mistakes that led to record deaths among the elderly by falsely claiming that he had ordered an earlier lockdown for care homes.[75]

Obfuscation is in this context a strategy that relied on the deliberate employment of lies, half-truths, and manipulated facts not simply to conceal the truth of government failures but also to blur the very distinction between truth and falsehood and to replace the former with emotional investment in aspirational narratives.[76] This emphasis on the emotional appeal of fake stories draws attention to the ideological function of obfuscation as a spreader of "emo-truths"—that is, of personal views that are not true but "feel" authentic to the like-minded and, as such, have the power to bring people together around their preexisting ideological attachments.[77]

Social media platforms, in particular Twitter, were central to the reproduction of Trumpian emo-truths and the formation of his affective communities of outrage, and they simultaneously used such "truths" to generate enormous profits for themselves.[78] Even though disinformation was also fueled by bots and users' evasion of the platforms' fact-checking technologies,[79] it was Trump's mass-mediated discourse that acted as the most decisive amplifier of all. Indeed, as a study of 38 million articles around the world demonstrates, "mentions of President Trump within the context of COVID-19 misinformation comprise by far the largest single component of the infodemic," occupying no less than 37.9 percent of the overall misinformation conversation.[80] The use of Twitter by Trump, "the most conspiracy-minded president in modern history,"[81] not only reinforced his supporters' fictitious beliefs but also sought to undermine public understandings of the stay-at-home recommendations made by his own White House. By tweeting "LIBERATE MICHIGAN," "LIBERATE MINNESOTA," and "LIBERATE VIRGINIA" to his 77 million followers in April 2020, Trump incited a backlash against expert-informed public-health advice, and in a call for insurrection against federal leaders of the opposition party, he encouraged his far-right supporters—the vast majority of whom were "white, cisgender, heterosexual, Protestant and native-born U.S. citizens"—to break the lockdowns of the first wave.[82] Although his followers were only a "minority," their "tweets including anti-mask hashtags were significantly more likely to use toxic language" and, generally, "tactics of verbal aggression" than pro-lockdown hashtags, thereby amplifying a far-right counternarrative of resistance to COVID-19 measures along the lines of the appropriated refrain "my body, my choice."[83] This rearticulation of rights as libertarian freedom in the redemptive narrative of authoritarian populism is, according to Jack Bratich, a "microfascist" practice of "necropopulism" that "under the banner of specific types of people (White, masculinized, Christian), seeks to extinguish the life that allows any people to persist."[84]

With the exception of his early weeks of normalization, Johnson eschewed the obfuscation effects of such platformized necropopulism, even though some of his "rebel" Conservative Party members of Parliament joined the far-right politician Nigel Farage—whose "Get Brexit Done" message Johnson used in his electoral victory in 2019—in antilockdown protests around the country.[85] Johnson himself implicitly endorsed a similar libertarian discourse of freedom when his reluctant introduction of public-health measures framed them as evil, albeit inevitable, restrictions that limited "the ancient, inalienable right of freeborn people of the United Kingdom to go to the pub."[86] This was similarly evident in his naming of July 4, 2020, the day that pubs and restaurants first reopened in England, as "Freedom Day" and further obvious in his equally apologetic message when he reintroduced restrictive measures in September 2020: "It is very difficult to ask the British population uniformly to obey guidelines in the way that is necessary," Johnson said, because he was "deeply, spiritually reluctant to make any of these impositions, or infringe anyone's freedom," given that "virtually every advance, from free speech to democracy, has come from this country."[87] So deeply embedded is the libertarian instinct of individual freedom among his compatriots, a "reluctant" Johnson suggested, that even a temporary constraint upon their liberty to dine out felt "very difficult." What remained persistently absent in this discourse was an assertive defense of public-health measures that would spell out the government's moral commitment to saving people's lives and would robustly defend its COVID-19 mitigation measures while addressing legitimate civil concerns about the impact of the restrictions on people's rights.[88]

To conclude, despite their significant differences, both leaders mobilized equivalent strategies of communication, all of which drew on a toxic discourse of tough masculinity that at first denied the severity of contagion while it continued to obfuscate information around it; then subsequently minimized the suffering of the people, ignoring dramatic inequalities in illness and death rates among social groups and vilifying some of those groups as responsible for their suffering; and finally employed a libertarian discourse of freedom that legitimized the grievances of antimask and antivaxx groups. This libertarian discourse, in turn, enabled and in the United States actively encouraged a necropopulist activism of reverse victimhood among a far-right minority, drawing attention away from the pandemic's massive risks to life and further endangering those already at risk.

THE SUPPRESSION OF COMPASSION: PAIN AND CRUELTY

In this chapter, I brought insights from my history of the concept of victimhood, as developed in chapter 1, and of the victim as a historical figure of modernity, from chapter 2, into the present moment to analyze the Anglo-American populist communication of the pandemic as an exemplary politics of pain in the twenty-first century. My assumption has been that insofar as authoritarian populism considers victimhood to be a crucial terrain of struggle for hegemony, that populism can be regarded as a historical-specific mutation of liberal modernity and, as such, participates in and capitalizes on modernity's communicative politics of pain.

Born within emotional capitalism, where "the people" functions as a linguistic signifier of liberal democratic politics and its promise of redemption from suffering, the distinctiveness of authoritarian populism lies in weaponizing the suffering of the people against them so that it ends up undermining liberalism and inflicting more pain on the most vulnerable. Inspired by research that takes its starting point in the antagonism between the people as victims and their "enemies," I thus proceeded to analyze the symbolic strategies through which populism articulated pain with redemption to create its own vocabulary of victimhood during the first wave of the pandemic.

Under the lens of normalization, the possibility of pandemic suffering was denied, rendering the languages of pain unnecessary, and preventive measures rather than the virus were instead seen as a form of pain and a threat to normal life. In militarization, pandemic pain was restored as a threat to public health in the form of the virus as enemy, but with redemption taking the form of an introverted nationalist narrative that suppressed the languages of pain and ignored but also partly vilified those most vulnerable to the virus—namely, racialized minorities, migrants, and frontline workers—as well as those clinically at risk. Finally, obfuscation construed pandemic restrictions as a form of pain that would be redeemed through the return of freedom: an appropriation of the language of rights that cast those opposing such measures as the true victims of the pandemic.

Together, those strategies worked as a form of mass gaslighting, a concerted effort to mislead the national community and distort the experience of pain among the victims while strengthening the populists' own political power over them.[89] In the face of record numbers of unnecessary deaths in both countries, populist gaslighting did not just ignore people's grief but also revealed whose lives are defined to really matter most and whose do not. For even though denial, unfeeling language, and the tactics of deceit were harmful for all, it was, let us recall, specifically racialized and gendered poor communities that silently paid a disproportionately high price,[90] while it was white, far-right groups that spoke out most loudly of their own supposed suffering.

Insofar as populist gaslighting legitimized and amplified such acts of reverse victimhood, then, it has been more than a mechanism of social forgetting. It has also been a mechanism of voice and community making for those minoritarian[91] white supremacists who resisted lockdowns and mask wearing as forms of emasculating oppression and weaponized the language of rights to the service of their own "limitless White desire."[92] Driven by entitlements around who owns public spaces and who dominates others, this reverse victimhood reproduced a "presumption of unfair treatment, persecution, and disproportionate suffering because of one's Whiteness" that demonstrated a profound contempt toward socially and clinically vulnerable bodies.[93]

Those minoritarian communities were predominantly visible online, using tags and hashtags to create frequent viral waves of sentiment on Twitter and Facebook,[94] and their online virality was instrumental to the amplification of white grievance during the pandemic, particularly in the United States.[95] It was the platforms' algorithms and recommendation systems, geared as they are to prioritize hostile language and outrage at great profit, that helped spread these groups' inflammatory far-right rhetoric far beyond the groups' restricted online networks. Further boosted by Trump's "LIBERATE" tweets, these minoritarian voices ended up touching upon "a far larger iceberg of right-wing resentment that [was] stewing at home as they read and transmit[ted] the tweets and Facebook posts, the 'truth' as they [saw] it, insisting the coronavirus lockdowns or mask mandates [were] violating their freedom and liberty,"[96] and eventually flooded the streets of major cities in antilockdown marches and protest rallies. Contrasting the invisible labor of racialized communities during lockdowns with the annoyed boredom of far-right protesters, Kumarini Carreira da Silva speaks precisely of this entitled white victimhood as a form of "thoughtless, mundane cruelty, that emerges from a much longer history, which includes settler colonialism and slavery" and that lies at the heart of "contemporary systems of value for human life."[97]

This amoral disregard for the lives of others, shockingly explicit in authoritarian populism but, as chapter 2 reminded us, also silently present in the very tissue of Western modernity, exposes the politics of pain as a double-edged sword of emotional capitalism—a structure mutable enough to be used at the service of empathy as much as of cruelty. The paradox of victimhood, as I identified it at the start of this chapter, may then not be a paradox at all in that what appears to be a contradictory position of claiming to care and letting die is, in fact, constitutive of the Janus face of liberal pain. Cruelty emerges in and through pain as a dual politics of communication capable of collective compassion and noble commemoration as much as a necropolitics of forgetting, erasure, and mass gaslighting. In the final chapter of this book, I turn to the question of what exactly this dual politics of pain and cruelty consists of and how we can challenge it.

4

HOW CAN VICTIMHOOD BE RECLAIMED?

A powerful person has committed an offense; this offense is an injustice for someone . . . who cannot really fight or take revenge, and who is in a profoundly unequal situation. So, what can [the witness] do? [They] can do one thing: [they] can speak, at risk and danger to [themselves], [they] can stand up before the person who committed the injustice and speak.

—Michel Foucault, *The Government of Self and Others*

VICTIMHOOD AS LEGACY AND STRUGGLE

"There can be nothing higher or more critical than the defense of innocent, unborn life," U.S. state representative Jim Olsen, a Republican, said on May 19, 2022, in the Oklahoma House.[1] This was a mere five weeks before the overturning of the *Roe v. Wade* legal precedent of 1973 by the U.S. Supreme Court, rendering the right to abortion conditional on the federal politics of states. The idea of the fetus as a victim that needs to be defended, as "innocent, unborn life," lies at the heart of the rationale for this overturning. As Feminists for Life, a pro-life organization, proclaimed, "When someone asks about exceptions for rape and incest, we must also consider how that makes those feel who were conceived through sexual assault," and, quoting the words of a graduate student described as a "rape child," it asserted: "I have a right to be here." Pitching the actual pain of people enduring rape against the imagined pain of an aborted embryo, this rhetoric of the unborn child—verbalized here by an adult, pro-life activist—mobilizes a politics of pain to invest the pro-life cause in the language of rights: the right to survive. This same pro-life rhetoric turns those who decide to have an abortion into perpetrators. By depriving unborn embryos of their right to exist, those people are seen to commit a form of violence that is comparable to the violence of rape: "She would never pass on the violence that was perpetrated against her to her own unborn child," the pro-life site declares of a rape victim's decision to continue with their pregnancy. "Now *that* is the strength of a woman!," it concludes, echoing a (post)feminist vocabulary of empowerment in its reference to the "strength of a woman."[2]

This reversal of victimhood is, of course, not new. We encountered it in chapter 3 as a communicative strategy of authoritarian populism, which, by treating the far-right antimaskers as an "oppressed" group seeking "liberation," swapped the suffering of the vulnerable, those most open to the risks of COVID-19, for the inconvenience of those who felt oppressed by having to wear a mask. We also identified it in chapter 2 not as a contemporary feature of political discourse but as a broader pattern of communication that highlighted the victimhood of Western soldiers in the "war on terror" over the victimhood of unarmed civilians in the global South—whose killing by those soldiers was euphemized as "collateral damage." And we further noted this reversal in chapter 1 with Brett Kavanaugh's performance of outrage regarding what he considered to be a defamatory campaign that threatened his promotion to the Supreme Court when he was accused of sexual assault by Christine Blasey Ford.

Full circle to this chapter, it is Kavanaugh again who, together with others, took the historic decision to overturn the *Roe v. Wade* legal precedent: "The bodies of girls, women, and other people who can get pregnant," as Kate Manne observes, are now "being policed and controlled by a legally sanctioned, court-appointed, supremely powerful alleged assailant."[3]

Just as in 2018 Kavanaugh claimed victimhood for an unrealized harm against him so as to discredit the woman publicly accusing him of attempted rape, so in 2022 he claimed a hypothetical form of victimhood, that of an aborted fetus as the object of murder,[4] to discredit pro-choice people as criminals and deprive those pregnant of the right to have control over their bodies.

Victimhood as Legacy

My first argument in this book—namely, that victimhood is not a stable identity but a contingent and malleable speech-act, *a linguistic claim* to suffering that bears no necessary relationship to the structural vulnerabilities the claimant may be experiencing—speaks precisely to these historical realities of reverse victimhood and their role in sustaining societal hierarchies of life and livelihood. Because of the overturning of *Roe v. Wade*, for instance, everyone who can get pregnant is subject to the law's intimate policing of specifically their bodies, but Black and poor persons in particular once again bear the brunt of state surveillance and because of their lack of access to safe options take life risks in making decisions about their pregnancy: "'Abortion-vulnerable' is racially coded and classed too"; as Susan Cohen shows, "we know Black women are five times more likely than white women to get abortions, while Latina women are twice as likely as white women to do so."[5] We also know that abortion has long been consolidated among the poor. As Jenna Jerman, Rachel Jones, and Tsuyoshi Onda show, "In 2014, three-fourths of abortion patients were low income—49% living at less than the federal poverty level, and 26% living at 100–199% of the poverty level."[6]

Similarly, we earlier saw how authoritarian populism spoke of the "people" as a unified national "front" against the pandemic "enemy" yet reproduced power divisions between a white middle-class relatively protected from COVID-19 and "essential workers"—that is, largely working-class, ethnic-minority, and migrant populations that suffered the consequences of their daily contact with the virus.[7] The history of this systemic inequality goes further back to earlier struggles around soldierly bodies and their voices of war. Such struggles, let us recall, hegemonized white over Black suffering, rendering the pain of the latter invisible and irrelevant to public memory.

This centering of victimhood helped us then highlight how race and gender, central as they are in the *experience* of pain, remain hidden in the *communication* of pain in ways that legitimize unequal, patriarchal, and colonial social orders. At the heart of this legacy in the communication of victimhood is what in chapter 2 I identified as a disconnection or disarticulation between body and pain. This means that those bodies who suffer the most are not necessarily able to speak out on their suffering because the languages of pain may not be accessible to them even though those languages are always open to appropriation by other bodies with more symbolic capital. It is exactly this unmooring of bodies from their circumstances of vulnerability, gendered, classed, or racialized, that the Supreme Court's "pro-life" decision reinforces. By employing the vocabulary of victimhood to give voice to the fetus as "unborn life" with the right to live, this ruling decouples pregnant bodies from their own circumstances of vulnerability, with all the risks to life these circumstances entail.[8] In so doing, it further deprives these bodies of the capacity to decide what is best for them and to protect themselves.

That this suppression of rights co-opts a "pro-woman" rhetoric, as the Feminists for Life example suggests,[9] highlights my second key argument in this book: even though vulnerability is not equally distributed among social groups, the political work of victimhood is to "universalize" the claims to suffering made by powerful voices while silencing claims by those less powerful speaking out about their suffering. Far from reflecting the human condition, victimhood, I have argued throughout, is a particular type of politics, a *politics of pain*, that not only selectively endows certain bodies with the capacity to speak out on their pain but in the process also invests those bodies with further legitimacy through the use of various narratives of justification, redemption, or critique—including the "pro-women" critique of abortion.[10] The aim of the politics of pain is, from this standpoint, to authorize certain bodies as human and worthy of emotion, here the fetus-as-body narrative, while dehumanizing and erasing others: the pregnant bodies that while being harmed remain under suspicion of harming others.[11] Indeed, this co-option of "feminist" critique at the service of the state's misogynistic, nativist agenda leads not simply to the stripping of pregnant people's rights but also to what I earlier referred to as their actual criminalization: "All pregnant women, not just those who try to end a pregnancy," as Lynn Paltrow and Jeanne Flavin say, "will face the possibility of arrest, detention, and forced intervention as well as threats to and actual loss of a wide range of rights associated with constitutional personhood."[12]

Insofar as it contributes to sustaining societal hierarchies, victimhood, this example suggests, should not be viewed simply as a communicative claim to pain but as an entire social logic of reproduction and change that is, in fact, constitutive of *emotional capitalism*. A twentieth-century mutation of the Western culture of sentimentality, emotional capitalism is founded upon an affective politics of communication that, as I argued in chapter 1, emerged through the languages of pain, trauma, and rights to produce the suffering self as a moral subject worthy of recognition. This subject accumulates symbolic capital by successfully claiming victimhood for itself, while creating its own exclusions and erasing those who do not fit within its own definition of the victim. Trauma and injury, I showed in chapter 2, greatly contributed to reshaping the white male self of the twentieth century away from stoicism and toward a self-expressive recognition of white men's own fragility; yet in this positive development, these same languages silenced or criminalized those experiencing enslaved and colonial or neocolonial pain—a silencing we also encountered more recently in the claiming of victimhood by authoritarian populists, wherein their promise of antilockdown liberation deleted compassion from their narrative of redemption.

Victimhood as Struggle

For all their exclusionary effects, however, the implications of those legacies of victimhood are more complex than the erasures they produce. This is because the politics of pain inherent in emotional capitalism, entangled as it may be with the interests of the powerful, is nonetheless still the only resource we have for shoring up emotions for the sufferer—empathy for them or outrage for their evil-doer—and so for nurturing cultures of solidarity, altruism, and protest against systems of oppression. As in my opening example of the Kavanaugh versus Blasey Ford stand-off, so it is in the overturning of *Roe v. Wade* that a politics of pain is germane not only to the pro-life narrative of the far-right establishment but also to its opposition. Not just the patriarchal politics of policing pregnant bodies, in other words, but also a feminist politics of resistance relies on appeals to empathy. If the former advocates against the right to body sovereignty, the latter pushes back and defends pregnant bodies as victims of the patriarchy. Likewise with outrage. The pro-life crowd's performative anger attacks those supposedly doing violence to "unborn children," but the pro-choice activists are equally vocal about their indignation regarding the law's misogyny. In June 2021, massive protests were mobilized in the United States and the world over to denounce the slashing of pregnant people's rights and demanding change: "Liberate abortion," a placard in a U.S. demonstration read. "It's time to start to ovary-act," said another.[13] "Grievances orient the action of social movements," Paolo Gerbaudo writes; "in a way they are the 'origin' or 'cause' of social movements. The grievance is a problem deemed to have detrimental effects on individuals and society at large."[14]

My third and final argument of the book, then, is that this *mutability of pain*, residing as it is in the slipperiness between *claims to victimhood* and *conditions of vulnerability*, lies at the heart of struggles for social change. In chapter 2, we saw how victimhood was never a linear or homogenous process of transformation from masculine reason to feminine emotion but precisely a site of struggle around the relationship between pain and the self. According to Stuart Hall, let us recall, social change is a relatively open process of articulation, where the languages of pain enter into ever-changing contestations over who claims to be a victim, from which position, and to what ends. Laurent Berlant, among others, has highlighted this transformative potential of empathy in her study of nineteenth-century culture of feminine and proto-feminist publics. Fellow feeling toward suffering "others" developed through routine literary encounters with the characters of sentimental novels, Berlant argues, and it was this sentimental education that encouraged women to share their own pain with one another in their own "intimate publics" outside the masculinist conversations of the public domain: "the motivating engine" behind such "publics," Berlant observes, "has been the desire to be *somebody* in a world where the default was being *nobody*, or worse, being presumptively *all wrong*: the intimate public legitimizes qualities, ways of being and entire lives that were otherwise deemed puny or disregarded."[15] As chapter 2 showed, however, it was eventually a parallel genealogy, namely the multi-institutional engagement with male suffering at war that propelled the public legitimization of the languages of pain from shell shock to PTSD.

Alongside empathy, the demand for rights has also been central to social change both in the form of collective struggles over workers' pay, women's right to vote, and civil rights in the late nineteenth century and the twentieth century—where, as Neil Stammers puts it, "ordinary people, working together in social movements, have always been a key originating source of human rights"[16]—and in the form of institutional protections for vulnerable persons in postwar global governance, or what I called in chapter 1, respectively, the *revolutionary* and the *reformative* versions of rights. In the second decade of the twenty-first century, we witnessed #MeToo, a massive online movement that used claims to gendered trauma and injury to bring together a global community of people against sexual violence.[17] We cannot say, course, that Me Too is not fraught with contradictions. Just like Berlant's sentimental publics centered the Black slave as a vehicle for the affirmation of an exclusively white sentimentality, so the Me Too publics produce their own exclusions by keeping the voices of marginalized survivors out of the movement's testimonials of suffering.[18] Nonetheless, both have opened up vital spaces for the articulation of pain as a mode of resistance to patriarchal violence, still promising, as Hester Baer contends, "possibilities . . . for new subjectivities and social formations."[19]

In the rest of this chapter, I navigate this space of cautious optimism to reflect on the limitations as much as on the promises of the politics of pain for social critique. Informed by the uses of victimhood as I have so far examined them, I first provide a rethinking of pain as a dual politics not only of compassion but also of cruelty (in the section "Pain and Cruelty") and subsequently propose a method for the critique of pain: a heuristics of victimhood that involves both the *sharpening of our awareness* about how cruelty operates today through specific linguistic tropes of victimhood and *the critical interrogation* of those tropes with a view to crafting new narratives of justice—narratives that combine the languages of pain and their emotions, empathy and anger, with explicit argument and informed judgment (in the section "Victimhood and Critique").

PAIN AND CRUELTY

The uses of the languages of pain by the powerful has already been theorized as "antivictimism." In her study of politics in the United States after September 11, 2001, Alyson Cole succinctly speaks of the weaponization of victimhood by the far Right so as to "persistently target racial politics, feminism and other forms of oppositional politics" and put forward their own brand of victimhood "by devising and promoting new groups of victims." For instance, Cole continues, "this movement recently succeeded in codifying fetuses' status as victims into law by amending legislation designed to reduce violence against women to include the Unborn Victims of Violence Act of 2004."[20]

Although Cole's study examines the rise of antivictimism at the turn of the twenty-first century, she and others locate its roots in the reactionary discontent with the legislative and social reforms that, following the U.S. civil rights and feminist struggles of the mid-1960s, worked in favor of those groups hitherto excluded. Feeling resentful of the ways these movements managed to push for broader structures of democratic inclusion for Black people and women, the conservative, white-supremacist parts of the middle class attacked oppressed groups for "playing the victimhood card" and then cast themselves instead as the "true victim" of the system. "As white men especially began to lose some of their systemic privileges in the wake of the minority rights and women's revolution," Robert Horwitz suggests, "they condemned the revolution as a politics of victimhood."[21] In this sense, the overturning of *Roe v. Wade* was an antivictimist project that was a long time coming and is now accomplished, for, under the guise of addressing what Judge Samuel J. Alito called "a critical moral question,"[22] this project managed to turn a partisan claim of the Evangelican far Right into a legal fact in many states.

The scope of the antivictimist agenda, however, is larger than its anti-abortion campaign and encompasses, among other programs, the authoritarian populisms we examined in chapter 3. By usurping the language of rights, far-right antivictimism ignores vulnerable groups' own right to life and instead attaches claims to pain to its own redemptive narrative: for instance, the promise of freedom in the midst of mass death. Further evident in Trump's and Johnson's macho performance of handshakes in the first COVID-19 wave, this narrative repeatedly enacted a specific version of manliness that combined the hardiness of stoicism in its indifference to illness and death with a toxic version of male fragility in its emotional outbursts of outrage and, in this way, encouraged a necropopulist sensibility that spoke of the people as victims but let people die en masse.[23] Although necropopulism was primarily a "suicidal" sensibility in that its performances were not just cruel to others but also "indifferent to [its] own persistence,"[24] my emphasis here falls on how such indifference goes beyond authoritarianism and is embedded in a broader necropolitical regime of postrecession/postpandemic capitalism that today more than ever endangers the structurally vulnerable.[25]

What this necropolitics of the present further encompasses is the relentless assault against Black lives in the United States, visualized most tragically in the viral video of George Floyd's murder;[26] in hostile anti-immigration practices, from Trump's policy to separate children from parents in 2018 to continuing border deaths to this day (with a U.S. record high of 728 deaths in 2021);[27] and in the overall rise in class inequalities that today are "probably higher than in any other society at any time in the past, anywhere in the world."[28] Necropolitics is similarly present in the United Kingdom, where migration policies have included, among others, the relocation of asylum seekers to Rwanda—an unprecedented violation of refugees' rights that puts their lives at serious risk;[29] where, because of sustained rollbacks in social and welfare support in 2010–2019, life expectancy has fallen for the first time since the Second World War, with prepandemic excess deaths already reaching a record 330,000; and where poverty has increased more than two-thirds over the past decade, to the point that 42 percent of families with three (or more) children are living below the poverty line.[30]

A more global outlook confirms this rise of inequality in the twenty-first century, so that in a range of countries the gap between the rich and the poor is for the first time on course to returning to levels previously seen at the time of the First World War: "It took two world wars to wipe away the past and significantly reduce the return on capital [against the growth of the economy]," says Thomas Piketty, but it is likely that this inequality will "again become the norm in the twenty-first century, as it had been throughout history until the eve of World War I."[31] With one of the greatest manifestations of inequality in the global South being the unequal distribution of COVID-19 vaccines during the 2020–2021 rollout, in which 71 percent of the eligible population in the WHO Africa region (i.e., excluding North Africa) still remained unvaccinated by October 2022.[32]

This necropolitical hegemony suggests not only that the onslaught against the structurally vulnerable exists side by side with the spread of the languages of pain but that it is in fact the latter, the very proliferation of these languages in antivictimist narratives, that legitimizes the former. In other words, the claimed victimhood of the privileged enables and legitimizes the onslaught against the vulnerable while keeping their suffering unheard—"compassionate conservatism" was, after all, the brand of both G. W. Bush, the "war on terror" U.S. president, and the U.K. Brexit Conservatives from David Cameron to Rishi Sunak, whose first speech as prime minister in October 2022 made a reference to his party's "capacity for compassion."[33]

In a manner reminiscent of the colonial dialectic of voicing and silencing I examined in chapter 2, here, too, claims to pain by "Us" entail unspeakable cruelty to "Them." And while the category "Them" has always been gendered and racialized, structural vulnerability is today increasingly widening to engulf populations that were previously shielded from its violence in the United Kingdom and beyond: "A decade of cuts has ripped apart the safety net. People on decent salaries hit by the COVID-19 fallout are in for a shock," wrote Polly Toynbee in an article for *The Guardian* entitled "The Middle Class Are About to Discover the Cruelty of Britain's Benefits System" in late March 2020.[34]

Cruelty is here an apt word choice. Defined by "two core features," as Brent Steele puts it, "the pain of others and the enjoyment in and of such pain,"[35] cruelty is, in this account, not the opposite of empathy but a potentiality inherent in the politics of pain itself. Indeed, as I have so far shown, cruelty is the current juncture of emotional capitalism that spins this politics in the direction of at once consolidating empathy for the privilege of the few and expanding cruelty for the many—what chapter 1 examined as the commodification and platformization of pain in postrecession/postpandemic neoliberalism.

The fusion of the languages of pain with market discourses evident in, among other things, the branding of humanitarianism as feel-good e-activism that avoids spectacles of suffering "others" manifested itself in different ways during the pandemic.[36] For instance, the populist strategy of normalization reflected a similar prioritization of the market and its economic imperative for continuous consumption over the mitigation of imminent mass suffering as a matter of national emergency. By insisting that "the economy will go on," both Johnson and Trump spoke through a neoliberal discourse of government that avoided any reference to COVID-19 and cast people primarily as consumers rather than as citizens committed to care for themselves and others. In a similar manner, "personal responsibility," which was the dominant postlockdown rhetoric in the United Kingdom, modeled the ideal citizen along the lines of a neoliberal entrepreneurialism driven by self-interest rather than by public commitment to care for one another and for the most vulnerable in society.

Likewise with social media platforms. Given that the right wing enjoyed "higher algorithmic amplification than the mainstream political left,"[37] particularly in the United States, where Trump led libertarian protests, fake news and trolling were significantly multiplied in populist online discourse on the pandemic. Disinformation campaigns, let us recall, spread politically motivated emo-truths, such as the "COVID as flu" myth, that led to mass gaslighting as well as to the contagion and death of people in the thousands, while at the same time far-right virality consolidated thin and dispersed offline communities of reverse victimhood into visible and loud protest movements in the streets. Whether by normalizing pain and privatizing social responsibility or by obfuscating reality and galvanizing communities of white resentment, the politics of cruelty capitalizes on this neoliberal platformization of pain so as to cause harm in new ways.[38]

In all these examples, however, cruelty emerges as more than a passive indulgence in the pain of others. It appears rather to enact "a conscious disregard—even contempt—for other people's pain," a "disregard" coming specifically "from those in a position of power to do something about the cause of distress."[39] From this standpoint, pandemic suffering may have been an extreme moment of mass suffering through which to highlight the cruelty of U.S. and U.K. populisms, but it is not a one-off instance. Rather, authoritarian populism is only one, albeit acute, manifestation of the global normalization of far-right cruelty beyond the Anglo-American world. From Hungary to India to Turkey and from Brazil to Italy, "the culture of cruelty," as Henry Giroux claims, "has taken on a sharper edge as it has moved to the center of political power, adopting an unapologetic embrace of nativism, xenophobia and white nationalist ideology, as well as an in-your-face form of racist demagoguery."[40]

Theorized by Enzo Traverso as "postfascism," this politics may lack the theoretical coherence of twentieth-century fascism, yet it is nonetheless reminiscent of that fascism in its reliance on illiberal leadership, lack of compassion, and contempt for humanity, all the while employing the languages of pain to normalize various forms of violence and to undermine democratic institutions.[41] More insidiously, Bratich argues, this post- or "microfascist" sensibility constitutes today a widespread affective sensibility of everyday life, manifesting itself online as "resentment, rage, shitposting (a will to freedom as transgressive and 'fun'), and strategic abjection (claims to victimhood)," while nurturing dispositions of nihilistic cynicism, an indifference to life, and a will to kill and be killed.[42]

By the same token, antivictimism, so far discussed as a rhetoric of the far Right, appears to be something more dangerous. It has become one, albeit perverse, manifestation of the communicative politics of pain through which emotional capitalism routinely reaffirms and reproduces itself today. It is for this reason that the question of *how* to resist the microfascist normalization of cruelty in public discourse is currently so urgent. How do we move on from here? How can we recognize and challenge the symbolic tropes of cruelty in our collective conversations? How can we interrogate those tropes and reclaim the languages of pain within narratives of justice?

VICTIMHOOD AND CRITIQUE

Emotional capitalism may have encouraged the formation of the liberal self as a moral subject whose pain is worthy of recognition, yet this self is at once also a subject of cruelty enacting and subjected to various forms of violence—from the white ignorance of colonial suffering to masculinist hierarchies of lives and livelihoods to pandemic necropopulism and its reproduction of these hierarchies in the present moment. This coupling of liberal pain with cruelty is impossible to fully disentangle. The two are inherently coemergent. Humanism and violence, altruism and domination, benevolence and enslavement, the civilizing mission and colonial expansion are parts of the same history of Western modernity. No one has theorized this more fully than postcolonial thinkers.[43] Speaking of how liberal humanism applies to colonial experience, Frantz Fanon, for instance, observed, "When I search of Man [sic] in the technique and style of Europe, that same Europe where they [are] never done talking of Man, and where they never stop proclaiming they [are] anxious for the welfare of Man . . . , I see only a succession of negations of man, and an avalanche of murders."[44] In the face of this duality of pain as a source of both benevolence and violence, what we can do, I propose, is apply the tools of social critique so as to question the politics of pain *from within* and *against itself* and to reclaim its languages, trauma and rights, so as to craft alternative narratives of redemption.

To this end, I adopt Edward Said's version of critique as a humanist project that, rather than upholding a "universal" notion of the human as white and male, seeks to uphold those who have historically fallen outside the remit of humanity and thus aspires to "speak about issues of injustice and suffering within a context that is amply situated in history, culture, and socio-economic reality."[45] I see this situated mode of critique as a fertile starting point for the interrogation of the politics of pain—a politics that, in contrast to Said's call for contextualization, presents dominant claims to victimhood as "universal" and in this way severs such claims from the contexts they appear in and from the selves that embody them. My critique of the politics of pain thus unfolds in two moves. The first involves the identification of the tropes of cruelty in public discourse as a way to sustain and sharpen our awareness about the subtle means by which the vocabulary of victimhood commits acts of symbolic violence in everyday life (in the subsection "The Symbolic Tropes of Cruelty").

The second move proposes a heuristics of victimhood, a set of questions, that can help us challenge narratives of antivictimism and guide us to reemploy the languages of pain in narratives of justice for the benefit of the structurally vulnerable (in the subsection "The Critical Interrogation of Victimhood").

The Symbolic Tropes of Cruelty

The identification of tropes of cruelty as a practice of critique draws attention to some of the concrete ways that the languages of pain are weaponized to legitimize microfascist agendas in public discourse. If the strategies of normalization, militarization, and obfuscation, discussed in chapter 3, are macrostrategies of political communication employed in the pandemic to misrepresent the violence of authoritarian governments that ruled in the name of victims, tropes of cruelty are microtechniques of language use that normalize microfascist dispositions to violence in the mundane contexts of daily encounters, while at the same time they "abnormaliz[e]," as Bart Cammaerts puts it, "social justice struggles like anti-racism, anti-sexism and pro-LGBTQ rights . . . as extreme deviant political positions."[46] Being aware of how these tropes perform the political work of antivictimism is an important step toward resisting that work. Keeping in mind that these tropes are *both* historically sedimented *and* relatively open to change, here is my open-ended inventory of some key tropes of cruelty in everyday use today: affective centering, idealization, linguistic reversal, semantic disidentification, euphemism, temporal projection, and universalization.

- *Affective centering*: This term refers to the compassionate centering of the already-privileged in stories about their infliction of violence and harm on vulnerable "others." The Blasey Ford–Kavanaugh example has already illustrated how the logic of affective centering operates when the languages of pain are mobilized not for the benefit of the female sufferer but at the advantage of a powerful, thrice accused, but never investigated man as the "true victim." An example of what Kate Manne calls "himpathy,"[47] this form of affective centering highlights the masculinist bias already inherent in the politics of pain—a bias manifesting itself as "a rhetorical template by which (usually white) men in positions of privilege could start taking up the mantle of victimhood as their own, often by claiming to be victims of (or, vulnerable to) false accusations of sexual harassment and assault by women."[48] More than this, by attending to the emotions of men, such narratives of victimhood simultaneously withdraw compassion from the femininities involved in the story, dissuading them from putting forward their own testimonies for fear of humiliation or punishment—as, indeed, was the case with Blasey Ford, who received numerous death threats after her testimony against Kavanaugh.

Like himpathy, the trope of the "Karen," originating in Black communities' tweets but now circulating beyond them, signals a parallel structure of affective centering wherein white female selves capitalize on their racial privilege to present themselves as victims of Black violence. Despite its longer history, the "Karen" as a trope that configures "entitled white supremacy and class privilege"[49] gained popularity in the spring of 2020 with a video testimony by a Black man, Christian Cooper, of a white woman who called the police while pretending to feel threatened by his presence—a case of "white female tears" weaponized to produce effects of cruelty against racial others.[50] By co-opting a traditional binary of gender roles, the female sufferer and the male abuser, within a racist narrative of Black criminality, affective centering here organizes its antivictimist argument around the stereotypical figure of the Black "thug" as a threat to a white woman.[51]

- *Idealization*: If himpathy skews storytelling toward an affective affinity with perpetrating masculinities, idealization projects a normative view of the female victim as a figure of pure innocence untouched by the messiness of social relations. A trope of maximal expectations, idealization sets the bar of virtuousness too high and requires that suffering femininities live up to this standard in order to be recognized as legitimate sufferers—with those who present themselves as messy, contradictory selves with emotional or nonlinear stories to tell not only remaining unheard but being accused as perpetrators.[52] Even though the myth that women's testimonies are largely "lies" predates modernity,[53] the modern construction of femininities as "tainted witnesses," Leigh Gilmore argues, is related to the valuing of masculinist contexts of judgment and their truth norms of objectivity and respectability as the ideal for all truth telling: "Truth," Gilmore explains, "is marked as a cultural production entwined with our notions of gender so completely that even the structural underpinnings of truth production are masculinist . . . from the formation of rules in confession to the installation of a man as judge."[54] And in part at least because of this systemically defined deficit in female credibility, a form of "testimonial" injustice,"[55] five in six women who are raped in the United Kingdom do not report it to the police.[56]

The Johnny Depp–Amber Heard trial in May 2022, where a lesser-known actress accused her Hollywood star husband of domestic violence and ended up being judged as guilty of defamation, is a case in point. Largely played out on the scene of social media, this was a trial where Depp was able to garner massive waves of platformized himpathy, whereas Heard, a tainted witness, failed to perform the "labor of believability" required of female victims and, as a result, also failed to "feel" credible and inspire trust and compassion.[57] The result was a relentless and overwhelming wave of misogyny masked as moral righteousness, where the obsessive spread of platformized hate—through memes, Tik Tok videos, tweets, and so on—turned Heard into "an online super-villain" that confirmed the sexist myth of women as liars.[58] By assuming believability to be a quality only of "pure" sufferers, the Depp–Heard trial illustrates how idealization works in tandem with himpathy as a trope of cruelty— one that at once vilifies women for not being perfect *and* centers men as bearers of testimonial privilege and objects of empathy (recall chapter 2) in line with preexisting hierarchies of victimhood. As Manne observed on the trial, "This is just what happens when a woman accuses a rich and powerful white man of sexual and domestic violence. . . . Such a woman must be a perfect victim—or maybe simply perfect—to avoid becoming the target of a smear campaign against her on the Internet."[59]

- *Linguistic reversal*: Rather than operating at the level of *storytelling*, as the previous two tropes did, this one operates at the level of *vocabulary* and relies on the reversal of the terms *victim* and *perpetrator* for a similar narrative effect: the recentering of empathy away from the former and toward the latter. Kyle Rittenhouse, a far-right white vigilante who in 2020 crossed state borders to kill two people protesting the killing of a Black man, Jakob Blake, was publicly called a "patriot" and a "hero" by top Republicans, including Trump ("I feel bad for this 17-year-old boy").[60] He was further protected by police officials, who claimed that he acted "in defense" of "small business owners."[61] Empathy is here, as before, attached to the killer, while it is denied to the dead: the judge did not allow for Rittenhouse's victims to be called "victims" in court because "the phrase is too 'loaded' and may sway the opinions of the jury."[62] Linguistic reversal constructs here a narrative that deprives the actual victims of their rightful representation as persons whose lives were violently taken by a far-right perpetrator and hence deserving of compassion. More than this, these victims were left vulnerable to a criminalizing language accusing them of being "arsonists," "looters," and "rioters"—a vocabulary allowed in court for use by Rittenhouse's defense.[63] An institutionally sanctioned act of reverse victimhood, this court narrative mobilized the languages of pain to flip the positions of victim and victimizer so as to vilify the dead—as the *Washington Post* wrote, to "put" them "on trial, to make it sound as though they got what they deserved."[64]

- *Semantic disidentification*: This trope refers to the decoupling of the languages of pain from their historical connotations associated with struggles for justice and their rearticulation in derogatory narratives of violence and oppression. Part of a broader repertoire of hate speech, terms such as *feminazi*, *human rights warrior*, *wokemob*, and *PC police*, among others, are used to delegitimize those speaking out on racial, gendered, or sexual violence—say, in Me Too testimonies—as too dogmatic to deserve attention, empathy, or solidarity.[65] Words such as *snowflakes* and *crybabies* are employed to similar effect, demoting victim testimonies to a form of feminine hypersensitivity that is "prone to taking offense" (at any provocation) and hence deserves no attention or compassion.[66]

Semantic disidentification works as a trope of cruelty by miscasting voices of suffering or protest as marginal or even inimical to dominant discourse with a view to canceling their potentially transformative power—a power associated with twentieth-century social struggles for voice, recognition, and justice.[67] By associating such voices with "moaners and whiners" as part of "a longer history of moralizing others,"[68] semantic disidentification is instrumental to far-right narratives of antivictimism and their construal of struggles for racial or gender-related justice as objects of contempt and humiliation.

• *Euphemism*: A distinct category of semantic disidentification, euphemism similarly aims to disembed language from its context, though this time a context of violence rather than of protest, and in this way to cleanse, soften, or altogether avoid references to the pain caused in this context. The vocabulary of "heroes" and "frontline workers" for first-contact professionals during the pandemic, for instance, operated as a trope of cruelty insofar as it concealed or beautified the lethal harms inflicted upon those professionals during the first wave; in the United Kingdom, this amounted to 119 deaths, 63 percent of whom were from racial minorities, during the first month alone after the March 2020 lockdown.[69] Given the decade-long neoliberal decimation of the United Kingdom's public-health institutions, the term *frontline* operates here as a "a smokescreen" that, as Sarah Farris and her colleagues argue, "deflects attention away from resource-starved health and social care infrastructures" and promotes what in chapter 3 we encountered as a nationalist narrative of self-sacrifice in the war against COVID-19.[70]

A different example of euphemistic articulation concerns the linguistic cluster of terms that includes *survivorship, resilience*, and *confidence*.[71] These terms have been widely used within therapeutic discourse as feminist, agentive vocabularies of empowerment to repudiate the identity of the victim in favor of the female self as a fighter under circumstances of traumatic violence and domestic abuse.[72] They can nonetheless also bear effects of cruelty when their widespread use in organizational and, more generally, popular cultures transposes a series of traumas and injuries caused by the failures of postrecession neoliberalism—including precarious employment, low pay, toxic work environments, and intimate relationships, among others—onto normative narratives of personal entrepreneurship, or what Shani Orgad and Rosalind Gill call the mantra of "dream big; take control; make a choice; and be confident!"[73] The cruelty of the use of the term *resilience* resides precisely in this paradox, where the injuries of neoliberalism are acknowledged yet protection from them is about personal training rather than about structural change, so that when some people eventually fail, they are said to have no one to blame but themselves.[74]

- *Temporal projection*: If in the euphemism of resilience cruelty produces pain by conjuring an imagined future of ever-receding success, in temporal projection pain resides in an imagined future of unsubstantiated fear—what Kathryn Higgins calls "white victimcould": "a structure of moral justification" that posits "the very possibility of harm (rather than the fact or even the likelihood of harm) . . . so as to position fearful white subjects as morally 'wronged.'"[75] In this way, victimcould effectively collapses the distinction between the hypothetically "injurable" and the "already injured," and instead of highlighting the actual and ongoing suffering of the systemically vulnerable, it casts those people as by default perpetrators of the imagined harms they are anticipated to commit and treats the felt reality of white fear as the only legitimate claim to victimhood.[76]

Narratives on border security are one example of the use of this trope in that they prioritize the protection of the global North over migrants from the global South escaping war, extreme poverty, and climate crisis: "Traumatized, impoverished and in need of aid, refugees, including legal immigrants," Jason Stanley writes, "[are] recast to fit racist stereotypes by leaders and movements committed to maintaining hierarchical group selection and using fascist politics."[77] The narrative produced by transexclusionary radical feminists, or TERFs, is another example of temporal projection in that it builds on existing accounts of victimhood associated with female vulnerabilities in patriarchal societies so as to project a hypothetical form of violence supposedly committed by transgender women onto an unlikely future so as to argue "that men may appear in public spaces as women in order to physically and sexually abuse women"—a narrative that ignores the multiple vulnerabilities of transitioning femininities and casts them instead as potential victimizers of cisgender women.[78]

- *Universalization*: Evident in hashtags such as #AllLivesMatter and #MenToo, the trope of universalization announces a radical expansion of compassion that includes *all* claims to pain in its caring fold independently of race, gender, sexuality, class, or ability. Launched as "responses" to the online justice Black Lives Matter and Me Too movements, these hashtags attempt to generalize the specificity of race- and gender-related suffering and in this way to blur the causal link between those claims and the historical experiences of violence they carry, whether the systematic destruction of Black life in the United States or the long-term openness of various femininities to masculinist violence. In this way, even though "the claim that all human life is valuable is not 'wrong,'" as Nikita Carney contends, the #All hashtag "intentionally erases the complexities of race, class, gender, and sexuality in the lives of people who suffer from systematic police brutality."[79]

The #All rhetoric upholds a liberal ethics of "common humanity" in line with postracial and postfeminist ideologies. Who can credibly claim that in principle some human lives matter more than others? Yet in the context of histories of racial and patriarchal violence we must also ask: Who can simultaneously claim that all lives have always been treated as equal to others? Far from denying that vulnerability is an existential feature of the human condition, the critique of universalization as a trope of cruelty aims rather at questioning the ways in which the rhetoric of #All reproduces ideologies of false equality. It shows how in covering up systemic patterns in the infliction of pain, universalization not only glosses over the traditional asymmetries that structure different groups' openness to violence but also ends up amplifying the tactical victimhood of those who under the guise of #All use the power they already have to voice their own grievance.

The Critical Interrogation of Victimhood

Tropes of cruelty organize claims to pain into moral narratives in ways that benefit privileged selves, usually white cis men, against female "tainted witnesses," political "snowflakes," and racial "threats": "Thinking about victimhood," Manne indeed confirms, "is fundamentally related to a victim/victimizer moral narrative, . . . essentially a simple, reductive morality tale, which allows for little variation or nuance."[80] If the recognition of how these tropes work to perpetuate hierarchies of suffering through such moral narratives is a crucial first step toward the critique of victimhood, the second step consists in establishing a critical method—what I call a "heuristics of victimhood"—to interrogate the public claims to pain that make these hierarchies legitimate in the first place. On the one hand, this critical method should enable us to question where claimed pain comes from and what effects it may have on those it involves; on the other hand, it should prompt us to exercise judgment rather than to rely only on emotion in our responses to claims to pain. The heuristic method, in other words, is meant to orient us not only toward *feeling for the claimant of the pain*, responding to appeals for recognition of their suffering, but also toward *understanding why we should feel for that suffering* and, where needed, engaging with the causal conditions of suffering to change them for the better.

THE HEURISTICS OF VICTIMHOOD

What are the questions that may drive the interrogation of victimhood? I propose that we begin with the following list, although, depending on context, these questions may be adapted to address their specific circumstances of discourse:

- Who is the victim and who is the perpetrator in this narrative?
- Which social positions (of class, gender, race, sexuality, ability) do the actors of suffering occupy?
- Who speaks and in which capacity, and who remains silenced?
- What truth claims to pain do the actors involved make, and how can these claims be scrutinized?
- What kinds of emotions do claims to pain attach to these actors?

- Who gains and who loses from these affective attachments?
- What kinds of communities do these attachments bring together?
- What kinds of exclusions do they presuppose and perpetuate?
- How do these exclusions intersect with positionalities of gender, race, sexuality, class, and ability?

By asking questions about the local contexts of claims to pain, the purpose of this heuristic method is to strip the communication of victimhood of its normative force. Stemming from the universal morality of modernity's culture of sympathy, let us recall, this norm takes pain to be an experience of "our" shared humanity but structures its claims in ways that already assign value to certain sufferers over others. The treatment of claims to pain as situated acts of speech open to our critical scrutiny instead of as emotional appeals on behalf of "our" humanity is thus meant to hold in check the consequences of this communicative bias that always works for the benefit of the privileged.

An example of this normativizing bias can be seen in the familiar overturning of *Roe v. Wade*. Its pro-life narrative centers on the unborn child as victim so as to incorporate the fetus into an ideal of shared humanity and, on this basis, to universalize the position of a particular political community, the white, masculinist, Evangelican far Right, as the only morally right and constitutionally legitimate response to abortions—part of a broader right-wing attack on women's rights that started much earlier.[81] That narrative was similar to the far Right's angry defense of Brett Kavanaugh in 2018, where the accusation against one particular man was cast as a structural vulnerability affecting all men; Trump's statement "It is a very scary time for young men in America" and Cornyn's assertion "Every female's got a father, some have a husband, some have a son" turned Kavanaugh's individual frustration into an instance of universal morality, what Banet-Weiser refers to as "a flipped dynamics" in the structure of "neoliberal patriarchy."[82] Both these acts of universalization constitute instances of *tactical victimhood* that rely on tropes of cruelty—idealization of the unborn "victim" in the pro-life narrative and himpathy for the male "victim" in Kavanaugh's case—so as represent the claimed pain of white masculinity as a structural question. At the same time, these same acts vilify the femininities they implicate in their claimed pain, in particular Black femininities, whose vulnerability is indeed structural: open to multiple risks of harm and death.

The #MeToo testimonials of sexual abuse constitute, in this context, a contrasting example of how situated claims to pain may instead operate as a corrective to the universalization of victimhood. Although the campaign was criticized precisely for individualizing the voices of critique,[83] nonetheless, from the standpoint of the heuristics it was #MeToo's cumulative and persistence particularization of women's suffering under patriarchy that tweet-on-tweet or "Me, too" over "Me, too" operated as a collective practice of resistance against the sexist norm that treats female victims with suspicion. Through the online proliferation of concrete circumstances of harassment or rape, such testimonials managed to challenge the masculinist norms of believability inherent in the politics of pain—norms that routinely reduce "women's accounts of harm into the 'He said/She said' pattern"[84]—and revealed the gendered bias inherent in the universalism of victimhood, whether such bias applies in the courts, in the press, in medical institutions, or in public debate.

This contextual scrutiny of victimhood provides an important critique of power in public discourse, but its value also resides in probing more deeply into the intersectional contexts of violence wherein people come to experience pain. Indeed, an important part of the heuristics of victimhood is the analysis of the *intersectionality* of pain because such claims often integrate compound experiences of suffering, depending on the positions of relative openness to violence they come from and thus on the relative privileges or vulnerabilities—of gender, race, class, sexuality, and ability—that the claimants embody. For all their work in challenging patriarchal norms of female believability, for example, the #MeToo and #BelieveWomen hashtags have also been accused of failing to capture how believability itself depends not only on gender-related structural vulnerabilities but also on those of race and class. "Whom are we to believe?," Amia Srinivasan asks with respect to the movement. "The white woman who says she was raped, or the black or brown woman who insists that her son is being set up? Carolyn Bryant or Mamie Till?"[85]

While such acts of public testimony, in other words, justly claim the right of all women to be believed, nonetheless movements such as #MeToo still operate within a dominant politics of pain and so inevitably perform their own universalizing work. They tend to privilege the voices of those women whose pain comes from positions of relative privilege, largely white middle-class women, while keeping already marginalized, minoritized, and working-class women in particular in a continuing void of silence: "The viral reach of the hashtag around the globe . . . makes clear that sexual violence is not only a U.S. white women's issue," writes Ashwini Tambe. "But if we look at U.S. media coverage of the movement and the most striking spokespersons as well as casualties in recent scandals, it is certainly white women's pain that is centered in popular media coverage."[86] It is these junctures of vulnerability—where being a woman leaves us all open to the physical violence of rape as much as to the symbolic violence of institutionalized suspicion, yet being a poor Black woman means that such violence multiplies risks to life— that the intersectional contextualization of pain brings to light;

to put it in Kimberlé Crenshaw's words, the heuristics of victimhood allows us to examine "*the particular manner* in which Black women are subordinated."[87]

The heuristics' intersectional lens by no means intends to delegitimize the pain of dominant actors on the ground that they come from positions of privilege alone. This would be a dehumanizing and unjust act. How could we possibly deny anyone their memories of traumatic childhood or the injuries inflicted on them by harmful social actors, structures, or institutions? Rather, following Said's call to contextualize suffering "in history, culture, and socio-economic reality," this lens seeks to examine, with some degree of approximation, how specific convergences of power with pain call up which types of self and which communities of recognition as well as to whose benefit and to whose harm—and to do this in order to identify how exactly such intersections participate in the legitimization or interruption of hierarchies of suffering and in the perpetuation or dismantling of structures of violence.

In summary, the heuristics of victimhood invite us to evaluate claims to pain as situated acts of power, where the distinction between systemic vulnerability and tactical victimhood does not appear as a clear and static binary but as a hybrid configuration along a continuum of social positions between privilege and vulnerability.[88] As a consequence, our analysis of the vocabulary of victimhood needs to approach such claims as more relative and precarious than they assert themselves to be and requires a critical orientation that patiently dissects the vocabulary's discursive operations, including its use of tropes of cruelty in public discourse. The heuristics comes, in this sense, a long way in recentering public attention away from the narrowly formulated questions of "true" or "fake" victim and toward a broader set of concerns that subsume truth to a broader agenda: whose suffering is complicated by which intersecting vulnerabilities and what this means for the claims to pain of the most vulnerable among us.

VICTIMHOOD AND JUSTICE

In its insistence on context and intersectionality, the heuristics presupposes our willingness to stop and think about *how* the communication of victimhood works. It requires a slow temporality of judgment. This temporality has the potential not only to contextualize claimed pain, as I have so far argued, but also to do the opposite: to lift claimed pain off its specificity and invite us to complement the question of *how* with the question of *why*. Here, the heuristics ask: Why is this suffering worthy of our emotion and attention? It is by posing the question of why that judgment comes into the affective politics of pain and introduces into public discourse the requirement for justice—a requirement that "*tests* those who suffer to determine what is just."[89] This idea of the just does not refer to an objective verdict of worthiness that exists "out there" but centers on "the test" itself as an intersubjective process. The critical work of the heuristics as a "test" is here about more than the interrogation of the local context of pain (and its matrix of privileges and vulnerabilities). It is also about an intellectual stance that resists the urgency of an immediate response. It is about "put[ting] aside any visceral reactions you have to what others are saying," as Loretta Ross puts it, and "requires you not to pay attention to your reaction but rather to devote your focus and respect to the person you're talking to."[90]

A key part of this process of judgment involves, in turn, the linking of the question of why with narratives of justice. Such narratives are already implicit in the ethos of the heuristics to understand where specific claims to pain come from and which particular intersections of vulnerability or privilege they articulate, or what we may also call the *explanatory* framework of the heuristics. But narratives of justice further require an explicit *justificatory* framework about why and how, on the basis of the explanation offered, we need to reform or transform the conditions of the structurally vulnerable who are implicated in the claims—a framework that challenges the neoliberal individualization of pain and creates the foundations for broad coalitions of social change. As I showed in chapter 1, such narratives of justice are a constitutive part of the history of human rights, with roots to *revolutionary* and *collectivist* struggles against organized systems of oppression, capitalism, patriarchy, and structural racism or to *reformative* efforts that seek to protect individuals from harmful institutions.

An example of a reformative narrative of justice at work is the painstaking intervention undertaken by a range of relevant stakeholders to protect children' rights in the digital age—a category of vulnerable persons whose voices are hardly heard in public discourse, yet their openness to violence increases as they gradually begin interacting with digital platforms. Echoing the heuristic sensibility, this research-driven, policy-oriented work began by contextualizing children's claims to digital harm across their national-cultural positions and socioeconomic intersections, and through rigorous justification it developed instruments for evaluating their openness to various forms of violence (lack of privacy, cyberbullying, and so on) across a spectrum of vulnerability and resilience. Resulting in concrete institutional change, the United Nations "General Comment 25 on Children's Rights in Relation to the Digital Environment" (March 2, 2021), the first-ever institutionalization of children's digital protection, "is a game-changer," explains Sonia Livingstone. "The General Comment will land on the desk of every government in the world. It clarifies what the digital environment means for children's civil rights and freedoms, their rights to privacy, nondiscrimination, protection, education, play and more. It also explains *why* States and other duty bearers must act and, within the limits of 10,700 words, *how* they should act."[91]

Reformative narratives of justice are necessary and important tools in the struggle to protect individual selves and groups from structural harms—for example, the structural harms of platform capitalism and digital oligopolies. Yet they are largely specialized, expert-driven actions that cannot on their own pose a political challenge to the forms of violence underlying the current social order. For the latter, we also require *collectivist* narratives of justice that avoid individualistic explanations of social suffering and demand concerted action that can transform the conditions of suffering in the first place. Such narratives may be regarded as dated in the present media landscape and its virality-driven economies of attention. Nonetheless, modernized for the present time, they remain indispensable not only to the fight against antivictimism and its far-right politics of cruelty but also to a much-needed vision of social change for the future.

Populated largely by commercialized and infotainment-driven genres of communicating pain, current discourse in media or politics, as I showed in chapter 1, tends to individualize narratives of trauma or human rights and to represent people's pain exclusively through personal stories of suffering, while diluting or simply deleting explanatory argument around the structural causes of pain. Liberal discourse, in particular, seems to prefer "ironic" styles of communication, where a commitment to injustice is the whole point of the message, but this commitment is hardly ever rendered explicit and is often articulated through a discourse of "detached knowingness, a self-conscious suspicion vis-à-vis all claims to truth ... a playful agnosticism."[92] My analysis of contemporary styles of humanitarian communication, for instance, shows how the branding of human rights causes in nongovernmental organization campaigns and celebrity advocacy, popular as they are among media users, tends to promote public engagement as a private matter of consumer choice and thus nurtures ambivalent models of informed citizenship, "at once, sceptical towards any moral appeal to solidary action and yet open to doing something about those who suffer."[93]

Similarly, Dannagal Young problematizes the use of irony in liberal politics, in particular the satirical genres in its U.S. manifestation, as a form of political critique that relies on justification and explanatory discourse while at the same time "downplaying its own moral certainty and issuing judgments through implication rather than proclamation."[94] By capitalizing on playfulness and ambiguity, such ironic genres have indeed become media-friendly, superpopular, and thus profitable modes of entertainment. At the same time, however, their formats, just like humanitarian branding, promote ambivalent forms of citizenship: an informed citizenry with a generalized distrust toward the political process and largely private responses to structural questions. "While [liberal citizens] have demonstrably little faith in politicians or people in government to do what is right[, they] have high confidence in their own ability to navigate their political world and make things happen," Young concludes.[95] Despite their critical edge, then, what is missing from these popular styles of liberal discourse is a belief in people acting together so as to change the conditions of structural injustice in their societies. What is missing, in other words, is collectivist narratives of justice.

This is urgently important in times of cruelty because the genres of liberal media, despite their popularity, can in no way compete with the ceaseless stream of far-right hate and outrage spreading both on television genres and social media and in platformized formats such as memes, gifs, and humorous videos. Contrasting the two, Young asserts that "irony is far more difficult than outrage to exploit for attaining large-scale political influence" because the latter capitalizes on "didactic, emotion-filled (typically hate- and anger-filled) speech . . . cloaked in moral certainty and purport[ing] to present an unequivocal truth."[96] Yet even if the present media ecology appears to stymie collectivist narratives of justification, it still offers some opportunity for alternatives. The podcast, the documentary, and the long read but also multimodal texts on Instagram, Twitter, Facebook, and TikTok already allow for diverse temporalities of critical thought online in ways that invite us to "reflect [on] the kaleidoscopic realities" of victimhood "instead of reducing it to monotones," to quote Loretta Ross,[97] and to open up possibilities for collective action.

Two positive examples of the generative uses of collectivist narratives of justice in public discourse come from the recent history of social movements in the United States and the United Kingdom. The first is the Black Lives Matter movement during the protests in Ferguson, Missouri, in 2014–2015, which at that time fashioned its narratives of justice not just around the death of Michael Brown and others who were killed after him but also, as Deen Freelon, Charlton McIlwain, and Meredith Clark argue, around a broader critique of institutional racism and concrete proposals to end police violence. By explicitly articulating the demands of the movement and why their implementation mattered, the Black Lives Matter narrative managed to recenter national conversations around the protests "away from a single-minded focus on individual police brutality incidents toward an understanding of the issue as systemic, racialized, and in dire need of remediation." As a result of using an explanatory narrative to contextualize Black pain within its circumstances of systemic injustice, the movement at its peak saw an unprecedented alliance of solidarities, where "Black celebrities and journalists, international media outlets, the White left, and Anonymous overwhelmingly sided with the protesters, against the police, or both," so that, "at least in that moment, the value of Black lives received massive affirmation from more than just the usual suspects."[98] A parallel example comes from the U.K. rail workers' trade union strikes in 2022–2023, a series of industrial-action initiatives that in unison with other professional sectors swept the crisis-ridden country in defense of working people's rights to decent salaries, better working conditions, and pensions. Starting from the union's specific dispute and situating the question of why strike action was necessary within a wider narrative of justification—the chronic impoverishment of working people in the country—this discourse turned a traditionally anti-union public in favor of the strikes and, despite hostile media coverage, gained increased support across the country.[99] "He [the union representative] has struck a chord with so many people," the journalist James Greig explained in *DAZED*, because, "he has a clear moral purpose, he focuses on the tangible experiences of the members he represents, and he articulates the underlying causes behind the UK's rampant economic injustice plainly and convincingly."[100]

Both examples suggest that the articulation of the languages of pain within narratives of justice is more than a civil pedagogy of moral recognition. It can also become a pedagogy of political coalition building. Whereas the potential of irony and outrage to galvanize new support is largely circumscribed by specific margins within their already-existing affective communities of recognition, the spelling out of why a claim to pain is unjust and what can be done about it potentially invites hitherto-undefined publics to make their own decisions as to whether this claim may be worthy of their attention or not. In this way, such publics also can "test[] those who suffer to determine what is just," in Boltanski's words, and come together into yet-to-be-formed political communities of action.

My emphasis on justification and judgment as part of a critique of victimhood is not meant to suggest that all claims to suffering require a collectivist response, for some may not. Nor is it meant to downplay reflexive introspection in therapeutic encounters or ignore the power of the emotions of the politics of pain—compassion and anger—in summoning political communities. Historic struggles against capitalist exploitation, patriarchal oppression, racist violence, and sexual marginalization, we may remember from chapter 1, have been seeped in empathy for people's suffering and indignation against their victimizers. The emphasis on narratives of justice is rather to remind us that judgment, argument, and justification are just as essential to the formation of longer-term political affiliations in ways that the affective attachments of platformized pain are not able to be.

For this reason, it is equally important that the critique of victimhood engages with the ongoing critique of social media platforms, capitalizing on the latter field's expansive work around digital harms, the injuries of datafication and algorithmic control, as well as platform regulation. I have often here returned to the platformization of pain and its toxic implications—namely, how social media organize online participation around invisible processes of data extraction and classification that reproduce the hierarchies already coded into their automated programs as well as how these media amplify emo-truths in ways that vilify, silence, and altogether exclude the most vulnerable voices of society. In both senses, social media, as Harsin says, "are ultimately designed to block the emergence of more inclusive social justice agendas or even the reorganization of the plane of political agency itself."[101] Elon Musk's acquisition of Twitter/X, which quickly doubled and tripled the platform's toxicity against gay people and Black Americans,[102] has dramatically highlighted the harm of market-driven business models on the nature of public discourse.

In this respect, I share Safiya Noble's and other scholars' concern regarding "how those who are already living with and under systemic oppression will be able to resist these conditions, and also organize for a fair and just society in which we can all flourish."[103] Efforts to reform platformized communication need to begin precisely from this concern. They need to focus on the vulnerable communities that "shoulder a greater share of the social, political, and emotional burden of online participation,"[104] and they must aim to challenge the profit-oriented models of big tech while promoting principles of public accountability in the ways that personal data are managed and advancing public interest in the ways online discourse is regulated.

As I write these final words, the role of platforms is more controversial and uncertain than ever before: "It's over. Facebook is in decline, Twitter in chaos. . . . It's never felt more plausible that the age of social media might end—and soon," proclaims Ian Bogost in the *Atlantic*.[105] Independently of how all this evolves in the future, my own argument on victimhood took its point of departure in our decade, the third decade of the twenty-first century, and so it relies as much on the ephemerality of the present juncture as it does on the durability of longer-term structures, specifically the politics of pain and its vocabulary of victimhood. Constitutive of emotional capitalism and its hierarchies of life, the communicative politics of pain has already changed drastically in the past hundred years. Throughout this centennial arc of immense human suffering and monumental social reform, this politics has slowly shifted the communication of victimhood toward increasingly individualized claims to pain, plunging the self into unequal struggles over whose suffering is worthy of moral recognition and in the process perpetuating historical silences over the traumas and injuries of the most vulnerable among us.

We cannot fully escape this legacy of emotional capitalism as a source of personal pain and societal suffering or of the language we use to talk about both. What we can do as we look ahead, however, is break with the taboo of Western modernity and its obligatory deference to the vocabulary of victimhood and instead pose the unthinkable question: *Why* should we care about *this* claim to suffering? It is this rigorous scrutiny of emotional capitalism, of its power relations and its communicative bias, that can help us reimagine the alternative vocabularies already present in the margins of the liberal polity. Now more than ever, it is time to reinvigorate the collectivist narratives of justice inherent in this polity, using them to highlight not everyone's pain in general but the pain of those who suffer most and turn that suffering into calls for solidarity. For without this work of reclaiming vulnerability for social change, the tactical uses of victimhood, to paraphrase Arendt,[106] can and will continue to change the world, but the most probable change will be to a world with more, not less, suffering.

NOTES

PREFACE AND ACKNOWLEDGMENTS

1. Hannah Arendt, *On Revolution* (1963; reprint, New York: Penguin, 2006); Luc Boltanski, *Distant Suffering: Morality, Media, and Politics*, trans. Graham D. Burchell (Cambridge: Cambridge University Press, 1999).
2. Eva Illouz, *Cold Intimacies: The Making of Emotional Capitalism* (Cambridge: Polity, 2007); and Illouz, *Saving the Modern Soul: Therapy, Emotions, and the Culture of Self-Help* (Berkeley: University of California Press, 2008).
3. Wendy Brown, *States of Injury: Power and Freedom in Late Modernity* (Princeton, NJ: Princeton University Press, 1995).
4. Judith Butler, Zeynep Gambetti, and Leticia Sabsay, eds., *Vulnerability in Resistance* (Durham, NC: Duke University Press, 2016).
5. Alyson M. Cole, *The Cult of True Victimhood: From the War on Welfare to the War on Terror* (Stanford, CA: Stanford University Press, 2007).

I. WHY VICTIMHOOD?

1. "#WhyIDidntReport: The Hashtag Supporting Christine Blasey Ford," BBC, September 23, 2018, https://www.bbc.co.uk/news/world-us-canada-45621124.
2. Alana Abramson, "Read the Letter from Christine Blasey Ford's Lawyers Requesting an FBI Inquiry Into Kavanaugh Allegation," *Time*,

September 18, 2018, http://time.com/5400239/christine-blasey-ford-investigation-letter/.

3. Kavanaugh, Cornyn, and Trump quoted in Maegan Vazquez, "Trump Is Casting Kavanaugh as a Victim. He's Felt the Same," CNN, October 3, 2018, https://edition.cnn.com/2018/10/03/politics/donald-trump-brett-kavanaugh-sexual-misconduct-allegations/index.html.

4. "Brett Kavanaugh's Supreme Court Confirmation Is Now the Ultimate Test of Political Power in 2018," *Time*, September 20, 2018, https://time.com/5401624/brett-kavanaugh-confirmation/; Emma Gray Ellis, "Blasey Ford–Kavanaugh Testimony Tells a Tale of Two Internets," *Wired*, September 27, 2018, https://www.wired.com/story/blasey-ford-kavanaugh-filter-bubbles/; Sheryl Gay Stolberg and Nicholas Fandos, "Brett Kavanaugh and Christine Blasey Ford Duel with Tears and Fury," *New York Times*, September 27, 2018, https://www.nytimes.com/2018/09/27/us/politics/brett-kavanaugh-confirmation-hearings.html.

5. Abramson, "Read the Letter from Christine Blasey Ford's Lawyers."

6. Kavanaugh quoted in Stolberg and Fandos, "Brett Kavanaugh and Christine Blasey Ford Duel with Tears and Fury."

7. Preexisting ideological alignments determined this decision, with Republican and Democratic senators supporting their respective party interests. As then senator Flake Abramson, the only Republican who acted outside his party box, put it, "Many members of this body, from both parties, have already made up their minds, on the record, in advance of this hearing. They will presumably hear what they want to hear and disregard the rest. One is tempted to ask, why even bother to have a hearing?"; see Burgess Everett, "Flake: Kavanaugh Vote Will Be 'Forever Steeped in Doubt,'" *Politico*, September 26, 2018, https://www.politico.com/story/2018/09/26/flake-committee-kavanaugh-843579=.

8. Christine Hauser, "The Women Who Have Accused Brett Kavanaugh," *New York Times*, September 26, 2018, https://www.nytimes.com/2018/09/26/us/politics/brett-kavanaugh-accusers-women.html.

9. See, for example, Yasmeen Serhan, "An American Spectacle Grabs Attention Overseas: The 'Supreme Ordeal' of the Kavanaugh Hearings Dominated Headlines Beyond the United States,"

Atlantic, September 28, 2018, https://www.theatlantic.com/international/archive/2018/09/how-the-world-saw-the-kavanaugh-hearing/571633/.

10. My reference to Western societies does not mean that victimhood is not a dominant feature of public cultures of the global South, particularly in authoritarian populist contexts. For instance, for Tayip Erdoğan's use of the victim trope for Turkey, see Omar al-Ghazzi, "We Will Be Great Again: Historical Victimhood in Populist Discourse," *European Journal of Cultural Studies* 24, no. 1 (2021): 45–59. For Narendra Modi in India, see Catarina Kinnvall, "Populism, Ontological Insecurity, and Hindutva: Modi and the Masculinization of Indian Politics," *Cambridge Review of International Affairs* 32, no. 3 (2019): 283–302. For Vladimir Putin in Russia, see Gulnaz Sharafutdinova, *The Red Mirror: Putin's Leadership and Russia's Insecure Identity* (Oxford: Oxford University Press, 2020). For a similar use of victimhood in the populism of the European Union countries of eastern Europe, such as Poland and Hungary, see Artur Lipiński and Gabriella Szabo, "Heroisation and Victimisation: Populism, Commemorative Narratives, and National Days in Hungary and Poland," *Journal of Contemporary European Studies* 32, no. 1 (2023): 345–62. My own research focus, however, falls on two major English-speaking societies of the Western world, the United Kingdom and the United States, simply because I have experiential access to their public discourse and can therefore speak more confidently about them.
11. Hughes quoted in Suzanne Moore, "On Talk Shows the Democracy of Pain Reigns Supreme," *New Statesman* 128, no. 4432 (1996): 17.
12. Didier Fassin and Richard Rechtman, *The Empire of Trauma: An Inquiry Into the Condition of Victimhood*, trans. Rachel Gomme (Princeton, NJ: Princeton University Press, 2009), 6.
13. Carolyn Dean, *The Moral Witness: Trials and Testimony After Genocide* (Ithaca, NY: Cornell University Press, 2019), 24.
14. In the United States, for instance, 82 percent of women reported experiencing some form of sexual harassment or assault, one in five experienced completed or attempted rape during their lifetimes, and one in three experienced completed or attempted rape between the ages of eleven and seventeen. In 2018, the year of the Blasey Ford public

testimony, only about 25 percent of women reported their assault to their police, with the percentage of false reporting down near 2 to 10 percent. See S. G. Smith et al., *The National Intimate Partner and Sexual Violence Survey (NISVS): 2015 Data Brief—Updated Release* (Atlanta, GA: National Center for Injury Prevention and Control, Centers for Disease Control and Prevention, 2018), https://www.nsvrc.org/sites/default/files/2021-04/2015data-brief508.pdf.

15. At least two hundred prominent men lost their jobs following public allegations of sexual harassment in the year after the Weinstein scandal and the first #MeToo wave in the United States, as opposed to fewer than thirty the previous year. Audrey Carlsen, Maya Salam, Cain Miller, Denise Lu, Ash Ngu, Jugal K. Patel, and Zach Wichter, "The Post- #MeToo Brought Down 201 Powerful Men. Nearly Half of Their Replacements Are Women," *New York Times*, October 23, 2018, https://www.nytimes.com/interactive/2018/10/23/us/metoo-replacements.html.

16. Arendt, *On Revolution*; Brown, *States of Injury*; Wendy Brown, "Wounded Attachments: Late Modern Oppositional Political Formations," *Political Theory* 21, no. 3 (1993): 390–410; Cole, *The Cult of True Victimhood*.

17. See, for instance, Bradley Campbell and Jason Manning's critique that the contemporary U.S. "culture of victimhood" among racialized minorities relies on those minorities' supposedly flawed relationship to truth. Bradley Campbell and Jason Manning, *The Rise of Victimhood Culture: Microaggressions, Safe Spaces, and the New Culture Wars* (New York: Palgrave Macmillan, 2018). By drawing on their analysis of similarities between these minorities' claims to "microaggressions" and what the authors call "the logic of false accusations," they argue that both work either by exaggerating or by avoiding documenting the violence the minorities claim to have been victimized by. Like false accusers, "microaggression complainants," they conclude, "seek to build a persuasive case by documenting a number of small offences, arguing that even if each one is small, added together they become serious" (106). By focusing on the micro-contexts of argumentation, however, what the authors omit from their analysis is the macrolevel of invisible structures of violence that racialized and other minoritized groups

experience in their daily lives and that affect their social contexts in ways that are real to them but may not be evident to observers in local interactions. This is one of the reasons why questions of claimed pain and victimhood should be approached as a *political* rather than an exclusively epistemological question. For a similar argument on the gendered politics of believability and doubt in the context of sexual abuse accusations and controversies, see Sarah Banet-Weiser and Kathryn Claire Higgins, *Believability: Sexual Violence, Media, and the Politics of Doubt* (Cambridge: Polity, 2023).

18. Arthur Brooks, "The Real Victims of Victimhood," *New York Times*, December 26, 2015, https://www.nytimes.com/2015/12/27/opinion/sunday/the-real-victims-of-victimhood.html.

19. Nancy Bermeo and Larry M. Bartels, eds., *Mass Politics in Tough Times: Opinions, Votes, and Protest in the Great Recession*, illus. ed. (Oxford: Oxford University Press, 2014); William Davies, "Destination Unknown," *London Review of Books* 14, no. 11 (2022), https://www.lrb.co.uk/the-paper/v44/n11/william-davies/destination-unknown.

20. Joseph Stiglitz, "COVID Has Made Global Inequality Much Worse," *Scientific American*, March 1, 2022, https://www.scientificamerican.com/article/covid-has-made-global-inequality-much-worse/. See also Richard Partington, "Rising Asset Wealth and Falling Real Wages 'Drive Inequality in Britain,'" *The Guardian*, November 9, 2022, https://www.theguardian.com/business/2022/nov/09/rising-asset-wealth-and-falling-real-wages-drive-inequality-in-britain.

21. Paulo Gerbaudo, "The Pandemic Crowd: Protest in the Time of COVID-19," *Journal of International Affairs* 73, no. 2 (2020): 65, https://www.jstor.org/stable/26939966. This periodization follows the analysis by the sociologist Mike Savage, who begins his study on inequality with a contrast between the first decade of the twenty-first century, characterized by a "heady millennial excitement about the promise of economic and social advance," and the current moment rooted "in the fallout from the austerity politics unleashed across the world in the aftermath of the 2008 financial crash" in combination with "the sense of malaise provoked . . . by growing divisions in such areas as social mobility, health, politics and well-being." Mike Savage, *The Return of*

Inequality: Social Change and the Weight of the Past (Cambridge, MA: Harvard University Press, 2021), 2.

22. Peter Dahlgren, "Media, Knowledge, and Trust: The Deepening Epistemic Crisis of Democracy," *Javnost—the Public* 25, nos. 1–2 (2018): 20–27, https://doi.org/10.1080/13183222.2018.1418819.
23. Lawrence Grossberg, *Under the Cover of Chaos: Trump and the Battle for the American Right* (London: Pluto, 2018), 248.
24. Nicolas Demertzis, "Emotions and Populism," in *Emotion, Politics, and Society*, ed. Paul Hoggett, Simon Clarke, and Simon Thompson (London: Palgrave Macmillan, 2006), 111.
25. Brown, "Wounded Attachments," 401.
26. For critical discussions of victimhood as resentment in left-wing populism during the Euro-crisis moment, see, for instance, Yannis Stavrakakis and Giorgos Katsambekis, "Left-Wing Populism in the European Periphery: The Case of SYRIZA," *Journal of Political Ideologies* 19, no. 2 (2014): 119–42; Roman Gerodimos, "Greece's Ongoing Tragedy," *Political Insight* 6, no. 3 (2015): 26–27, https://doi.org/10.1111/2041-9066.12111; Gerodimos, "Humiliation, Shame, and Violence: Honor, Trauma, and Political Extremism Before and After the 2009 Crisis in Greece," *International Forum of Psychoanalysis* 31, no. 1 (2022): 34–45; Nicolas Demertzis, *The Political Sociology of Emotions: Essays on Trauma and Ressentiment* (London: Routledge, 2020); Andriani Retzepi, Angelos Nastoulis, and Panayis Panagiotopoulos, "The 'Deserved' Victimhood of Far-Left Terrorism: Shame, Guilt, and Status Reversal," in *Interdisciplinary Applications of Shame/Violence Theory*, ed. Roman Gerodimos (London: Palgrave Macmillan, 2022), 177–89.
27. Jason Stanley, *How Fascism Works: The Politics of Us and Them*, illus. ed. (New York: Random House, 2018), 73.
28. Richard Saull, "Racism and Far Right Imaginaries Within Neo-liberal Political Economy," *New Political Economy* 23, no. 5 (2018): 588.
29. Arlie Russell Hochschild, *Strangers in Their Own Land: Anger and Mourning on the American Right*, illus. ed. (New York: New Press, 2016), 421.
30. John Sides, "Resentful White People Propelled Trump to the White House—and He Is Rewarding Their Loyalty," *Washington Post*,

August 3, 2017, https://www.washingtonpost.com/news/monkey-cage/wp/2017/08/03/resentful-white-people-propelled-trump-to-the-white-house-and-he-is-rewarding-their-loyalty/; Emily Badge, "Estranged in America: Both Sides Feel Lost and Left Out," *New York Times*, April 10, 2018, https://www.nytimes.com/2018/10/04/upshot/estranged-america-trump-polarization.html. For the link between neoliberalism and the far Right in academic literature, see Sean Phelan, "Neoliberalism, the Far Right, and the Disparaging of 'Social Justice Warriors,'" *Communication, Culture, & Critique* 12, no. 4 (2019): 455–75; Lilie Chouliaraki and Myria Georgiou, *The Digital Border: Migration, Technology, Power* (New York: New York University Press, 2022).

31. Sarah Banet-Weiser, "Popular Feminism: Male Victimhood," *Los Angeles Review of Books*, February 22, 2019, https://lareviewofbooks.org/article/popular-feminism-male-victimhood/#!.
32. Jan Van Dijk, "Free the Victim: A Critique of the Western Conception of Victimhood," *International Review of Victimology* 16, no. 1 (2009): 1–33.
33. Yevgen Galona, "From Ritual to Metaphor: The Semantic Shift in the Concept of 'Victim' and Medieval Christian Piety," *International Review of Victimology* 24, no. 1 (2018): 83–98, https://doi.org/10.1177/0269758017732923.
34. Dean, *The Moral Witness*.
35. Paul Frosh and Amit Pinchevski, "Introduction: Why Witnessing? Why Now?," in *Media Witnessing: Testimony in the Age of Mass Communication*, ed. Paul Frosh and Amit Pinchevski (London: Palgrave Macmillan, 2009), 1–22.
36. Dean, *The Moral Witness*.
37. Shoshana Felman and Dori Laub, *Testimony: Crises of Witnessing in Literature, Psychoanalysis, and History* (New York: Routledge, 1992).
38. Annette Wieviorka, *The Era of the Witness* (Ithaca, NY: Cornell University Press, 2006).
39. Anna Hunter, "The Holocaust as the Ultimate Trauma Narrative," in *Trauma and Literature*, ed. J. Roger Kurtz (Cambridge: Cambridge University Press, 2018), 66.
40. Amit Pinchevski, *Transmitted Wounds: Media and the Mediation of Trauma* (Oxford: Oxford University Press, 2019).

41. Sandra Ristovska, "Witnessing and the Failure of Communication," *Communication Review* 17, no. 2 (2014): 150, https://doi.org/10.1080/10714421.2014.901062; see also Fassin and Rechtman, *The Empire of Trauma*.
42. Dean, *The Moral Witness*. For the legal framework, see United Nations Office on Genocide Prevention and the Responsibility to Protect, "Ratification of the Genocide Convention," convention signed December 9, 1948, https://www.un.org/en/genocideprevention/genocide-convention.shtml.
43. Shoshana Felman, "Theaters of Justice: Arendt in Jerusalem, the Eichmann Trial, and the Redefinition of Legal Meaning in the Wake of the Holocaust," *Critical Inquiry* 27, no. 2 (2001): 465, https://www.jstor.org/stable/1344248.
44. Felman, "Theaters of Justice," 465.
45. Daniel Levy and Natan Sznaider, "The Politics of Commemoration: The Holocaust, Memory, and Trauma," in *Handbook of Contemporary European Social Theory*, ed. Gerard Delanty (London: Routledge, 2006), 292.
46. Aimé Césaire, *Discourse on Colonialism* (New York: New York University Press, 2001), 36.
47. Dominick LaCapra, *Writing History, Writing Trauma* (Baltimore, MD: Johns Hopkins University Press, 2014), 174.
48. Stef Craps, *Postcolonial Witnessing: Trauma out of Bounds* (London: Palgrave Macmillan, 2013).
49. Jeffrey C. Alexander, "On the Social Construction of Moral Universals: The 'Holocaust' from War Crime to Trauma Drama," *European Journal of Social Theory* 5, no. 1 (2002): 6, https://doi.org/10.1177/1368431002005001001.
50. Aimé Césaire formulates the exceptionality of the Holocaust as the "founding trauma" of Western modernity as a matter of race—that is, of white-on-white violence rather than white-on-Black violence, as in colonial suffering: "The crime in itself, the crime against man, it is not the humiliation of man as such, it is the crime against the white man, the humiliation of the white man, and the fact that he applied to Europe colonialist procedures which until then had been reserved exclusively for the Arabs of Algeria, the coolies of India and the blacks of Africa." Césaire, *Discourse on Colonialism*, 164.

1. WHY VICTIMHOOD? 149

51. Craps, *Postcolonial Witnessing*, 12. Barbie Zelizer makes a similar point with respect to the proliferation of Holocaust-like photographic aesthetics in the photojournalism of atrocity, where she demonstrates how the widespread use of visual templates of the Holocaust in other atrocities around the world aim at evoking the Holocaust to amplify the dramatic impact of each atrocity but end up erasing the particularities of their diverse contexts: "Paradoxically," she argues, "it may be that Holocaust photos have helped us remember the Holocaust so as to forget contemporary atrocity." Barbie Zelizer, *Remembering to Forget: Holocaust Memory Through the Camera's Eye* (Chicago: University of Chicago Press, 1998), 13.
52. Michael Rothberg, *Multidirectional Memory: Remembering the Holocaust in the Age of Decolonization* (Stanford, CA: Stanford University Press, 2009).
53. Jean-François Lyotard, *The Postmodern Condition: A Report on Knowledge* (Manchester: Manchester University Press, 1984).
54. Illouz, *Cold Intimacies*, 4.
55. Eva Illouz, *Oprah Winfrey and the Glamour of Misery: An Essay on Popular Culture* (New York: Columbia University Press, 2003); Illouz, *Cold Intimacies*; Illouz, *Saving the Modern Soul*; Illouz, "The Culture of Management: Self-Interest, Empathy, and Emotional Control," in *An Introduction to Social Entrepreneurship: Voices, Preconditions, Contexts*, ed. Rafael Ziegler (Cheltenham, U.K.: Edward Elgar, 2009), 107–32.
56. Cathy Caruth, *Unclaimed Experience: Trauma, Narrative, and History* (Baltimore, MD: Johns Hopkins University Press, 2016).
57. Yannis Stavrakakis, "Jacques Lacan: Negotiating the Psychosocial in and Beyond Language," in *The Routledge Handbook of Language and Politics*, ed. Ruth Wodak and Bernhard Forchtner (London: Routledge, 2017), 83.
58. Juliet Mitchell, "Trauma, Recognition, and the Place of Language," *Diacritics* 28, no. 4 (1998): 121–33, https://doi.org/10.1353/dia.1998.0035.
59. Jeffrey C. Alexander, "Social Subjectivity: Psychotherapy as Central Institution," *Thesis Eleven* 96 (2009): 131.
60. Frank Furedi, *Therapy Culture: Cultivating Vulnerability in an Uncertain Age* (London: Routledge, 2003), 12.
61. Illouz, *Cold Intimacies*, 108.

62. Nikolas Rose, *Powers of Freedom: Reframing Political Thought* (Cambridge: Cambridge University Press, 1999).
63. For Adam Smith, being lovely and not being hateful are the two key affective drives of the good citizen: "Man [sic] naturally desires not only to be loved but to be lovely." He further says, "He naturally dreads, not only to be hated but to be hateful." See Adam Smith, *The Theory of Moral Sentiments* (1759; reprint, Oxford: Oxford University Press, 1976), 113. While this quote suggests that tender-hearted responsiveness has always been central to the norms of liberal citizenship, it is, in particular, the pain of the other that lies at the heart of this civic norm. For, as Smith explains, "the other person's agonies, when they are thus brought home to ourselves[,] . . . begin at last to affect us and we then tremble and shudder at the thought of what he feels" (*The Theory of Moral Sentiments*, 9). See also Natan Sznaider, "The Sociology of Compassion: A Study in the Sociology of Morals," *Journal for Cultural Research* 2, no. 1 (1998): 122.
64. Smith, *The Theory of Moral Sentiments*, 9. See also David Marshall, "Adam Smith and the Theatricality of Moral Sentiments," *Critical Inquiry* 10, no. 4 (1984): 592–613, https://www.jstor.org/stable/1343313; and Emma Rothschild, "The Theory of Moral Sentiments and the Inner Life," *Adam Smith Review* 5 (2010): 2425–36.
65. Boltanski, *Distant Suffering*, 88.
66. Frantz Fanon, *The Wretched of the Earth*, trans. Constance Farrington (New York: Grove, 1963), 250.
67. Lilie Chouliaraki, *The Spectatorship of Suffering* (London: Sage, 2006); Chouliaraki, *The Ironic Spectator: Solidarity in the Age of Posthumanitarianism* (New York: Wiley, 2013).
68. Catherine Rottenberg, "Neoliberal Feminism and the Future of Human Capital," *Signs: Journal of Women in Culture and Society* 42, no. 2 (2017): 329–48, https://doi.org/10.1086/688182.
69. Eva Illouz, "'That Shadowy Realm of the Interior': Oprah Winfrey and Hamlet's Glass," *International Journal of Cultural Studies* 2, no. 1 (1999): 119, 123, emphasis in original, https://doi.org/10.1177/136787799900200106.
70. David Krasner, "Book Review: *Oprah Winfrey and the Glamour of Misery: An Essay on Popular Culture* by Eva Illouz," *African American Review* 38, no. 3 (2004): 540.

71. Rosalind Gill and Shani Orgad, "The Shifting Terrain of Sex and Power: From the 'Sexualization of Culture' to #MeToo," *Sexualities* 21, no. 8 (2018): 1323, https://doi.org/10.1177/1363460718794647.
72. Catherine Rottenberg, "Can #MeToo Go Beyond White Neoliberal Feminism? Who Can Say #MeToo and Who Will Be Heard?," *Al Jazeera*, December 17, 2017, https://www.aljazeera.com/opinions/2017/12/13/can-metoo-go-beyond-white-neoliberal-feminism.
73. Bryan Turner, *Vulnerability and Human Rights* (University Park: Pennsylvania State University Press, 2006).
74. Samuel Moyn, *The Last Utopia: Human Rights in History* (Cambridge, MA: Harvard University Press, 2010), 26, 200.
75. Nancy Naples, "To Interpret the World and to Change It: An Interview with Nancy Fraser," *Signs: Journal of Women in Culture and Society* 29, no. 4 (2004): 1103–24, https://www.journals.uchicago.edu/doi/full/10.1086/382631.
76. Katherine M. Franke, "Becoming a Citizen: Reconstruction Era Regulation of African American Marriages," *Yale Journal of Law & the Humanities* 11 (1991): 251.
77. W. E. B. Du Bois, *Black Reconstruction in America: Toward a History of the Part Which Black Folk Played in the Attempt to Reconstruct Democracy in America, 1860–1880* (1935; reprint, London: Routledge, 2012), xv.
78. Kate Nash, "The Cultural Politics of Human Rights and Neoliberalism," *Journal of Human Rights* 18, no. 5 (2019): 491.
79. Samuel Moyn, *Not Enough: Human Rights in an Unequal World* (Cambridge, MA: Belknap Press of Harvard University Press, 2018), 7.
80. Moyn, *The Last Utopia*, 227.
81. Michael Meranze, "Distant Suffering: Morality, Media, and Politics," *History Workshop Journal* 53, no. 1 (2002): 254, https://doi.org/10.1093/hwj/53.1.252.
82. Boltanski, *Distant Suffering*, 63.
83. Mervi Pantti and Karin Wahl-Jorgensen, "On the Political Possibilities of Therapy News: Social Responsibility and the Limits of Objectivity in Disaster Coverage," *Communication Studies* 1, no. 1 (2007): 18.
84. Roland Burke, "Emotional Diplomacy and Human Rights at the United Nations," *Human Rights Quarterly* 39 (May 2017): 295.

85. Beata A. Safari, "Intangible Privacy Rights: How Europe's GDPR Will Set a New Global Standard for Personal Data Protection," *Seton Hall Law Review* 47 (2016): 809.
86. Moyn, *The Last Utopia*.
87. Chouliaraki, *The Ironic Spectator*, 13.
88. Arendt, *On Revolution*, 90.
89. Boltanski, *Distant Suffering*, 18.
90. Stuart Hall, "On Postmodernism and Articulation: An Interview with Stuart Hall," ed. Lawrence Grossberg, *Journal of Communication Inquiry* 10, no. 2 (1986): 53.
91. Erin Hanafy, "Christine Blasey Ford's Testimony Showed That Vulnerability Is Actually a Superpower," *Well+Good*, September 27, 2018, https://www.wellandgood.com/good-advice/christine-blasey-ford-vulnerability-strength/; Megan Garber, "For Christine Blasey Ford to Be Believable, She Had to Be 'Likable,'" *Atlantic*, September 27, 2018, https://www.theatlantic.com/entertainment/archive/2018/09/christine-blasey-ford-pernicious-demand-be-likable/571555/.
92. Hanafy, "Christine Blasey Ford's Testimony."
93. Alice Marwick and Robyn Caplan, "Drinking Male Tears: Language, the Manosphere, and Networked Harassment," *Feminist Media Studies* 18, no. 4 (2018): 543–59.
94. Grossberg, *Under the Cover of Chaos*, 248–49.
95. Simon Kemp, "Digital 2021 October Global Statshot Report," *DataReportal—Global Digital Insights*, October 2021, https://datareportal.com/reports/digital-2021-october-global-statshot.
96. Merlyna Lim, "Clicks, Cabs, and Coffee Houses: Social Media and Oppositional Movements in Egypt, 2004–2011," *Journal of Communication* 62, no. 2 (2012): 231, https://doi.org/10.1111/j.1460-2466.2012.01628.x.
97. Alyson Cole and Sumru Atuk, "What's in a Hashtag? Feminist Terms for Tweeting in Alliance," *philoSOPHIA: A Journal of Continental Feminism* 9, no. 1 (2019): 26–52.
98. Marwick and Caplan, "Drinking Male Tears," 543.
99. Laura García-Favaro and Rosalind Gill, "'Emasculation Nation Has Arrived': Sexism Rearticulated in Online Responses to Lose the Lads' Mags Campaign," *Feminist Media Studies* 16 (November 2015): 388, https://doi.org/10.1080/14680777.2015.1105840.

100. Molly Dragiewicz et al., "Technology Facilitated Coercive Control: Domestic Violence and the Competing Roles of Digital Media Platforms," *Feminist Media Studies* 18, no. 4 (2018): 621, https://doi.org/10.1080/14680777.2018.1447341.
101. José van Dijck, *The Culture of Connectivity: A Critical History of Social Media* (Oxford: Oxford University Press, 2013).
102. Muchazondida Mkono, "'Troll Alert!': Provocation and Harassment in Tourism and Hospitality Social Media," *Current Issues in Tourism* 21, no. 7 (2015): 791–804, https://doi.org/10.1080/13683500.2015.1106447.
103. Van Dijck, *The Culture of Connectivity*, 13.
104. Alexander Brown, "What Is Hate Speech? Part 1: The Myth of Hate," *Law and Philosophy* 36 (August 2017): 419–68, https://doi.org/10.1007/s10982-017-9297-1.
105. Sonia Livingstone and Peter K. Smith, "Annual Research Review: Harms Experienced by Child Users of Online and Mobile Technologies: The Nature, Prevalence and Management of Sexual and Aggressive Risks in the Digital Age," *Journal of Child Psychology and Psychiatry* 55, no. 6 (2014): 635, https://doi.org/10.1111/jcpp.12197.
106. Shari Kessel Schneider et al., "Cyberbullying, School Bullying, and Psychological Distress: A Regional Census of High School Students," *American Journal of Public Health* 102, no. 1 (2012): 175, https://www.academia.edu/11327868/Cyberbullying_School_Bullying_and_Psychological_Distress_A_Regional_Census_of_High_School_Students.
107. The two are of course interconnected. Nonetheless, it is useful to separate them analytically: trauma speaks of harm primarily within the nexus of victim-perpetrator-benefactor, whereas injury deindividualizes victimhood and places personal pain within a broader sociopolitical context.
108. Nicola Henry and Anastasia Powell, "Embodied Harms: Gender, Shame, and Technology-Facilitated Sexual Violence," *Violence Against Women* 21, no. 6 (2015): 758, https://doi.org/10.1177/1077801215576581.
109. For digital parenting initiatives, see Giovanna Mascheroni and Donell Holloway, *The Internet of Toys: Practices, Affordances, and the Political Economy of Children's Smart Play* (London: Palgrave Macmillan, 2019); and for practicing "digital detox," see Trine Syvertsen and Gunn Enli, "Digital Detox: Media Resistance and the Promise of Authenticity,"

Convergence 26, nos. 5–6 (2020): 1269–83, https://doi.org/10.1177/1354856519847325. On new digital rights discourses and interventions, see Sonia Livingstone, "Developing Social Media Literacy: How Children Learn to Interpret Risky Opportunities on Social Network Sites," *Communications* 39 (September 2014): 283–303, https://doi.org/10.1515/commun-2014-0113; and Sonia Livingstone and Amanda Third, "Children and Young People's Rights in the Digital Age: An Emerging Agenda," *New Media & Society* 19, no. 5 (2017): 657–70, https://doi.org/10.1177/1461444816686318.

110. Deborah Lupton and Ben Williamson, "The Datafied Child: The Dataveillance of Children and Implications for Their Rights," *New Media & Society* 19, no. 5 (2017): 780–94, https://doi.org/10.1177/1461444816686328.

111. Shoshana Zuboff, "Big Other: Surveillance Capitalism and the Prospects of an Information Civilization," *Journal of Information Technology* 30, no. 1 (2015): 76, 85, https://doi.org/10.1057/jit.2015.5.

112. The embeddedness of communicative acts in society's power relations is a common assumption in a number of critical and post-structuralist hermeneutic approaches, which ask the question of how claims to suffering participate in the formation of subjectivity and community. See Lois McNay, "Suffering, Silence, and Social Weightlessness: Honneth and Bourdieu on Embodiment and Power," in *Embodied Selves*, ed. Stella Gonzalez-Arnal, Gill Jagger, and Kathleen Lennon (London: Palgrave Macmillan, 2012), 230; Judith Butler, *Precarious Life: The Powers of Mourning and Violence* (London: Verso, 2004); and Chouliaraki, *The Spectatorship of Suffering*.

113. McNay, "Suffering, Silence, and Social Weightlessness," 230.

114. Robin Pogrebin and Kate Kelly, "Brett Kavanaugh Fit in with the Privileged Kids. She Did Not," *New York Times*, September 14, 2019, https://www.nytimes.com/2019/09/14/sunday-review/brett-kavanaugh-deborah-ramirez-yale.html.

115. For the patriarchal politics of believability, see Leigh Gilmore, *Tainted Witness: Why We Doubt What Women Say About Their Lives* (New York: Columbia University Press, 2017); and Banet-Weiser and Higgins, *Believability*.

116. John Cassidy, "The Other Problem with Brett Kavanaugh's Supreme Court Nomination: Privilege," *The New Yorker*, September 21, 2018,

https://www.newyorker.com/news/our-columnists/how-brett-kavanaughs-hobbled-nomination-puts-american-privilege-on-trial; Stephanie Kirchgaessner, "FBI Director Faces New Scrutiny Over Investigation of Brett Kavanaugh," *The Guardian*, September 14, 2021, https://www.theguardian.com/us-news/2021/sep/14/brett-kavanaugh-fbi-investigation-documents. See also "FBI Failed to Fully Investigate Kavanaugh Allegations, Say Democrats," *The Guardian*, July 22, 2021, https://www.theguardian.com/us-news/2021/jul/22/brett-kavanaugh-sexual-misconduct-allegations-fbi-senators.
117. Sara Ahmed, *The Cultural Politics of Emotion* (Edinburgh: Edinburgh University Press, 2004), 120, emphasis in original.
118. Tami Amanda Jacoby, "A Theory of Victimhood: Politics, Conflict, and the Construction of Victim-Based Identity," *Millennium* 43, no. 2 (2015): 517, https://doi.org/10.1177/0305829814550258.
119. Meghan Chakrabarti, "In 'Thick,' Tressie McMillan Cottom Looks at Beauty, Power, and Black Womanhood in America," *On Point*, WBUR, January 21, 2019, https://www.google.co.uk/amp/s/amp.wbur.org/onpoint/2019/05/27/thick-tressie-mcmillan-cottom.
120. Edward W. Said, *Orientalism* (New York: Pantheon, 1978), xxiii.
121. In a *Guardian* article in 2002, Eric Hobsbawm summarized his own argument on "the age of catastrophe" as follows: "The 20th century was the most murderous in recorded history. The total number of deaths caused by or associated with its wars has been estimated at 187m, the equivalent of more than 10% of the world's population in 1913. Taken as having begun in 1914, it was a century of almost unbroken war, with few and brief periods without organised armed conflict somewhere. It was dominated by world wars: that is to say, by wars between territorial states or alliances of states." See Eric Hobsbawm, "War and Peace," *The Guardian*, February 3, 2003, https://www.theguardian.com/education/2002/feb/23/artsandhumanities.highereducation.
122. Caruth, *Unclaimed Experience*, 12.

2. WHO USED TO BE A VICTIM?

1. Peter Jackson, *They Shall Not Grow Old*, documentary (WingNut Films, 2018). See also Richard Brody, "'They Shall not Grow Old' Reviewed: The Indelible Voices in Peter Jackson's Documentary," *The*

New Yorker, February 19, 2019, https://www.newyorker.com/culture/the-front-row/they-shall-not-grow-old-reviewed-the-indelible-voices-in-peter-jacksons-first-world-war-documentary.

2. Thomas Gibbons-Neff, "Haunted by Their Decisions in War," *Washington Post*, March 6, 2015, https://www.washingtonpost.com/opinions/haunted-by-their-decisions-in-war/2015/03/06/db1cc404-c129-11e4-9271-610273846239_story.html?utm_term=.6a14a7c0adb.

3. Tyler Boudreau, "The Morally Injured," *Massachusetts Review* 52, nos. 3–4 (2011): 754, https://www.jstor.org/stable/23210143. For a similar history of the shift from silent suffering to the recognition of trauma, albeit with a different focus and argument, see Fassin and Rechtman, *Empire of Trauma*.

4. Santanu Das, "Colors of the Past: Archive, Art, and Amnesia in a Digital Age," *American Historical Review* 124, no. 5 (2019): 1772, https://doi.org/10.1093/ahr/rhz1021.

5. Das, "Colors of the Past," 1775. See also Vasja Badalič, *The War Against Civilians: Victims of the "War on Terror" in Afghanistan and Pakistan* (Cham, Switzerland: Springer International, 2019).

6. Joanna Bourke, "Fear and Anxiety: Writing About Emotion in Modern History," *History Workshop Journal* 55 (February 2003): 111–33, https://doi.org/10.1093/hwj/55.1.111; Yuval Noah Harari, *Renaissance Military Memoirs: War, History, and Identity, 1450–1600* (Suffolk, U.K.: Boydell and Brewer, 2004).

7. Thousands of women served in the First and Second World Wars (and even earlier in the Crimean War and the U.S. Civil War), but they did so mostly as nurses and auxiliary staff. Women were first allowed to join U.S. military service academies in the 1970s—though their engagement in air and naval combat missions did not take place until the 1990s. Today, 16 percent of the U.S. Army combat force and 11.8 percent of the U.K. force are female. See Lori Robinson and Michael O'Hanlon, "Women Warriors: The Ongoing Story of Integrating and Diversifying the American Armed Forces," Brookings Institute Report, 2020, https://www.brookings.edu/essay/women-warriors-the-ongoing-story-of-integrating-and-diversifying-the-armed-forces/; Meghan Harding, "Representation of Women in the Armed Forces," U.K. House of Commons Library, 2021, https://

commonslibrary.parliament.uk/representation-of-women-in-the-armed-forces/.

8. My reference to the predominantly male nature of war suffering relies on an established definition of hegemonic masculinity. According to Frank Barrett, "The term 'hegemonic masculinity' refers to a particular idealized image of masculinity in relation to which images of femininity and other masculinities are marginalized and subordinated. The hegemonic ideal of masculinity in current Western culture is a man who is independent, risk-taking, aggressive, heterosexual and rational." Frank J. Barrett, "The Organizational Construction of Hegemonic Masculinity: The Case of the US Navy," *Gender, Work, & Organization* 3, no. 3 (1996): 130, https://doi.org/10.1111/j.1468-0432.1996.tb00054.x. Although the notion of the "hegemonic" always suggests the historical possibility of emerging alternatives—a process of change that I follow throughout this chapter—Kimberly Hutchings argues that there is, in fact, a more constant, constitutive relationship between this form of masculinity and war insofar as "the formal properties of masculinity enable it to act as a prism through which to see, and make sense of, war." Kimberly Hutchings, "Making Sense of Masculinity and War," *Men and Masculinities* 10, no. 4 (2008): 390, https://doi.org/10.1177/1097184X07306740.

9. For relevant literature on war trauma and remasculinization, see, among other sources, Jason Crouthamel, "Male Sexuality and Psychological Trauma: Soldiers and Sexual Disorder in World War I and Weimar Germany," *Journal of the History of Sexuality* 17 (February 2008): 60–84, for the First World War; Christina Sharon Jarvis, *The Male Body at War: American Masculinity and Embodiment During World War II* (University Park: Pennsylvania State University Press, 2000), for the Second World War; Susan Jeffords, "Debriding Vietnam: The Resurrection of the White American Male," *Feminist Studies* 14, no. 3 (1988): 525–43, for Vietnam; and Thomas Bjerre, "From Warrior Heroes to Vulnerable Boys: Debunking 'Soldierly Masculinity' in Tim Hetherington's Infidel Photos," in *Visualizing War: Emotions, Technologies, Communities*, ed. Anders Engberg-Pedersen and Kathrin Maurer (London: Routledge, 2017), 146–64, for twenty-first-century wars.

10. Elaine Showalter, "Hysteria, Feminism, and Gender" in Sander Gilman et al., *Hysteria Beyond Freud* (Berkeley: University of California Press, 1993), 286–344.
11. Suzie Grogan, *Shell Shocked Britain: The First World War's Legacy for Britain's Mental Health*, illus. ed. (Barnsley, U.K.: Pen & Sword, 2014), 80.
12. Ruth Leys, "Traumatic Cures: Shell Shock, Janet, and the Question of Memory," in *Tense Past: Cultural Essays in Trauma and Memory*, ed. Paul Antze and Michael Lambek (London: Routledge, 1996), 110.
13. Alison S. Fell and Christine E. Hallett, *First World War Nursing: New Perspectives* (London: Routledge, 2013), 3.
14. Sharon Ouditt, *Fighting Forces, Writing Women: Identity and Ideology in the First World War* (London: Routledge, 2020).
15. Grogan, *Shell Shocked Britain*, 101. For the link between domestic violence and war trauma today, see Rachel Pain, "Intimate War," *Political Geography* 44 (January 2015): 64–73, https://doi.org/10.1016/j.polgeo.2014.09.011.
16. Diane Enns, *The Violence of Victimhood* (University Park: Pennsylvania State University Press, 2012), 81.
17. Arlene Stein, "Feminism, Therapeutic Culture, and the Holocaust in the United States: The Second-Generation Phenomenon," *Jewish Social Studies* 16, no. 1 (2009): 30, https://doi.org/10.2979/jss.2009.16.1.27. For a critique of the second wave's victimhood narrative, see Brown, *States of Injury*.
18. Cathy Humphreys and Stephen Joseph, "Domestic Violence and the Politics of Trauma," *Women's Studies International Forum* 27 (2004): 561, https://doi.org/10.1016/j.wsif.2004.09.010. See also Judith L. Herman, *Trauma and Recovery: The Aftermath of Violence—from Domestic Abuse to Political Terror* (New York: Basic, 1992).
19. Rosemary Kellison, *Expanding Responsibility for the Just War: A Feminist Critique* (Cambridge: Cambridge University Press, 2018), 5. For the need for a decolonial expansion of Western conceptualizations of war rape as "moral injury," see Carina M. Uchida, "Constraints on Rape as a Weapon of War: A Feminist and Post-colonial Revision," *E-International Relations*, November 20, 2018, https://www.e-ir.info/2018/11/20/constraints-on-rape-as-a-weapon-of-war-a-feminist

-and-post-colonial-revision/. For a feminist critique of "moral injury" as patriarchal practice, see Carol Gilligan, "Moral Injury and the Ethic of Care: Reframing the Conversation About Differences," *Journal of Social Philosophy* 45, no. 1 (2014): 89–106, https://doi.org/10.1111/josp.12050.

20. There is already a significant body of interdisciplinary work on the colonial dynamics of Western armies in the world wars and Vietnam. See, for instance, Santanu Das, ed., *Race, Empire, and First World War Writing* (Cambridge: Cambridge University Press, 2011); Daniel Kryder, *Divided Arsenal: Race and the American State During World War II* (Cambridge: Cambridge University Press, 2001); and James E. Westheider, *Fighting on Two Fronts: African Americans and the Vietnam War* (New York: New York University Press, 1997). Yet existing studies on the cultural construction of soldierly victimhood largely do not adopt a race-based perspective. For instance, see Leys, "Traumatic Cures"; Eric Leed, *No Man's Land: Combat and Identity in World War 1* (Cambridge: Cambridge University Press, 1979); Leed, "Fateful Memories: Industrialized War and Traumatic Neuroses," *Journal of Contemporary History* 35, no. 1 (2000): 85–100, https://doi.org/10.1177/002200940003500108; Joanna Bourke, "Effeminacy, Ethnicity, and the End of Trauma: The Sufferings of 'Shell-Shocked' Men in Great Britain and Ireland, 1914–39," *Journal of Contemporary History* 35, no. 1 (2000): 57–69, https://www.jstor.org/stable/261181; Bourke, "Fear and Anxiety"; Paul Fussell, *The Great War and Modern Memory* (London: Sterling , 2009); and Jay Winter, *Sites of Memory, Sites of Mourning: The Great War in European Cultural History* (Cambridge: Cambridge University Press, 1998).
21. Karen Halttunen, "Humanitarianism and the Pornography of Pain in Anglo-American Culture," *American Historical Review* 100, no. 2 (1995): 320, https://doi.org/10.2307/2169001.
22. John Stuart Mill, "Civilization," in *Essays on Politics and Culture*, ed. Gertrude Himmelfarb (New York: Basic, 1963), 64.
23. For the transformation of modern masculinity in relation to changes in social class and the dynamics of social movements since the eighteenth century, see George Lachmann Mosse, *The Image of Man: The Creation of Modern Masculinity* (Oxford: Oxford University Press, 1998).

For the hybridity of twentieth-century masculinities, see Robert A. Nye, "Western Masculinities in War and Peace," *American Historical Review* 112, no. 2 (2007): 421, https://www.jstor.org/stable/4136608. For the dominant presence of toxic masculinity today, see Paul Elliott Johnson, "The Art of Masculine Victimhood: Donald Trump's Demagoguery," *Women's Studies in Communication* 40, no. 3 (2017): 229–50, https://doi.org/10.1080/07491409.2017.1346533. For the mix of stoic masculinity and vulnerability in contemporary media representations of soldiers, see Bjerre, "From Warrior Heroes to Vulnerable Boys."

24. Ana Carden-Coyne, "Masculinity and the Wounds of the First World War: A Centenary Reflection," *Revue française de civilisation britannique*, online publication, May 1, 2015, https://doi.org/10.4000/rfcb.305.

25. Elaine Scarry, *The Body in Pain: The Making and Unmaking of the World* (Oxford: Oxford University Press, 1987), 63.

26. Harari, *Renaissance Military Memoirs*, 104. On the seventeenth-century culture of chivalry, see Leo Braudy, *From Chivalry to Terrorism: War and the Changing Nature of Masculinity* (New York: Knopf, 2003).

27. Harari, *Renaissance Military Memoirs*, 140.

28. Christopher Coker, *Humane Warfare* (London: Routledge, 2001); Moyn, *The Last Utopia*.

29. The Crimean War (1853–1856) was, in fact, the first industrialized conflict of the modern era, and its shockingly high death toll (19 percent of the combatants as opposed to 11 percent in the First World War) led to the establishment of the first integrated military hospitals, to which Florence Nightingale greatly contributed. See Orlando Figes, *Crimea* (London: Penguin, 2011); and Yakup Bektas, "The Crimean War as a Technological Enterprise," *Notes and Records: Royal Society Journal of the History of Science* 71, no. 3 (2017): 233–62. It also led to the establishment of the Red Cross by Henry Dunant, the first humanitarian organization in aid of wounded combatants that worked independently of conflict sides in battlefields around the world. See James Crossland, *War, Law, and Humanity: The Campaign to Control Warfare, 1853–1914* (London: Bloomsbury, 2018). However, the widespread and enduring commemoration practices of the American war—as opposed to the Crimean one, also known as an "off the charts" war—has determined

this chapter's focus. See Anne Louise Berridge, "Off the Chart: The Crimean War in British Public Consciousness," *19: Interdisciplinary Studies in the Long Nineteenth Century* 20 (2015): 1–23, https://doi.org/10.16995/ntn.726.

30. Christon I. Archer, *World History of Warfare* (Lincoln: University of Nebraska Press, 2002), 413–14.
31. Quoted in DeAnne Blanton and Lauren Cook Wike, *They Fought Like Demons: Women Soldiers in the American Civil War* (Baton Rouge: Louisiana State University Press, 2002), 194.
32. Gugliotta Guy, "New Estimate Raises Civil War Death Toll," *New York Times*, April 2, 2012, https://www.nytimes.com/2012/04/03/science/civil-war-toll-up-by-20-percent-in-new-estimate.html.
33. On this code, see Braudy, *From Chivalry to Terrorism*.
34. Jessica Meyer, "Separating the Men from the Boys: Masculinity and Maturity in Understandings of Shell Shock in Britain," *Twentieth Century British History* 20, no. 1 (2009): 5, https://doi.org/10.1093/tcbh/hwn028.
35. Drew Gilpin Faust, *This Republic of Suffering* (New York: Knopf Doubleday, 2008), xiv, 189.
36. Charles Mills, "White Ignorance," in *Race and Epistemologies of Ignorance*, ed. Shannon Sullivan and Nancy Tuana (Albany: State University of New York Press, 2007), 11–38.
37. Faust, *This Republic of Suffering*, 47.
38. Margaret Humphreys, *Intensely Human: The Health of the Black Soldier in the American Civil War*, illus. ed. (Baltimore, MD: Johns Hopkins University Press, 2008), 6.
39. David W. Blight, "'For Something Beyond the Battlefield': Frederick Douglass and the Struggle for the Memory of the Civil War," *Journal of American History* 75, no. 4 (1989): 1158, https://doi.org/10.2307/1908634.
40. Isabel Wilkerson, *Caste: The Origins of Our Discontents* (New York: Random House, 2020), xx.
41. W. E. B. Du Bois, *Worlds of Color* (1925; reprint, Edinburgh: Mainstream/Random House, 1961), 352.
42. Mills, "White Ignorance."
43. Derek H. Alderman and Rebecca Dobbs, "Geographies of Slavery: Of Theory, Method, and Intervention," in "Geographies of Slavery,"

ed. Derek H. Alderman and G. Rebecca Dobbs, special issue, *Historical Geography* 39 (2011): 29–40.
44. Gaines M. Foster, *Ghosts of the Confederacy: Defeat, the Lost Cause, and the Emergence of the New South, 1865–1913* (1985; reprint, New York: Oxford University Press, 1987), 196.
45. Nye, "Western Masculinities in War and Peace," 421.
46. Edgar Jones and Simon Wessely, "A Paradigm Shift in the Conceptualization of Psychological Trauma in the 20th Century," *Journal of Anxiety Disorders* 21, no. 2 (2007): 164–75, https://doi.org/10.1016/j.janxdis.2006.09.009.
47. Michael Roper, "Between the Psyche and the Social: Masculinity, Subjectivity, and the First World War Veteran," *Journal of Men's Studies* 15, no. 3 (2008): 254.
48. George Lachmann Mosse, *Nationalism and Sexuality: Respectability and Abnormal Sexuality in Modern Europe* (Madison: University of Wisconsin Press, 1985).
49. John T. MacCurdy, *The Psychology of War* (1918; reprint, Minneapolis, MN: Franklin Classics, 2018), quoted in Bourke, "Effeminacy, Ethnicity, and the End of Trauma," 58.
50. Leed, *No Man's Land*, 164.
51. F. G. Chandler, "Memories of August 1917: Extract from a Doctor's Diary," *London Hospital Gazette*, 1918, 4, Imperial War Museum, London, quoted in Edgar Jones, "The Psychology of Killing: The Combat Experience of British Soldiers During the First World War," *Journal of Contemporary History* 41, no. 2 (2006): 231, https://www.jstor.org/stable/30036384.
52. Leon C. Standifer, *Not in Vain: A Rifleman Remembers World War II* (Baton Rouge: Louisiana State University Press, 1992), 30–31, quoted in Leed, "Fateful Memories," 86.
53. Leed, "Fateful Memories," 95.
54. Bourke, "Effeminacy, Ethnicity, and the End of Trauma."
55. Mark Micale, *Approaching Hysteria: Disease and Its Interpretations* (Princeton, NJ: Princeton University Press, 1995), 168; the insertion "like women before them" is my addition. The Canadian doctor Harold McGill, who treated shell-shocked soldiers returning from the Western Front, described this split as follows: "The victims were men

of the finest moral courage[, which in fact] set the stage for the development of shell-shock. The man's whole physical nature revolted from the sights and sounds of a bombardment. This was much intensified if he was with troops holding a static position and obliged to sit still and take punishment without the opportunity of striking back. The thoughts and the sights of jagged pieces of steel tearing through living human flesh were appalling. All the man's natural physical impulses prompted him to take shelter, and to run away if necessary. On the other hand, his spiritual courage, his faith to his duty and his discipline forced him to remain. The result was a conflict under which the nervous system collapsed and the soldier became a gibbering maniac." Harold W. McGill, *Medicine and Duty: The World War I Memoir of Captain Harold W. McGill, Medical Officer, 31st Battalion, C.E.F.*, ed. Marjorie Barron Norris (Calgary, Canada: University of Calgary Press, 2007), 172.

56. Crouthamel, "Male Sexuality and Psychological Trauma."
57. As Elaine Showalter has shown, in 1916 "war neurosis" cases made up 40 percent of the British war casualties, and by 1918 there were already twenty mental hospitals treating psychiatric military cases in Britain. See Showalter, "Hysteria, Feminism, and Gender," 321.
58. Fussell, *The Great War and Modern Memory*; Winter, *Sites of Memory, Sites of Mourning*.
59. The chivalric ideal of the noble, self-sacrificial soldier is mocked by Wilfred Owen in his poem "Dulce et decorum est" (1920) and immortalized by the literary canon of British, French, and German First World War veterans. See Samuel Hynes, *The Soldiers' Tale: Bearing Witness to Modern War* (New York: Allen Lane, 1997).
60. Scarry, *The Body in Pain*, 77.
61. Emma Hutchison, *Affective Communities in World Politics* (Cambridge: Cambridge University Press, 2016).
62. Michael Roper, "Between Manliness and Masculinity: The 'War Generation' and the Psychology of Fear in Britain, 1914–1950," *Journal of British Studies* 4, no. 2 (2005): 348.
63. Robert Hemmings, "'The Blameless Physician': Narrative and Pain, Sassoon and Rivers," *Literature and Medicine* 24, no. 1 (2005): 114, https://doi.org/10.1353/lm.2005.0026.

64. Winter, *Sites of Memory, Sites of Mourning*; Jay Winter, *Remembering War: The Great War Between Memory and History in the 20th Century*, annotated ed. (New Haven, CT: Yale University Press, 2006); Winter, "Foreword: Historical Remembrance in the Twenty-First Century," in "Historical Remembrance in the Twenty-First Century," ed. Jay Winter, special issue, *Annals of the American Academy of Political and Social Science* 617, no. 1 (2015): 6–13, https://doi.org/10.1177/0002716207312761.
65. Roger Luckhurst, *The Trauma Question* (London: Routledge, 2008), 5.
66. Fiona Reid, *Broken Men: Shell Shock, Treatment, and Recovery in Britain, 1914–1930*, illus. ed. (London: Continuum, 2010), 14.
67. Jacqueline Jenkinson, "'All in the Same Uniform?' The Participation of Black Colonial Residents in the British Armed Forces in the First World War," *Journal of Imperial and Commonwealth History* 40, no. 2 (2012): 207–30, https://doi.org/10.1080/03086534.2012.697611.
68. Hilary Buxton, "Imperial Amnesia: Race, Trauma, and Indian Troops in the First World War," *Past & Present* 241, no. 1 (2018): 225, https://doi.org/10.1093/pastj/gty023.
69. Trevor Dodman, "'Belated Impress': River George and the African American Shell Shock Narrative," *African American Review* 44 (January 2011): 149–66, https://doi.org/10.1353/afa.2011.0023.
70. Thomas Lacquer, "Memory and Naming in the Great War," in *Commemorations: The Politics of National Identity*, ed. John R. Gillis (1994; reprint, Princeton, NJ: Princeton University Press, 1996), 150–67.
71. Imperial War Graves Commission, response to the "Historical Inequalities in the Commemoration of the Dead" report (2020), composed by an independent Special Committee of experts and chaired by Sir Tim Hitchens, https://www.cwgc.org/non-commemoration-report/our-response/.
72. Michèle Barrett, *Casualty Figures: How Five Men Survived the First World War* (London: Verso, 2007), 465. Behind the erasure, new evidence coming to light as late as 2014 about the experience of Indian troops in the Western Front, namely Indian soldiers' or sepoys' letters back home, paint a complex and touching portrait of those soldiers whose war service had been long forgotten and unappreciated: "It is important," argues Santanu Das, "to go beyond the stereotype of the Indian sepoy as the loyal *izzat*-driven subject or the naive, hapless

victim of war, and to see him as a complex, intelligent individual, negotiating between different cultures, institutions and people." Santanu Das, "The Indian Sepoy in the First World War," British Library Archive, February 6, 2014, https://www.bl.uk/world-war-one/articles/the-indian-sepoy-in-the-first-world-war. Similarly, it was only in 2016—after ninety-seven years in the dark—that the records of 320,000 Punjab soldiers were discovered and examined: "Punjab," the chair of the U.K. Punjab Heritage Association said, "was the main recruiting ground for the Indian army during world war one [sic]. And yet the contribution of the individuals has largely been unrecognised. In most cases, we didn't even know their names." Quoted in Rajeev Syal, "Records of 320,000 Punjab Soldiers from First World War Uncovered," *The Guardian*, November 10, 2021, https://amp.theguardian.com/world/2021/nov/10/records-of-320000-punjab-soldiers-from-first-world-war-uncovered.

73. Imperial War Graves Commission, response to the "Historical Inequalities in the Commemoration of the Dead" report.
74. Although racial segregation in the U.S. Army officially ended in 1948, when President Truman issued an executive order for equality of treatment in the U.S. Armed Forces (http://www.Army.Mil/blackamericans), discrimination in the army continued through to Vietnam and still exists today. See Westheider, *Fighting on Two Fronts*.
75. Ron Eyerman, *Memory, Trauma, and Identity* (London: Palgrave Macmillan, 2019).
76. Hynes, *The Soldiers' Tale*, 178.
77. For the impact that the televising of the Vietnam War had on public opinion on war, see Daniel Hallin, *The Uncensored War: The Media and Vietnam* (Berkeley: University of California Press, 1989); and Michael Mandelbaum, "Vietnam: The Television War," *Daedalus* 111, no. 4 (1982): 157–69.
78. David E. Kaiser, *American Tragedy: Kennedy, Johnson, and the Origins of the Vietnam War* (Cambridge, MA: Harvard University Press, 2000); Charles R. Figley, *Stress Disorders Among Vietnam Veterans: Theory, Research* (London: Routledge, 2014).
79. Peter Arnett, *Live from the Battlefield: From Vietnam to Baghdad: 35 Years in the World's War Zones* (New York: Simon & Schuster, 1994).

80. Stathis Kalyvas and Matthew Adam Kocher, "The Dynamics of Violence in Vietnam: An Analysis of the Hamlet Evaluation System (HES)," *Journal of Peace Research* 46, no. 3 (2009): 338, https://www.jstor.org/stable/25654409.
81. Braudy, *From Chivalry to Terrorism*, 529.
82. Coker, *Human Warfare*, 35–36.
83. Hynes, *The Soldiers' Tale*, 180.
84. Stephen Howard, "The Vietnam Warrior: His Experience, and Implications for Psychotherapy," *American Journal of Psychotherapy* 30, no. 1 (1976): 124.
85. Eyerman, *Memory, Trauma, and Identity*, 167.
86. On the use of napalm, see Robert M. Neer, *Napalm* (Cambridge, MA: Harvard University Press, 2013).
87. Fassin and Rechtman, *The Empire of Trauma*, 95.
88. Chad Williams, "World War I in the Historical Imagination of W. E. B. Du Bois," *Modern American History* 1, no. 1 (2018): 3–22.
89. Kalyvas and Kocher, "The Dynamics of Violence in Vietnam," 338.
90. Irving M. Allen, "Posttraumatic Stress Disorder Among Black Vietnam Veterans," *Psychiatric Services* 37, no. 1 (1986): 55.
91. Daniel Lucks, "African American Soldiers and the Vietnam War: No More Vietnams," *The Sixties* 10, no. 2 (2017): 197, https://doi.org/10.1080/17541328.2017.1303111.
92. Martin Luther King Jr., "The World House," in *Where Do We Go from Here: Chaos or Community?* (1967), introduction by Vincent Harding, foreword by Coretta Scott King (Boston, MA: Beacon, 2010), 201.
93. Jonathan Rosenberg, *How Far the Promised Land? World Affairs and the American Civil Rights Movement from the First World War to Vietnam* (Princeton, NJ: Princeton University Press, 2006), 5. The link between human rights as a principle of universal humanity and Black liberation struggles was present in the early rhetoric of Frederick Douglass: "Human rights," he wrote, "stand upon a common basis; and by all the reason that they are supported, maintained and defended, for one variety of the human family, they are supported, maintained and defended for *all* the human family; because all mankind have the same wants, arising out of a common nature." Frederick Douglass, "The Claims of the Negro Ethnologically Considered" (1854), in *The Speeches of*

2. WHO USED TO BE A VICTIM? ❧ 167

Frederick Douglass: A Critical Edition, ed. John R. McKivigan, Julie Husband, and Heather L. Kaufman (New Haven, CT: Yale University Press, 2018), 147. This same link was also present in the writing of W. E. B. Du Bois, who joined the Niagara Movement as "the first black organisation which aggressively and unconditionally demanded human rights for their people." See Elliott Rudwick, "The Niagara Movement," *Journal of Negro History* 42, no. 3 (1957): 177. Du Bois, a founding figure of the NAACP, also sowed the seeds for pan-Africanism, a movement that globalized the struggle of Black people across continents. See W. E. B. Du Bois, *On Sociology and the Black Community*, ed. Dan Green and Edwin Driver (Chicago: University of Chicago Press, 1978), 23–27. For a detailed account of the tensions and splits in the Civil Rights Movement between the radical Black Liberation movement (Malcolm X) and the NAACP (King) during the 1960s and the Vietnam conflict, see Jonas Gilbert, *Freedom's Sword: The NAACP and the Struggle Against Racism in America, 1909–1969* (New York: Routledge, 2006).

94. The judicial understanding of trauma was first established in the Eichmann trial around the Holocaust, as I have already mentioned, but this trial concerned Jewish and other minority-group survivors rather than soldiers.

95. Illouz, *Cold Intimacies*, 59. For the financial implications of recognizing the PTSD sufferer as a traumatized person in need of treatment but also as a legal subject entitled to state protection and compensation, see Jones and Wessely, "A Paradigm Shift." Zachary Steel, Catherine Bateman Steel, and Derrick Silove argue that PTSD "offered mental health researchers and human rights advocates alike a new tool to document and quantify the psychological consequences associated with human rights abuses and organized violence." Zachary Steel, Catherine R. Bateman Steel, and Derrick Silove, "Human Rights and the Trauma Model: Genuine Partners or Uneasy Allies?," *Journal of Traumatic Stress* 22, no. 5 (2009): 360, https://doi.org/10.1002/jts.20449.

96. See, for instance, Illouz, "'That Shadowy Realm of the Interior.'"

97. Moyn quoted in Robert Kaplan, "*Humane: How the United States Abandoned Peace and Reinvented War* by Samuel Moyn," *New York Times*,

September 21, 2021, https://www.nytimes.com/2021/09/14/books/review/humane-samuel-moyn.html.
98. Hew Strachan, *The Direction of War: Contemporary Strategy in Historical Perspective* (Cambridge: Cambridge University Press, 2013).
99. Coker, *Human Warfare*, 453.
100. More recent wars, such as the post–Arab Spring coalition against Libya or, selectively, against Syria, similarly occurred in the name of the "responsibility to protect" United Nations doctrine, meant to assuage Gaddafi's and Assad's attacks against their own people (Strachan, *The Direction of War*). All these "humanitarian" conflicts need to be seen as part of a post–Cold War world order that no longer relies on superpower rivalries but on the governance of a multipolar network of particular state powers promoting a security mandate through professional armies and under the formal jurisdiction of supranational institutions such as the United Nations, the North Atlantic Treaty Organization, and the European Union. See Grant Marlier and Neta Crawford, "Incomplete and Imperfect Institutionalisation of Empathy and Altruism in the 'Responsibility to Protect' Doctrine," *Global Responsibility to Protect* 5 (January 2013): 397–422, https://doi.org/10.1163/1875984X-00504003.
101. Coker, *Human Warfare*, 133.
102. Mathew Coleman, "Immigration Geopolitics Beyond the Mexico–US Border," *Antipode* 39, no. 1 (2007): 54–76, https://doi.org/10.1111/j.1467-8330.2007.00506.x.
103. Walt Napier, "A Short History of Integration in the US Armed Forces," U.S. Department of Defense, July 1, 2021, https://www.af.mil/News/Commentaries/Display/Article/2676311/a-short-history-of-integration-in-the-us-armed-forces/&cd=17&hl=el&ct=clnk&gl=uk.
104. Arundhati Roy, "Noam Chomsky, Neoliberalism, and the New War on Iraq," *Contemporary Justice Review* 6, no. 4 (2003): 321, emphasis in the original, https://doi.org/10.1080/1028258032000144767.
105. Boudreau, "The Morally Injured."
106. Mady Stovall, Lissi Hansen, and Michelle van Ryn, "A Critical Review: Moral Injury in Nurses in the Aftermath of a Patient Safety Incident," *Journal of Nursing Scholarship* 52, no. 3 (2020): 320.

107. Wood quoted in Kenneth MacLeish, "On 'Moral Injury': Psychic Fringes and War Violence," *History of the Human Sciences* 31, no. 2 (2018): 128, https://doi.org/10.1177/0952695117750342.
108. Julia Welland, "Compassionate Soldiering and Comfort," in *Emotions, Politics, and War*, ed. Linda Åhäll and Thomas Gregory (London: Routledge, 2015), 125.
109. Alison O'Connor, "Coming Home to the Arts: Theatre as Reconnection," paper presented at the Culture, Health, and Wellbeing International Conference, June 20–22, 2017, Bristol, U.K., https://pure.southwales.ac.uk/en/publications/coming-home-to-the-arts-theatre-as-reconnection.
110. Brock and Litini quoted in Adam Eriksen, "Demons of War. A Silent Killer for Soldiers: Moral Injury," *Sojourners*, June 25, 2015, https://sojo.net/articles/demons-war. See also Rita Brock and Gabriella Litini, *Soul Repair: Recovering from Moral Injury After War* (Boston, MA: Beacon, 2013); and O'Connor, "Coming Home to the Arts."
111. Rebecca Sanders, "Human Rights Abuses at the Limits of the Law: Legal Instabilities and Vulnerabilities in the 'Global War on Terror,'" *Review of International Studies* 44, no. 1 (2018): 2–23.
112. Elizabeth Spelman, *Fruits of Sorrow: Framing Our Attention to Suffering* (Boston, MA: Beacon, 2001), 118, quoted in Welland, "Compassionate Soldiering and Comfort," 125.
113. Elke Schwarz, "Prescription Drones: On the Techno-biopolitical Regimes of Contemporary 'Ethical Killing,'" *Security Dialogue* 47, no. 1 (2016): 59–75, https://www.jstor.org/stable/26293585.
114. See Andrew Hoskins, "Digital War," in *Routledge Handbook of Humanitarian Communication*, ed. Lilie Chouliaraki and Anne Vestergaard (London: Routledge, 2022), 66–86.
115. For the numbers given here, see Costs of War on Terror, online project, Watson Institute of International and Public Affairs, Brown University, https://watson.brown.edu/costsofwar/.
116. David Kennedy, "Modern War and Modern Law," *International Legal Theory* 12, no. 55 (2006): 471–94, https://heinonline.org/HOL/Page?handle=hein.journals/intltr12&id=61&div=&collection=.
117. For continuing racist practices in the U.K. Army, see, for instance, Balissa Greene, "A Study of the British Army: White, Male, and

Little Diversity," *LSE Blog*, December 16, 2016, https://www.lse.ac.uk/News/Research-Highlights/Society-media-and-science/British-Army. On the U.S. Army, see, among other sources, Kat Stafford and James Laporta, "Military Still Grappling with Racism, Extremism, Investigation Finds," *Newshour*, PBS, December 29, 2021, https://www.pbs.org/newshour/nation/military-still-grappling-with-racism-and-extremism-investigation-finds.

118. Eric Hobsbawm, *Age of Extremes: A History of the World, 1914–1991* (1994; reprint, London: Abacus, 1995); Hobsbawm titles part 1 of his book "The Age of Catastrophe."

119. Scarry, *The Body in Pain*.

120. Theodor Meron, *The Humanization of International Law* (Leiden, Netherlands: Martinus Nijhoff, 2006).

121. Fiona McQueen, "Male Emotionality: 'Boys Don't Cry' Versus 'It's Good to Talk,'" *NORMA* 12, nos. 3–4 (2017): 205–19, https://doi.org/10.1080/18902138.2017.1336877. Campaigns for veterans' mental health in both the United Kingdom and the United States focus precisely on the detrimental impact of this core tension between expressing and denying emotion in relation to traumatic experiences in war. See, for instance, "Mental Health in the Military: Where Are We Now?," *PsychCentral*, May 24, 2022, https://psychcentral.com/ptsd/mental-health-in-the-military; and "Royals Push for More Military Mental Health Awareness," *ForcesNet*, February 28, 2018, https://www.forces.net/news/royals-push-more-military-mental-health-awareness.

122. Kate Manne, *Entitled: How Male Privilege Hurts Women* (New York: Crown, 2020); Tressie McMillan Cottom, "Where Platform Capitalism and Racial Capitalism Meet: The Sociology of Race and Racism in the Digital Society," *Sociology of Race and Ethnicity* 6, no. 4 (2020): 441–49, https://doi.org/10.1177/2332649220949473.

3. WHO IS A VICTIM TODAY?

1. "Speech: Prime Minister's Statement on Coronavirus (COVID-19)," Gov.UK, March 12, 2020, https://www.gov.uk/government/speeches/pm-statement-on-coronavirus-12-march-2020.

2. Johnson quoted in Tim Adams, "A Year After Johnson's Swaggering Greenwich Speech, 100,000 Dead," *The Guardian*, January 31, 2021, https://www.theguardian.com/politics/2021/jan/31/a-year-after-johnsons-swaggering-greenwich-speech-and-100000-dead.
3. Trump quoted in Brad Brooks, "Like the Flu? Trump's Coronavirus Messaging Confuses Public, Pandemic Researchers Say," Reuters, March 13, 2020, https://www.reuters.com/article/us-health-coronavirus-mixed-messages-idUSKBN2102GY.
4. Trump quoted in Aaron Blake and J. M. Rieger, "Timeline: The 201 Times Trump Has Downplayed the Coronavirus Threat," *Washington Post*, November 3, 2020, https://www.washingtonpost.com/politics/2020/03/12/trump-coronavirus-timeline/.
5. World Health Organization, WHO Coronavirus (COVID-19) Dashboard, https://covid19.who.int/. U.K. deaths include those of Northern Ireland.
6. U.K. House of Commons Science and Technology Committee and Health and Social Care Committee, "Coronavirus: Lessons Learned to Date," 2021, https://committees.parliament.uk/publications/7496/documents/78687/default/; see also U.K. COVID-19 Public Inquiry, 2023, https://covid19.public-inquiry.uk/, covering the inquiry that took place in the fall of 2023 and further exposed the depths of incompetence, indifference, and corruption that defined the nation's response to the pandemic. Congressional investigation quoted in Rich Mendez, "Trump Officials Bragged About Pressuring CDC to Alter COVID-19 Reports, Emails Reveal," CNBC, April 9, 2021, https://www.cnbc.com/2021/04/09/trump-officials-bragged-about-pressuring-cdc-to-alter-covid-reports-emails-reveal-.html.
7. Nazrul Islam et al., "Excess Deaths Associated with COVID-19 Pandemic in 2020: Age and Sex Disaggregated Time Series Analysis in 29 High Income Countries," *British Medical Journal* 373, no. 1137 (2021), https://www.bmj.com/content/373/bmj.n1137.
8. See, for example, Sheryl Gay Stolberg and Noa Weiland, "Study Finds 'Single Largest Driver' of Coronavirus Misinformation: Trump," *New York Times*, September 30, 2020, https://www.nytimes.com/2020/09/30/us/politics/trump-coronavirus-misinformation.html; "The COVID-19 Infodemic," collective editorial, *Lancet: Infectious Diseases*

20, no. 8 (2020): 875, https://www.thelancet.com/journals/laninf/article/PIIS1473-3099(20)30565-X/fulltext; and Laurie Garrett, "COVID-19: The Medium Is the Message," *Lancet* 395, no. 10228 (2020): 942–43, https://www.thelancet.com/journals/lancet/article/PIIS0140-6736(20)30600-0/fulltext.

9. Even though authoritarian populist governments have been dominant across several countries around the world, they all did not produce a unitary response to the pandemic—with some, unlike the United States and the United Kingdom, employing explicitly protectionist policies. For such variations among populist governments, see, for instance, Pippa Norris, "Varieties of Populist Parties," *Philosophy & Social Criticism* 45, nos. 9–10 (2019): 981–1012, https://doi.org/10.1177/0191453719872279. The United Kingdom and the United States, despite their historical, political, and cultural differences, shared a similar orientation to what Rogers Brubaker calls "anti-intellectualism, libertarian anti-statism, and myths of self-reliance," all of which shaped their discourses and policies on COVID-19. Rogers Brubaker, "Paradoxes of Populism During the Pandemic," *Thesis Eleven* 164, no. 1 (2021): 74, https://doi.org/10.1177/0725513620970804.

10. The first wave of the COVID-19 pandemic is officially defined as March–June 2020, when the first U.K. national lockdown and most U.S. lockdowns took place, but the communicative strategies that defined this specific time slot extend both before it (normalization) and after it (obfuscation), so I have here drawn on Johnson and Trump texts produced in the period February to September 2020—whether these texts are public addresses, press conference statements, or news interviews. Further local (in the United States and the United Kingdom) and national lockdowns (in the United Kingdom) also took place until April 2021, but they do not form part of my analysis.

11. See, for instance, Steven Levitsky and Daniel Ziblatt, *How Democracies Die* (New York: Crown, 2018); Timothy Snyder, *On Tyranny: Twenty Lessons from the Twentieth Century* (New York: Crown/Random House, 2017); Snyder, *The Road to Unfreedom* (New York: Crown/Random House, 2018); Grossberg, *Under the Cover of Chaos*; Aurelien Mondon and Aaron Winter, *Reactionary Democracy: How Racism and the Populist Far Right Became Mainstream* (London: Verso, 2020); and

Ruth Ben-Ghiat, *Strongmen: How They Rise, Why They Succeed, How They Fall* (London: Profile, 2000).

12. Mondon and Winter, *Reactionary Democracy*, 5. On the persisting power of authoritarian populism, see Tom Nichols, "The Authoritarian Right Is Regrouping," *Atlantic*, November 29, 2022, https://www.theatlantic.com/newsletters/archive/2022/11/the-authoritarian-right-is-regrouping/672286/; Nichols, "Never Trump Means Never: Opposing Trumpism Is About More Than Rejecting One Man," *Atlantic*, November 28, 2022, https://www.theatlantic.com/newsletters/archive/2022/11/never-trump-means-never/672295/; Ido Vock, "Europe's Far-Right Parties Are Learning from One Another," *New Statesman*, December 3, 2022, https://www.newstatesman.com/world/europe/2022/12/europe-far-right-parties-cas-mudde; Pedro Marques, "To the Far Right: Bella Ciao. Will Europe Manage to Survive the Attacks on Democracy from Within?," *Politico*, November 18, 2022, https://www.politico.eu/article/giorgia-meloni-italy-prime-minister-democracy-attacks-european-union/.
13. Pippa Norris and Ronald Inglehart, *Cultural Backlash: Trump, Brexit, and Authoritarian Populism* (Cambridge: Cambridge University Press, 2019), 8.
14. Francisco Panizza, introduction to *Populism and the Mirror of Democracy*, ed. Francisco Panizza (London: Verso, 2005), 3.
15. Note that without referring to populism's relationship to the legacy of the politics of pain, as I do here, Michael Kazin defines populism in a similar manner as "a persistent yet mutable style of political rhetoric with roots deep in the nineteenth century," which is capable of combining the people's "collective grievances and optimistic hopes." Michael Kazin, *The Populist Persuasion: An American History* (Ithaca, NY: Cornell University Press, 1995), 5–6.
16. For the link between redemption and pragmatism as constitutive of the political discourse of liberalism, see Margaret Canovan, "Trust the People! Populism and the Two Faces of Democracy," *Political Studies* 47, no. 1 (1999): 2–16, https://doi.org/10.1111/1467-9248.00184. Canovan arrives at the two terms by reworking Michael Oakeshott's "two faces of democracy" argument—namely, the politics of faith and the politics of skepticism—and using them to theorize populism as an

articulatory possibility internal to democratic politics. See Michael Oakeshott, *The Politics of Faith and the Politics of Scepticism*, ed. Timothy Fuller (New Haven, CT: Yale University Press, 1996), 21–38. For a reformulation of Canovan's definition that approaches populism's relationship to liberal politics in terms of "spectral recurrences" as both "a visitation" and "a haunting," see Benjamín Arditi, "Populism as a Spectre of Democracy: A Response to Canovan," *Political Studies* 52, no. 1 (2003): 135–43, https://doi.org/10.1111/j.1467-9248.2004.00468.x. Treating populism as an "internal periphery of democratic politics," like Canovan, Arditi captures the duality of populism in his reformulation: "Populism," he says, "can be a dimension of representation and a mode of participation lodged in the rougher edges of democracy, but also something more disturbing, as it can thrive in political democracies while it morphs into democracy's nemesis" (143).

17. Filipe Carreira da Silva and Mónica Brito Vieira, "Populism and the Politics of Redemption," *Thesis Eleven* 149, no. 1 (2018): 21, https://doi.org/10.1177/0725513618813374.

18. Nadia Urbinati, *Me the People: How Populism Transforms Democracy* (Cambridge, MA: Harvard University Press, 2019), 47.

19. "Trump Inauguration: President Vows to End 'American Carnage,'" *BBC News*, January 21, 2017, https://www.bbc.co.uk/news/world-us-canada-38688507; "Prime Minister Johnson's Brexit Address," Reuters, February 1, 2020, https://www.reuters.com/article/uk-britain-eu-johnson-address-idUSKBN1ZU31M. See also Ruth Wodak, *The Politics of Fear: What Right-Wing Populist Discourses Mean* (Los Angeles: Sage, 2015); Wodak, *The Politics of Fear: The Shameless Normalization of Far-Right Discourse*, 2nd ed. (Los Angeles: Sage, 2020); and Wodak, "Crisis Communication and Crisis Management During COVID-19," *Global Discourse* 11, no. 3 (2021): 329–53.

20. Nicolas Demertzis and Ron Eyerman, "COVID-19 as Cultural Trauma," *American Journal of Cultural Sociology* 8, no. 3 (2020): 428–50, https://doi.org/10.1057/s41290-020-00112-z.

21. Brubaker, "Paradoxes of Populism During the Pandemic," 80.

22. The articulation of pragmatism with redemption during the pandemic took different forms in different political discourses across national contexts around the world. Other national discourses of public health,

for instance, opted for pragmatic articulations of pain that fully acknowledged the threat of the virus but without abandoning a hopeful, redemptive vision of saving lives. They did so by not accepting deaths as inevitable but by seeking to act proactively so as to combat the virus through public-health measures that mitigated transmission: "Leaders such as Ardern, Merkel, and Taiwan's president Tsai Ingwen," say Carol Johnson and Blair Williams, have been praised for their "effective messaging and decisive action," which differed from "the bombastic approaches of several of the world's most prominent male leaders." Rather than slipping into the cynical fatalism of Johnson's statement, these leaders' narratives of redemption were not about sacrificing but about protecting the people. See Carol Johnson and Blair Williams, "Gender and Political Leadership in a Time of COVID," *Politics & Gender* 16, no. 4 (2020): 946, https://doi.org/10.1017/S1743923X2000029X. See also Timon Forster and Mirko Heinzel, "Reacting, Fast and Slow: How World Leaders Shaped Government Responses to the COVID-19 Pandemic," *Journal of European Public Policy* 28, no. 8 (2021): 1299–320, https://doi.org/10.1080/13501763.2021.1942157. For New Zealand's response in the first wave of the pandemic, see Michael Baker and Andrew Anglemyer, "Successful Elimination of COVID-19 Transmission in New Zealand," *New England Journal of Medicine* 383 (2020): e56, https://www.nejm.org/doi/full/10.1056/NEJMc2025203. For Germany's response, see Michael Baker, Nick Wilson, and Andrew Anglemyer, "Excess Mortality due to COVID-19 in Germany," *Journal of Infection* 81, no. 5 (2020): 797–801, https://www.nejm.org/doi/full/10.1056/NEJMc2025203. For Taiwan, see Jennifer Summers et al., "Potential Lessons from the Taiwan and New Zealand Health Responses to the COVID-19 Pandemic," *Lancet Regional Health* 4 (November 2020), https://www.sciencedirect.com/science/article/pii/S2666606520300444.

23. For the performativity of populism, see Benjamin Moffitt and Simon Tormey, "Rethinking Populism: Politics, Mediatisation, and Political Style," *Political Studies* 62, no. 2 (2014): 381–97, https://doi.org/10.1111/1467-9248.12032; Yannis Stavrakakis et al., "Populism, Anti-populism, and Crisis," *Contemporary Political Theory* 17 (2018): 4–27; Angelos Kissas, "Performative and Ideological Populism: The Case of

Charismatic Leaders on Twitter," *Discourse & Society* 31, no. 3 (2020): 268–84, https://doi.org/10.1177/0957926519889127. For the use of *articulation* in a discursive theory of populism, see Ernesto Laclau, "Populism: What's in a Name?," in *Populism and the Mirror of Democracy*, ed. Panizza, 103–14. Speaking of the open-endedness of the discursive articulations of populism, Laclau says that "nothing anticipates, in their isolated contents, the ways in which they [political signifiers] will be differentially or equivalentially articulated" because "that will depend on the historical context" ("Populism," 109).

24. Patrick Cockburn, "Donald Trump's Megalomania and Boris Johnson's Incompetence Have Increased the Coronavirus Death-Toll," *Independent*, May 15, 2020, https://www.independent.co.uk/voices/trump-boris-johnson-coronavirus-death-toll-a9517321.html.

25. The report on COVID-19 from the Organization for Economic Cooperation and Development (OECD) in 2022 is explicit on this point: "The young, the low educated, migrants, racial/ethnic minorities and low-wage workers were over-represented in jobs that cannot be done remotely and were therefore exposed to a higher risk of infection or job loss when the pandemic began. Many of those employed in these at-risk jobs were the frontline workers who continued to work in their physical workplace and in contact with other people throughout the pandemic to deliver essential goods and services. Indeed, the crisis has highlighted the extent to which society depends upon frontline workers who are often employed in low-paid jobs whose quality matches neither the importance of the work, nor the hazards involved. Other workers in at-risk jobs suffered particularly large losses in employment and income. In particular, both migrants and workers from racial/ethnic minorities were hit harder initially and are recovering more slowly." See "OECD Policy Responses to Coronavirus. The Unequal Impact of COVID-19: A Spotlight on Frontline Workers, Migrants, and Racial/Ethnic Minorities," *OECD*, March 17, 2022.

26. It is beyond the scope of my argument to offer a genealogy of such earlier versions of populism, but Eric Bonner's account, among others, appears to suggest (albeit in different language) that both past and present versions can be seen to be similarly located within the premises of emotional capitalism. See Eric Bonner, "From Modernity to Bigotry,"

in *Critical Theory and Authoritarian Populism*, ed. Jeremiah Morelock (London: University of Westminster Press, 2018), 85–105. Specifically, Bonner's argument on nineteenth- and twentieth-century modernity centers on the "bigot" as an emerging figure of political discontent on the grounds of lost privilege and describes the mechanism of reverse victimhood as central to the bigot's politics of grievance. This fundamental sense of conceiving the political subject of modernity in terms of discontent and outrage and hence of grasping politics through the dynamics of suffering and privilege suggests that the affective communication of populism is rooted in emotional capitalism.

27. In the United Kingdom, for instance, lockdown skeptics (but not necessarily far-right activists) made up only 16 percent of the population, one of the lowest percentages in Europe, as shown in Eir Nolsoe, "Britons Are Among the Least Lockdown Sceptical Nationalities in a Survey of 20 European Countries," YouGov, August 17, 2021, https://yougov.co.uk/topics/politics/articles-reports/2021/08/17/how-many-europeans-are-sceptical-lockdowns-and-hea. In the United States, where the political landscape was much more polarized, the first wave similarly saw a majority supporting lockdown measures (on March 26, 2020, 71 percent of the population supported lockdown, with a larger share among the Democrats and Democratic-leaning independents, 81 percent, than Republicans and Republican Party leaners, 61 percent). See Pew Research Center, "Public Views of the Coronavirus's Impact on the U.S.," March 26, 2020, https://www.pewresearch.org/politics/2020/03/26/public-views-of-the-coronaviruss-impact-on-the-u-s/. An online far-right-motivated antilockdown movement, however, began to get organized already in April 2020. Consisting of militia groups (such as the Wolverine Watchman in Michigan), the Proud Boys, and members of the QAnon movement, as the Institute of Strategic Dialogue reports, "the anti-lockdown movement is best described as localised, state-level opposition," which mobilized these dispersed groups in local rallies: "These rallies offered citizens and more extreme groups the opportunity to protest outside state Capitols with firearms and accompanying military gear" (Institute of Strategic Dialogue, "Anti-lockdown Activity: United States Country Profile," The Future of Extremism, 2021, https://www.isdglobal.org/wp-content/uploads/2022

/03/Anti-lockdown-U.S.-briefing.pdf). For a comment on the amplification of these minority voices, see Jamelle Bouie, "The Anti-lockdown Protesters Have a Twisted Conception of Liberty," *New York Times*, May 8, 2020, https://www.nytimes.com/2020/05/08/opinion/sunday/anti-lockdown-protesters.html.

28. Trump quoted in "Why It's Too Early to Compare COVID-19 with the Flu," PBS, February 28, 2020, https://www.pbs.org/newshour/health/why-its-too-early-to-compare-covid-19-with-the-flu; Boris Johnson, interview on *This Morning*, ITV, March 5, 2021, https://www.youtube.com/watch?v=vOHiaPwtGl4.

29. Zoe Tidman, "Coronavirus: Trump Shakes Hands with Crowd of Supporters Despite White House Telling Elderly to Avoid Contact," *Independent*, March 11, 2020, https://www.independent.co.uk/news/world/americas/us-politics/coronavirus-trump-handshake-florida-white-house-us-cases-outbreak-a9393281.html.

30. Ruth Garland and Darren Lilleker, "From Consensus to Dissensus: The UK's Management of a Pandemic in a Divided Nation," in *Political Communication in the Time of Coronavirus*, ed. Peter Aelst and Jay G. Blumler (New York: Routledge, 2021), 17–32.

31. Stephen Grey and Andrew MacAskill, "RPT Special Report. Johnson Listened to His Scientists About Coronavirus—but They Were Slow to Sound the Alarm," Reuters, April 7, 2020, https://www.reuters.com/article/health-coronavirus-britain-path/rpt-special-report-johnson-listened-to-his-scientists-about-coronavirus-but-they-were-slow-to-sound-the-alarm-idUKL4N2BV54X.

32. Johnson, interview on *This Morning*, March 5, 2021. On "herd immunity," see, for instance, Secunder Kermani, "Coronavirus: Whitty and Vallance Faced 'Herd Immunity' Backlash, Emails Show," *BBC News*, September 23, 2020, https://www.bbc.co.uk/news/uk-politics-54252272; Ed Yong, "The UK's 'Herd Immunity' Debacle," *Atlantic*, March 20, 2020, https://www.theatlantic.com/health/archive/2020/03/coronavirus-pandemic-herd-immunity-uk-boris-johnson/608065/; "The Government's Herd Immunity Plan Is Callous and Dangerous. Readers Respond to Boris Johnson's Apparent Strategy to Tackle the COVID-19 Outbreak," *The Guardian*, March 15, 2020, https://www.theguardian.com/world

/2020/mar/15/the-governments-herd-immunity-plan-is-callous-and-dangerous; C. O'Grady, "The U.K. Backed Off on Herd Immunity. To Beat COVID-19, We'll Ultimately Need It," *National Geographic*, March 20, 2020, https://www.nationalgeographic.com/science/article/uk-backed-off-on-herd-immunity-to-beat-coronavirus-we-need-it; and Christian Aschwanden, "The False Promise of Herd Immunity for COVID-19," *Nature*, October 21, 2020, https://www.nature.com/articles/d41586-020-02948-4. On the White House's reluctance to adopt this approach, see Julian Borgen, "Trump Team Thought UK Officials 'out of Their Minds' Aiming for Herd Immunity, Book Says," *The Guardian*, August 22, 2021, https://www.theguardian.com/world/2021/aug/19/us-trump-johnson-herd-immunity-aftershocks-book.

33. Gavin Yanem and Clare Wenham, "The U.S. and U.K. Were the Two Best Prepared Nations to Tackle a Pandemic—What Went Wrong?," *Time*, July 1, 2020, https://time.com/5861697/us-uk-failed-coronavirus-response/.

34. For the United Kingdom, see Tom Gillespie, "COVID-19: More Than 20,000 Lives Could Have Been Saved If First Lockdown Was Introduced a Week Earlier," *Sky News*, June 23, 2020, https://news.sky.com/story/Covid-19-more-than-20-000-lives-could-have-been-saved-if-first-lockdown-was-introduced-a-week-earlier-report-says-12340094. For the United States, see "Earlier Coronavirus Lockdown Could Have Saved 36,000 Lives," *BBC News*, May 22, 2020, https://www.bbc.co.uk/news/world-us-canada-52757150.

35. Report quoted in "UK's 'Policy Approach of Fatalism' Early in Pandemic Was Major Error, Lawmakers Say," Reuters, October 12, 2021, https://www.reuters.com/world/uk/uks-policy-approach-fatalism-early-pandemic-was-major-error-lawmakers-say-2021-10-11/.

36. Austin Hubner, "How Did We Get Here? A Framing and Source Analysis of Early COVID-19 Media Coverage," *Communication Research Reports* 38, no. 2 (2021): 118, https://doi.org/10.1080/08824096.2021.1894112.

37. Brigitte Nerlich and Rusi Jaspal, "Social Representations of 'Social Distancing' in Response to COVID-19 in the UK Media," *Current Sociology* 69, no. 4 (2021): 574, https://doi.org/10.1177/0011392121990030.

38. Rose, *Powers of Freedom*; Nikolas Rose, "Still 'Like Birds on the Wire'? Freedom After Neoliberalism," *Economy and Society* 46, nos. 3–4 (2017): 303–23, https://doi.org/10.1080/03085147.2017.1377947.

39. Trump quoted in Matthew Perrone and Calvin Woodward, "Trump Claims Rising Suicides If U.S. Stays Shut," Associated Press, March 24, 2020, https://apnews.com/article/ap-fact-check-virus-outbreak-donald-trump-us-news-politics-34f0d353e3cf9b507bed8815ff25b21b. Also see U.S. National Center of Statistics data demonstrating that, in fact, suicides declined during the pandemic: "Suicide in the U.S. Declined During the Pandemic," *CDC*, November 5, 2021, https://www.cdc.gov/nchs/pressroom/podcasts/2021/20211105/20211105.htm.

40. Amalesh Sharma and Sourav Bikash Borah, "COVID-19 and Domestic Violence: An Indirect Path to Social and Economic Crisis," *Journal of Family Violence* 37, no. 5 (2022): 759–65, https://doi.org/10.1007/s10896-020-00188-8.

41. Regarding (sections of) the libertarian Left, which, from a different problematic on the boundaries between the state and individual freedom, also supported an antilockdown stance, see Giorgio Agamben, *Where Are We Now? The Epidemic as Politics* (London: Rowman and Littlefield, 2021). For a critical discussion of the libertarian position, see, among other sources, Gerard Delanty, "Six Political Philosophies in Search of a Virus: Critical Perspectives on the Coronavirus Pandemic," *LEQS Paper* 156 (2020): 5–24, https://www.lse.ac.uk/european-institute/Assets/Documents/LEQS-Discussion-Papers/LEQSPaper156.pdf.

42. Johnson quoted in Kevin Rawlinson, "'This Enemy Can Be Deadly': Boris Johnson Invokes Wartime Language," *The Guardian*, March 17, 2020, https://www.theguardian.com/world/2020/mar/17/enemy-deadly-boris-johnson-invokes-wartime-language-coronavirus.

43. Sara Dada et al., "Words Matter: Political and Gender Analysis of Speeches Made by Heads of Government During the COVID-19 Pandemic," *BMJ Global Health* 6, no. 1 (2021): e003910, https://doi.org/10.1136/bmjgh-2020-003910; Brian Bennett and Tessa Berenson, "'Our Big War': As Coronavirus Spreads, Trump Refashions Himself as a Wartime President," *Time*, March 19, 2020, https://time.com/5806657/donald-trump-coronavirus-war-china/.

44. Trump quoted in "Coronavirus: Trump Puts U.S. on War Footing to Combat Outbreak," BBC Canada, March 19, 2020, https://www.bbc.co.uk/news/world-us-canada-51955450.
45. Elena Semino, "'Not Soldiers but Fire-Fighters'—Metaphors and COVID-19," *Health Communication* 36, no. 1 (2021): 51, https://doi.org/10.1080/10410236.2020.1844989.
46. Inés Olza et al., "The #ReframeCOVID Initiative: From Twitter to Society Via Metaphor," *Metaphor and the Social World* 11 (September 2021): 98–120, https://doi.org/10.1075/msw.00013.olz.
47. Julia Sonnevend, "A Virus as an Icon: The 2020 Pandemic in Images," *American Journal of Cultural Sociology* 8 (2020): 451–61.
48. For instance, "UK Government Evokes Wartime Blitz Spirit for Fight Against Coronavirus," Reuters, March 15, 2020, https://www.reuters.com/article/health-coronavirus-britain-idUSL8N2B80B1; and "Why Has Britain Become Numb to the Horror of Deaths Caused by Incompetence?," *The Guardian*, January 7, 2021, https://www.theguardian.com/commentisfree/2021/jan/07/britain-deaths-incompetence-coronavirus-boris-johnson.
49. Sam Wood, "The Reality of Blitz Spirit During COVID-19," University of Kent News Centre, 2021, https://www.kent.ac.uk/news/society/25315/expert-comment-the-reality-of-blitz-spirit-during-covid-19.
50. Lisa McCormick, "Marking Time in Lockdown: Heroization and Ritualization in the UK During the Coronavirus Pandemic," *American Journal of Cultural Sociology* 8, no. 3 (2020): 324–51, https://doi.org/10.1057/s41290-020-00117-8.
51. Clip from Trump rally on Devan Cole and Tara Subramanim, "Trump on COVID Death Toll: 'It Is What It Is,'" CNN, September 3, 2020, https://edition.cnn.com/2020/08/04/politics/trump-covid-death-toll-is-what-it-is/index.html.
52. Rob Merrick, "Boris Johnson Accused of Lacking Compassion for Coronavirus Victims After Making 'Calvin Klein Briefs' Joke," *Independent*, July 15, 2020, https://www.independent.co.uk/news/uk/politics/boris-johnson-keir-starmer-calvin-klein-briefs-pmqs-coronavirus-a9620371.html.
53. Jayson Harsin, "Toxic White Masculinity, Post-truth Politics, and the COVID-19 Infodemic," *European Journal of Cultural Studies* 23, no. 6

(2020): 1062, https://doi.org/10.1177/1367549420944934; Christina Cauterucci, "The Masculine Bluster of Trump's Coronavirus Hand-Shaking Tour," *Slate*, March 13, 2020, https://slate.com/news-and-politics/2020/03/trump-still-shaking-hands-coronavirus-handshake.amp.

54. Purnell quoted in Robert Mendick and Harry Yorke, "The Inside Story of Boris Johnson's Coronavirus Battle," *Telegraph*, April 6, 2020, https://www.telegraph.co.uk/politics/2020/04/06/inside-story-boris-johnsons-coronavirus-battle/.

55. Elisabeth Mahase, "COVID-19: Neglect Was One of Biggest Killers in Care Homes During Pandemic, Report Finds," *BMJ*, December 2021, https://www.bmj.com/content/375/bmj.n3132.

56. Trump quoted in Quin Forgey, "'It Affects Virtually Nobody': Trump Downplays Virus Threat to Young People," *Politico*, September 22, 2020, https://www-politico-com.translate.goog/news/2020/09/22/trump-downplays-coronavirus-threat-young-people-419883?_x_tr_sl=en&_x_tr_tl=el&_x_tr_hl=el&_x_tr_pto=op,sc. For instances of dehumanizing hierarchy in the United Kingdom, see Savitri Hensman, "Whose Views, and Lives, Truly Count? The Meaning of Co-production Against a Background of Worsening Inequalities," in *COVID-19 and Co-production in Health and Social Care Research, Policy, and Practice*, vol. 1: *The Challenges and Necessity of Co-production*, ed. Peter Beresford et al. (Cambridge: Policy, 2021), 19–27; and Caroline Hood and Alice Butler-Warke, "Living on the Edge: Spatial Exclusion Rendered Visible by the COVID-19 Pandemic," *Discover Society*, April 28, 2020, https://archive.discoversociety.org/2020/04/28/living-on-the-edge-spatial-exclusion-rendered-visible-by-the-covid-19-pandemic/.

57. Cockburn, "Donald Trump's Megalomania and Boris Johnson's Incompetence."

58. Delan Devakumar et al., "Racism and Discrimination in COVID-19 Responses," *Lancet*, April 11, 2020, https://www.thelancet.com/journals/lancet/article/PIIS0140-6736(20)30792-3/fulltext; David Smith, "Trump Falsely Ties Climbing COVID-19 Cases to Black Lives Matter Protests," *The Guardian*, July 23, 2022, https://www.theguardian.com/us-news/2020/jul/22/trump-coronavirus-briefing-black-lives-matter-protests.

59. Peter Walker, Rajiv Syal, and Heather Stewart, "Boris Johnson Under Pressure to Apologise for Care Home 'Insult,'" *The Guardian*, July 7,

2020, https://www.theguardian.com/society/2020/jul/07/care-home-chief-denounces-clumsy-and-cowardly-boris-johnson-comments.
60. Samantha G. Farris et al., "A Qualitative Study of COVID-19 Distress in University Students," *Emerging Adulthood* 9, no. 5 (2021): 462–78, https://doi.org/10.1177/21676968211025128. The "clap for our carers" campaign was an initiative involving people around the country stepping out on their doorstep and clapping for a few minutes to show gratitude for the work of the U.K. National Health System. It lasted for ten weeks during the first COVID-19 wave starting March 26, 2020. See the campaign's website at https://clapforourcarers.co.uk/.
61. David Cox, "Pandemic Reflections," *International Journal of Community and Social Development* 2, no. 3 (2020): 349–54, https://doi.org/10.1177/2516602620959506.
62. Jasper Jolly, "Number of Billionaires in UK Reached New Record During COVID Crisis," *The Guardian*, May 21, 2021, https://www.theguardian.com/business/2021/may/21/number-of-billionaires-in-uk-reached-new-record-during-covid-pandemic; Helen Wood and Beverley Skeggs, "Clap for Carers? From Care Gratitude to Care Justice," *European Journal of Cultural Studies* 23, no. 4 (2020): 641–47, https://doi.org/10.1177/1367549420928362.
63. Shani Orgad and Radha Sarma Hegde, "Crisis-Ready Responsible Selves: National Productions of the Pandemic," *International Journal of Cultural Studies* 25, nos. 3–4 (2022): 287–308, https://doi.org/10.1177/13678779211066328.
64. Farris et al., "A Qualitative Study of COVID-19 Distress."
65. "COVID-19—Break the Cycle of Inequality," editorial, *Lancet*, February 1, 2021, https://www.thelancet.com/journals/lanpub/article/PIIS2468-2667(21)00011-6/fulltext.
66. Clyde Yancy, "COVID-19 and African Americans," *JAMA* 323, no. 19 (April 15, 2020): 1891–92, https://jamanetwork.com/journals/jama/fullarticle/2764789; Peter Dizikes, "Study: Sex Differences in COVID-19 Mortality Vary Across Racial Divides," *MIT News*, April 21, 2021, https://news.mit.edu/2021/sex-covid-19-mortality-0421.
67. Denise Obinna, "Essential and Undervalued: Health Disparities of African American Women in the COVID-19 Era," PubMed, January 20, 2021, https://pubmed.ncbi.nlm.nih.gov/33190539/. For a

demographic breakdown of essential workers, see Hye Jin Rho, Hayley Brown, and Shawn Fremstad, "A Basic Demographic Profile of Workers in Frontline Industries," U.S. Center for Economic and Policy Research, April 7, 2020, https://cepr.net/a-basic-demographic-profile-of-workers-in-frontline-industries/. For an overview of research on the racism driving both employment-related exposure to COVID-19 deaths and the medical and cultural narratives and practices driving Black people's disproportionate rates of hospitalizations and deaths from COVID-19 in the United States during the first wave, see "There Is No Stopping COVID-19 Without Stopping Racism," *BMJ Opinion*, June 5, 2020, https://blogs.bmj.com/bmj/2020/06/05/there-is-no-stopping-covid-19-without-stopping-racism/.

68. "Speech: Prime Minister's Statement on Coronavirus."
69. For instance, "the PAC [Public Accounts Committee] highlighted an estimated loss of 26 billion pounds through fraud and repayment default from loans handed to businesses to help cope with the pandemic." See "UK Will Be Exposed to Paying Pandemic Cost Risks for Decades—Report," Reuters, July 25, 2021.
70. Grey and MacAskill, "RPT Special Report. Johnson Listened to His Scientists About Coronavirus."
71. Trump quoted in Daniel Wolfe and Daniel Dale, "'It's Going to Disappear': A Timeline of Trump's Claims That COVID-19 Will Vanish," CNN, October 31, 2020, https://edition.cnn.com/interactive/2020/10/politics/covid-disappearing-trump-comment-tracker/. For the case and death numbers, see Steven Woolf, Derek Chapman, and Roy Sabo, "Excess Deaths from COVID-19 and Other Causes," *JAMA* 324, no. 15 (2020): 1562–64, https://jamanetwork.com/journals/jama/fullarticle/2771761.
72. World Health Organization, *Infodemic*, https://www.who.int/health-topics/infodemic#tab=tab_1.
73. Joe Sommerlad, "Ivermectin: Why Are U.S. Anti-vaxxers Touting a Horse Dewormer as a Cure for COVID?," *Independent*, September 7, 2020, https://www.independent.co.uk/news/health/ivermectin-covid-joe-rogan-anti-vaxx-b1915539.html; Jeff Tollefson, "How Trump Damaged Science—and Why It Could Take Decades to Recover," *Nature*, October 5, 2020, https://www.nature.com/articles/d41586-020-02800-9.

74. Sommerlad, "Ivermectin"; Stephen Buranyi, "Scathing COVID-19 Book from *Lancet* Editor—Rushed but Useful," book review of Richard Horton, *The COVID-19 Catastrophe: What's Gone Wrong and How to Stop It Happening Again*, *Nature*, June 18, 2020, https://www.nature.com/articles/d41586-020-01839-y.
75. "Exclusive: Review Contradicts Boris Johnson on Claims He Ordered Early Lockdown at UK Care Homes," Reuters, May 15, 2020, https://www.reuters.com/article/us-health-coronavirus-britain-carehomes-idUSKBN22R1O2.
76. Ignas Kalpokas, "On Guilt and Post-truth Escapism: Developing a Theory," *Philosophy & Social Criticism* 44, no. 10 (2018): 1127–47, https://doi.org/10.1177/0191453718794752.
77. Harsin, "Toxic White Masculinity."
78. Since 2019, online antivaccine accounts, for instance, "increased their following by at least 7.8 million people," realizing U.S.$1 billion in annual revenues for social media firms. Talha Burki, "The Online Anti-vaccine Movement in the Age of COVID-19," *Lancet Digital Health*, October 2020, https://www.thelancet.com/journals/landig/article/PIIS2589-7500(20)30227-2/fulltext.
79. Karen Hao, "How Facebook and Google Fund Global Misinformation," *MIT Technology Review*, November 11, 2021, https://www.technologyreview.com/2021/11/20/1039076/facebook-google-disinformation-clickbait/; Taylor Shelton, "A Post-truth Pandemic?," *Big Data & Society* 7, no. 2 (2020): 1–6, https://doi.org/10.1177/2053951720965612.
80. Sarah Evanega et al., "Coronavirus Misinformation: Quantifying Sources and Themes in the COVID-19 'Infodemic,'" *Journal of Medical Internet Research*, preprint publication, October 19, 2020, https://doi.org/10.2196/preprints.25143.
81. Matthew J. Hornsey et al., "Donald Trump and Vaccination: The Effect of Political Identity, Conspiracist Ideation, and Presidential Tweets on Vaccine Hesitancy," *Journal of Experimental Social Psychology* 88 (May 2020): article 103947, https://doi.org/10.1016/j.jesp.2019.103947.
82. Owen Dyer, "COVID-19: Trump Stokes Protests Against Social Distancing Measures," *BMJ*, April 21, 2020, https://www.bmj.com

/content/369/bmj.m1596; Francesca Bolla Tripodi, *The Propagandists' Playbook: How Conservative Elites Manipulate Search and Threaten Democracy* (New Haven, CT: Yale University Press, 2022), 5.
83. Paola Pascual-Ferrá et al., "Toxicity and Verbal Aggression on Social Media: Polarized Discourse on Wearing Face Masks During the COVID-19 Pandemic," *Big Data & Society*, Online First, June 10, 2021, https://doi.org/10.1177/20539517211023533; Dyer, "COVID-19."
84. Jack Bratich, "'Give Me Liberty or Give Me COVID!': Anti-lockdown Protests as Necropopulist Downsurgency," *Cultural Studies* 35, nos. 2–3 (2021): 264, https://doi.org/10.1080/09502386.2021.1898016.
85. For the antilockdown stance present in the Conservative Party's COVID Recovery Group, a rebel group that opposed Boris Johnson's second and third lockdown restrictions, see "Coronavirus: Scores of Rebel Tory MPs Launch Anti-lockdown Campaign Group," *Sky News*, November 11, 2020, https://news.sky.com/story/coronavirus-scores-of-rebel-tory-mps-launch-anti-lockdown-campaign-group-12129631. Paolo Gerbaudo also offers an account of the ways in which the U.K. antilockdown movement was heavily informed by U.S. politics. The ten-thousand-strong Unite for Freedom march in central London in late April 2021, for instance, included many messages of support for Trump, QAnon, and the police as well as opposition to Bill Gates–sponsored vaccine programs, 5G infrastructure, and globalization in general. See Gerbaudo, "The Pandemic Crowd."
86. Johnson quoted in "Ancient British Rights to a Drink in the Pub Have to Be Suspended: Johnson," Reuters, March 20, 2020, https://www.reuters.com/ /article/us-health-coronavirus-britain-pubs/ancient-british-rights-to-a-drink-in-the-pub-have-to-be-suspended-johnson-idUSKBN21732F/. See also Darren G. Lilleker and Thomas Stoeckle, "The Challenges of Providing Certainty in the Face of Wicked Problems: Analysing the UK Government's Handling of the COVID-19 Pandemic," *Journal of Public Affairs* 2733 (2021): 1–10, https://www.ncbi.nlm.nih.gov/pmc/articles/PMC8420585/#pa2733-note-0003. The U.K. government's initial plan was backed by its "nudge" unit, an advisory experts group informed by the behavioral sciences that implements alternatives to standard government interventions (e.g., in markets) to influence the choices people make in their everyday lives

without imposing or taking away their capacity to make decisions. The strategy was summed up in a *Guardian* article. Dr. David Halpern, a psychologist who heads the Behavioural Insights Team, said on *BBC News*: "There's going to be a point, assuming the epidemic flows and grows, as we think it probably will do, where you'll want to cocoon, you'll want to protect those at-risk groups so that they basically don't catch the disease and by the time they come out of their cocooning, herd immunity's been achieved in the rest of the population." Quoted in Sarah Boseley, "Herd Immunity: Will the UK's Coronavirus Strategy Work?," *The Guardian*, March 13, 2020, https://www.theguardian.com/world/2020/mar/13/herd-immunity-will-the-uks-coronavirus-strategy-work.

87. Johnson quoted in Julian Baggini, "'Freedom-Loving Brits'? It's Not That Simple, Prime Minister," *The Guardian*, September 23, 2020, https://www.theguardian.com/commentisfree/2020/sep/23/freedom-loving-brits-prime-minister-state-conservative. See also Health Secretary Matt Hancock's statement on COVID-19: "In recent weeks, we have had to impinge on historic liberties to protect our NHS and our loved ones, and yet our goal must be freedom. Freedom from the virus, yes—and we will not lift measures until it is safe to do so. But also we care about the restoration of social freedom and economic freedom too. Each citizen's right to do as they please." "Health and Social Care Secretary's Statement on Coronavirus (COVID-19): 1 May 2020," Gov.UK, May 1, 2020, https://www.gov.uk/government/speeches/health-and-social-care-secretarys-statement-on-coronavirus-covid-19-1-may-2020.

88. Julie Leask, Claire Hooker, and Catherine King, "Media Coverage of Health Issues and How to Work More Effectively with Journalists: A Qualitative Study," *BMC Public Health* 10, no. 1 (2010): 1–7. This libertarian discourse of freedom was further evident in Johnson's focus on the individual as the sole controller of the virus—for instance, in his introduction of the NHS's main postlockdown strategy in May–November 2020: "Stay alert. Control the virus. Save lives." Fully resonant with a neoliberal logic of individual autonomy, this discourse promoted an ideal "entrepreneurial" self-defined by its capacity for self-regulation and self-management (wash hands, stay indoors), while

shifting attention away from the state's responsibilities to mobilize its own welfare structures in order to care for and protect its citizens. See Orgad and Hedge, "Crisis-Ready Responsible Selves."
89. Paige L. Sweet, "The Sociology of Gaslighting," *American Sociological Review* 84, no. 5 (2019): 851–75.
90. "The Impact of COVID-19 on Women," United Nations Policy Brief, 2020, https://www.unwomen.org/en/digital-library/publications/2020/04/policy-brief-the-impact-of-covid-19-on-women. This unequal exposure to COVID-19 illness and death has already been explored within the context of preexisting structural inequalities, which shaped gender and racial disparities throughout the pandemic. See, among other sources, Rory C. O'Connor et al., "Mental Health and Well-Being During the COVID-19 Pandemic: Longitudinal Analyses of Adults in the UK COVID-19 Mental Health & Wellbeing Study," *British Journal of Psychiatry: The Journal of Mental Science* 218, no. 6 (2021): 326–33, https://doi.org/10.1192/bjp.2020.212; Obinna, "Essential and Undervalued"; Ann Caroline Danielsen et al., "How Cumulative Statistics Can Mislead: The Temporal Dynamism of Sex Disparities in COVID-19 Mortality in New York State," *International Journal of Environmental Research and Public Health* 19, no. 21 (2022): article 14066, https://doi.org/10.3390/ijerph192114066; Vanessa Williams, "Disproportionately Black Counties Account for Over Half of Coronavirus Cases in the U.S. and Nearly 60% of Deaths, Study Finds," *Washington Post*, May 20, 2020, https://www.washingtonpost.com/nation/2020/05/06/study-finds-that-disproportionately-black-counties-account-more-than-half-covid-19-cases-us-nearly-60-percent-deaths/.
91. With variations, the majority in both countries belonged to the pro-vaccine categories of strongly supporting the vaccines or supporting them with concerns (United Kingdom, 76 percent; United States, 60 percent). Only 7 percent of the U.S. population and 3 percent of the U.K. population were categorically antivaccine. Timothy Gravelle et al., "Estimating the Size of 'Anti-vax' and Vaccine Hesitant Populations in the US, UK, and Canada: Comparative Latent Class Modeling of Vaccine Attitudes," *Human Vaccines and Immunotherapeutics* 18, no. 1 (2022), https://doi.org/10.1080/21645515.2021.2008214.

92. Kevin Grove et al., "The Uneven Distribution of Futurity: Slow Emergencies and the Event of COVID-19," *Geographical Research* 60, no. 1 (2022): 13, https://doi.org/10.1111/1745-5871.12501.
93. Josh Smicker, "COVID-19 and 'Crisis as Ordinary': Pathological Whiteness, Popular Pessimism, and Pre-apocalyptic Cultural Studies," *Cultural Studies* 35, nos. 2–3 (2021): 293, https://doi.org/10.1080/09502386.2021.1898038.
94. Thomas Magelinski and Kathleen M. Carley, "Detecting Coordinated Behavior in the Twitter Campaign to Reopen America," paper presented at the Center for Informed Democracy & Social-Cybersecurity Annual Conference, Carnegie Mellon University, Pittsburg, PA, 2020, https://www.cmu.edu/ideas-social-cybersecurity/events/conference-archive/2020papers/magelinski_ideas_abstract_reopen.pdf.
95. Eric Klinenberg and Melina Sherman, "Face Mask Face-Offs: Culture and Conflict in the COVID-19 Pandemic," *Public Culture* 33, no. 3 (2021): 441–66, https://doi.org/10.1215/08992363-9262919.
96. Jen Schradie, "'Give Me Liberty or Give Me COVID-19': Antilockdown Protesters Were Never Trump Puppets," *Communication and the Public* 5, nos. 3–4 (2020): 128, https://doi.org/10.1177/2057047320969433.
97. Kumarini Carreira da Silva, "COVID-19 and the Mundane Practices of Privilege," *Cultural Studies* 35, nos. 2–3 (2021): 243, https://doi.org/10.1080/09502386.2021.1898034.

4. HOW CAN VICTIMHOOD BE RECLAIMED?

1. Olsen quoted in Kate Zernike, Mitch Smith, and Luke Vander Ploeg, "Oklahoma Legislature Passes Bill Banning Almost All Abortions," *New York Times*, May 19, 2022, https://www.nytimes.com/2022/05/19/us/oklahoma-ban-abortions.html.
2. Serrin Foster, "What About Rape? What If It Was Your Daughter Who Was Raped?," Feminists for Life, n.d., emphasis in original, https://www.feministsforlife.org/what-about-rape/.
3. Kate Manne, "Women's Lives, Rapists' Laws: Remembering Who Brett Kavanaugh Is, One of the Men Now Presiding Over the Bodies of Girls, Women, and Others Who Can Get Pregnant," *More to Hate*,

June 25, 2022, https://katemanne.substack.com/p/womens-lives-rapists-laws?utm_source=email.
4. Richard Stith, "Abortion Is More Than a Murder. Nietzsche vs Christ," *New Oxford Review* 72 (November 2005), https://www.newoxfordreview.org/documents/abortion-is-more-than-murder/.
5. Susan A. Cohen, "Abortion and Women of Color: The Bigger Picture," *Policy Review* 11, no. 3 (2008): 5, https://www.guttmacher.org/sites/default/files/article_files/gpr110302.pdf.
6. Jenna Jerman, Rachel K. Jones, and Tsuyoshi Onda, "Characteristics of U.S. Abortion Patients in 2014 and Changes Since 2008," Working Paper no. 29, Guttmacher Institute, New York, 2016, https://www.guttmacher.org/report/characteristics-us-abortion-patients-2014?utm_source=flin%20flon%20reminder&utm_campaign=flin%20flon%20reminder%3A%20outbound&utm_medium=referral. See also Carly Thomsen et al., "Presence and Absence: Crisis Pregnancy Centers and Abortion Facilities in the Contemporary Reproductive Justice Landscape," *Human Geography* 6, no. 1 (2023): 64–74, https://doi.org/10.1177/19427786221109959.
7. See note 25, chapter 3.
8. Daniel Grossman et al., "Change in Abortion Services After Implementation of a Restrictive Law in Texas," *Contraception* 90, no. 5 (2014): 496–501, https://doi.org/10.1016/j.contraception.2014.07.006.
9. Also as Justice Samuel Alito's own rationale for the overturning shows: see Catriona Stewart, "Overturning *Roe vs Wade*: Causing Women's Deaths Is Not 'Pro-life,'" *Herald Scotland*, July 3, 2020, https://www.heraldscotland.com/opinion/20119223.overturning-roe-vs-wade-causing-womens-deaths-not-pro-life/.
10. For the framing of claims to victimhood in moral narratives, see also Kate Manne, *Down Girl: The Logic of Misogyny* (Oxford: Oxford University Press, 2017), 223–28.
11. This exclusionary politics of pain also structures the public discourse of TERF (transexclusionary radical feminism) activists on transgender rights, where the argument that women are potential victims of trans men becomes the basis for depriving trans selves of their right to self-determination while othering and criminalizing them. See, among other sources, Sally Hines, "The Feminist Frontier: On Trans and Feminism," *Journal of Gender Studies* 28, no. 2 (2019): 145–57.

12. Lynn M. Paltrow and Jeanne Flavin, "Arrests of and Forced Interventions on Pregnant Women in the United States, 1973–2005: Implications for Women's Legal Status and Public Health," *Journal of Health Politics, Policy, and Law* 38, no. 2 (2013): 335, https://doi.org/10.1215/03616878-1966324.
13. Placards shown in Jim Powell, "Americans Take to Streets Across US to Protest for Abortion Rights—in Pictures," *The Guardian*, June 25, 2022, https://www.theguardian.com/world/gallery/2022/jun/25/abortion-rights-protest-roe-v-wade-us-in-pictures.
14. Gerbaudo, "The Pandemic Crowd," 65.
15. Lauren Berlant, *The Female Complaint: The Unfinished Business of Sentimentality in American Culture* (Durham, NC: Duke University Press, 2008), 3, emphasis in the original.
16. Neil Stammers, *Human Rights and Social Movements* (London: Pluto, 2009), 1.
17. Sara De Benedictis, Shani Orgad, and Catherine Rottenberg, "#MeToo, Popular Feminism, and the News: A Content Analysis of UK Newspaper Coverage," *European Journal of Cultural Studies* 22, nos. 5–6 (2019): 718–38, https://doi.org/10.1177/1367549419856831.
18. Rottenberg, "Neoliberal Feminism"; Shani Orgad and Rosalind Gill, *Confidence Culture* (Durham, NC: Duke University Press, 2021); Verity Trott, "Networked Feminism: Counterpublics and the Intersectional Issues of #MeToo," *Feminist Media Studies* 21, no. 7 (2021): 1125–42, https://doi.org/10.1080/14680777.2020.1718176.
19. Hester Baer, "Redoing Feminism: Digital Activism, Body Politics, and Neoliberalism," *Feminist Media Studies* 16, no. 1 (2016): 17, https://doi.org/10.1080/14680777.2015.1093070.
20. Cole, *The Cult of True Victimhood*, 4.
21. Robert Horwitz, "Politics as Victimhood, Victimhood as Politics," *Journal of Policy History* 30 (July 2018): 564, https://doi.org/10.1017/S0898030618000209.
22. Alito quoted in Aziz Huq, "Alito's Case for Overturning *Roe* Is Weak for a Reason," *Politico*, March 5, 2022, https://www.politico.com/news/magazine/2022/05/03/alito-case-roe-wade-weak-law-supreme-court-00029653.
23. Bratich, "'Give Me Liberty or Give Me COVID!,'" 261; Smicker, "COVID-19 and 'Crisis as Ordinary.'"

24. David Leonhardt, "Red COVID: COVID's Partisan Pattern Is Growing More Extreme," *New York Times*, September 27, 2021, https://www.nytimes.com/2021/09/27/briefing/covid-red-states-vaccinations.html. That indifference was manifested in the high numbers of deaths among antimask communities.
25. Gerbaudo, "The Pandemic Crowd"; William Davies, *The Limits of Neoliberalism: Authority, Sovereignty, and the Logic of Competition* (London: Sage, 2016).
26. Neal Schaffer, *The Age of Influence: The Power of Influencers to Elevate Your Brand* (New York: HarperCollins Leadership, 2020).
27. Melissa Block, "Strict Border Policies Contribute to Rising Immigrant Deaths," NPR, July 2, 2022, https://www.npr.org/2022/07/02/1109557989/strict-border-policies-contribute-to-rising-immigrant-deaths.
28. Thomas Piketty, "Capital in the Twenty-First Century: A Multidimensional Approach to the History of Capital and Social Classes," *British Journal of Sociology* 65, no. 4 (2014): 744. See also Gabriel Zucman, "Global Wealth Inequality," *Annual Review of Economics*, no. 11 (2019): 109–38. For an informative piece of journalism, see Nick Hanauer and David M. Rolf, "The Top 1% of Americans Have Taken $50 Trillion from the Bottom 90%—and That's Made the U.S. Less Secure," *Time*, September 17, 2020, https://time.com/5888024/50-trillion-income-inequality-america/.
29. United Nations High Commissioner for Refugees, "UK Migration and Economic Development Partnership with Rwanda," April 2022, https://www.unhcr.org/uk/uk-immigration-and-asylum-plans-some-questions-answered-by-unhcr.html.
30. Emily Head, "Life Expectancy Declining in Many English Communities Even Before Pandemic," *Imperial News*, October 12, 2021, https://www.imperial.ac.uk/news/231119/life-expectancy-declining-many-english-communities/; Veena Raleigh, "What Is Happening to Life Expectancy in England?," *Kings Fund*, August 10, 2022, https://www.kingsfund.org.uk/publications/whats-happening-life-expectancy-england; Paul Butler, "Over 330,000 Excess Deaths in Great Britain Linked to Austerity, Finds Study," *The Guardian*, October 5, 2022, https://www.theguardian.com/business/2022/oct/05/over-330000-excess-deaths-in-great-britain-linked-to-austerity-finds

-study; "Working Family Poverty Hits Record High, Fuelled by Rising Housing Costs and Childcare Challenges," Institute for Public Policy Research, May 26, 2021, https://www.ippr.org/news-and-media/press-releases/revealed-working-family-poverty-hits-record-high-fuelled-by-rising-housing-costs-and-childcare-challenges.
31. Piketty, "Capital in the Twenty First Century," 47.
32. Sophie Harman et al., "Global Vaccine Equity Demands Reparative Justice—Not Charity," *BMJ Global Health* 6 (2021): e006504, https://gh.bmj.com/content/bmjgh/6/6/e006504.full.pdf; see also World Health Organization, *COVID-19 Vaccine Delivery Partnership (2022): Situation Report* (Geneva: World Health Organization, October 2022), file:///C:/Users/Health%20Policy/Downloads/CoVDP-SitRep_Issue-8_October.pdf.
33. Allegra Stratton, "David Cameron: Tory Party Is 'Modern and Compassionate,'" *The Guardian*, October 2, 2011, https://www.theguardian.com/politics/2011/oct/02/cameron-tory-party-modern-compassionate; "Rishi Sunak's First Speech as Prime Minister," Conservatives, the Conservative Party's official website, October 25, 2022, https://www.conservatives.com/news/2022/rishi-sunak-s-first-speech-as-prime-minister.
34. Polly Toynbee, "The Middle Class Are About to Discover the Cruelty of Britain's Benefits System," *The Guardian*, March 24, 2020, https://www.theguardian.com/commentisfree/2020/mar/24/britain-benefits-rishi-sunak-claimants-austerity.
35. Brent J. Steele, "'The Cruelty of Righteous People': Niebuhr on the Urgency of Cruelty," *Journal of International Political Theory* 17, no. 2 (2021): 205, https://doi.org/10.1177/1755088221989745.
36. On feel-good e-activism, see Chouliaraki and Vestergaard, *Routledge Handbook of Humanitarian Communication*.
37. Ferenc Huszár et al., "Algorithmic Amplification of Politics on Twitter," *Proceedings of the National Academy of Sciences* 119 (January 2022): 1, https://doi.org/10.1073/pnas.2025334119.
38. Phelan, "Neoliberalism.'"
39. Debora Barros Leal Farias, Guilherme Casarões, and David Magalhães, "Radical Right Populism and the Politics of Cruelty: The Case of COVID-19 in Brazil Under President Bolsonaro," *Global Studies Quarterly* 2, no. 2 (2022): 3, https://doi.org/10.1093/isagsq/ksab048.

40. Henry A. Giroux, "The Culture of Cruelty in Trump's America," Truthout, 2017, https://truthout.org/articles/the-culture-of-cruelty-in-trump-s-america/. See also Wodak, *The Politics of Fear: What Right-Wing Populist Discourses Mean*; Michal Krzyzanowski and Ruth Wodak, "Right-Wing Populism in Europe & USA: Contesting Politics & Discourse Beyond 'Orbanism' and 'Trumpism,'" *Journal of Language and Politics* 16 (October 2017): 471–84, https://doi.org/10.1075/jlp.17042.krz.
41. Enzo Traverso, *The New Faces of Fascism: Populism and the Far Right* (London: Verso, 2019), 261.
42. Bratich, "'Give Me Liberty or Give Me COVID!,'" 261.
43. Said, *Orientalism*; Gayatri Chakravorty Spivak, "Three Women's Texts and a Critique of Imperialism," *Critical Inquiry* 12, no. 1 (1985): 243–61, https://www.jstor.org/stable/1343469; Achille Mbembe, "Necropolitics," *Public Culture* 15, no. 1 (2003): 11–40, https://doi.org/10.1215/08992363-15-1-11.
44. Fanon, *The Wretched of the Earth*, 252.
45. Edward Said, "Orientalism," *Counterpunch*, August 5, 2003, https://www.counterpunch.org/2003/08/05/orientalism/.
46. Bart Cammaerts, "The Abnormalisation of Social Justice: The 'Anti-woke Culture War' Discourse in the UK," *Discourse & Society* 33, no. 6 (2022): 730.
47. Manne, *Down Girl*, 88.
48. Sarah Banet-Weiser, "'Ruined Lives': Mediated White Male Victimhood," *European Journal of Cultural Studies* 24, no. 1 (2021): 60, https://doi.org/10.1177/1367549420985840.
49. Diane Negra and Julia Leyda, "Querying 'Karen': The Rise of the Angry White Woman," *European Journal of Cultural Studies* 24, no. 1 (2021): 352, https://doi.org/10.1177/1367549420947777.
50. Ruby Hamad, *White Tears / Brown Scars: How White Feminism Betrays Women of Color* (Melbourne: Melbourne University Press, 2019); Alison Phipps, "White Tears, White Rage: Victimhood and (as) Violence in Mainstream Feminism," *European Journal of Cultural Studies* 24, no. 1 (2021): 81–93, https://doi.org/10.1177/1367549420985852.
51. Calvin John Smiley and David Fakunle, "From 'Brute' to 'Thug': The Demonization and Criminalization of Unarmed Black Male Victims in America," *Journal of Human Behavior in the Social Environment* 26

(January 2016): 1–17, https://doi.org/10.1080/10911359.2015.1129256; Amia Srinivasan, *The Right to Sex: Feminism in the Twenty-First Century* (New York: Farrar, Straus and Giroux, 2021).

52. Srinivasan, *The Right to Sex*; Jessica Ringrose and Emma Renold, "Slut-Shaming, Girl Power, and 'Sexualisation': Thinking Through the Politics of the International Slutwalks with Teen Girls," *Gender and Education* 24, no. 3 (2012): 333–43.
53. Mary Beard, *Women & Power: A Manifesto* (London: Profile, 2017).
54. Leigh Gilmore, "Policing Truth: Confession, Gender, and Autobiographical Authority," in *Autobiography and Postmodernism*, ed. Gerald Peters, Kathleen Ashley, and Leigh Gilmore (Boston: University of Massachusetts Press, 1994), 54.
55. Debora Tuerkheimer, "Incredible Women: Sexual Violence and the Credibility Discount," *University of Pennsylvania Law Review* 166, no. 1 (2017): 1–56.
56. Criminal Injuries Helpline, *Sexual Assault Stats and Facts, 2023*, blog, https://criminalinjurieshelpline.co.uk/blog/sexual-assault-data-stats/.
57. Eliana Docterman, "The Depp–Heard Trial Perpetuates the Myth of the Perfect Victim," *Time*, June 2, 2022, https://time.com/6183505/amber-heard-perfect-victim-myth-johnny-depp/; Ashley Collman, "Amber Heard Lost Her Defamation Case with Johnny Depp Because She Wasn't Believable and Not as Big of a Star, Experts Say," *Insider*, June 2, 2022, https://www.insider.com/why-amber-heard-lost-her-defamation-trial-with-johnny-depp-2022-6.
58. Jessica Valenti, "The Memeification of Amber Heard: When Misogyny Is Masked as Moral Righteousness," *Abortion, Every Day*, June 2, 2022, https://jessica.substack.com/p/the-memeification-of-amber-heard?s=w.
59. Kate Manne, "Why the Internet Sided with Johnny Depp," *The Nation*, June 6, 2022, https://www.thenation.com/article/society/amber-heard-johnny-depp-defamation/.
60. Natasha N. Korecki and Christopher Cadelago, "With a Hand from Trump, the Right Makes Rittenhouse a Cause Célèbre," *Politico*, January 9, 2020, https://www.politico.com/news/2020/09/01/trump-rittenhouse-kenosha-support-407106.
61. Akin Olla, "The People Kyle Rittenhouse Shot Can't Be Called 'Victims,' a Judge Says. Surprised?," *The Guardian*, October 31, 2021,

https://www.theguardian.com/commentisfree/2021/oct/31/kyle-rittenhouse-shot-victims-judge.

62. Judge quoted in Paul Butler, "Are the Men Kyle Rittenhouse Killed Victims? Not According to the Judge," *Washington Post*, October 29, 2021, https://www.washingtonpost.com/opinions/2021/10/29/are-men-kyle-rittenhouse-killed-victims-not-according-judge/.

63. Butler, "Are the Men Kyle Rittenhouse Killed Victims?"

64. Butler, "Are the Men Kyle Rittenhouse Killed Victims?" For the linguistic criminalization of the Black body, see Smiley and Fakunle, "From 'Brute' to 'Thug.'"

65. Cammaerts, "The Abnormalisation of Social Justice."

66. Kaitlyn Regehr and Jessica Ringrose, "Celebrity Victims and Wimpy Snowflakes: Using Personal Narratives to Challenge Digitally Mediated Rape Culture," in *Mediating Misogyny: Gender, Technology, and Harassment*, ed. Jacqueline Ryan Vickery and Tracy Everbach (Cham, Switzerland: Springer, 2018), 361.

67. Ulrich Baer, "What 'Snowflakes' Get Right About Free Speech," *New York Times*, April 24, 2017, https://newseumed.org/sites/default/files/2019-06/What%20%E2%80%98Snowflakes%E2%80%99%20Get%20Right%20About%20Free%20Speech%20-%20The%20New%20York%20Times.pdf.

68. Phelan, "Neoliberalism," 467.

69. Tim Cook, Emira Kursumovic, and Simon Lennane, "Exclusive: Deaths of NHS Staff from COVID-19 Analysed," *HSJ: Health Services Journal*, April 22, 2020, https://www.hsj.co.uk/exclusive-deaths-of-nhs-staff-from-covid-19-analysed/7027471.article.

70. Sara Farris, Nira Yuval-Davis, and Catherine Rottenberg, "The Frontline as Performative Frame: An Analysis of the UK COVID Crisis," *State Crime Journal* 10, no. 2 (2021): 284.

71. Shani Orgad, "The Survivor in Contemporary Culture and Public Discourse: A Genealogy," *Communication Review* 12, no. 2 (2009): 132–61, https://doi.org/10.1080/10714420902921168; Cole, *The Cult of True Victimhood*; Brad Evans and Julian Reid, "Exhausted by *Resilience*: Response to the Commentaries," *Resilience* 3, no. 2 (2015): 154–59, https://doi.org/10.1080/21693293.2015.1022991; Orgad and Gill, *Confidence Culture*.

72. Kimmery Newsom and Karen Myers-Bowman, "'I Am Not a Victim. I Am a Survivor': Resilience as a Journey for Female Survivors of Child Sexual Abuse," *Journal of Child Sexual Abuse* 26, no. 8 (2017): 927–47; Sarah Banet-Weiser, *Empowered: Popular Feminism and Popular Misogyny*, illus. ed. (Durham, NC: Duke University Press, 2018).
73. Orgad and Gill, *Confidence Culture*, 15.
74. Jo Littler, *Against Meritocracy: Culture, Power, and Myths of Mobility* (London: Routledge, 2017).
75. Kathryn Claire Higgins, "Realness, Wrongness, Justice: Exploring Criminalization as a Mediated Politics of Vulnerability," PhD diss., London School of Economics and Political Science, 2022, 19.
76. Cole, *The Cult of True Victimhood*.
77. Stanley, *How Fascism Works*, 192. See also Chouliaraki and Georgiou, *The Digital Border*, on how a similar temporality of im/probability is central to the narrative of migration as a "crisis" for the West, thereby normalizing lethal border-protection policies that harm the most vulnerable.
78. Sally Hines, "Sex Wars and (Trans) Gender Panics: Identity and Body Politics in Contemporary UK Feminism," *Sociological Review* 6, no. 4 (2020): 713, https://doi.org/10.1177/0038026120934684; Ahmed, *The Cultural Politics of Emotion*.
79. Nikita Carney, "All Lives Matter, but so Does Race: Black Lives Matter and the Evolving Role of Social Media," *Humanity & Society* 40, no. 2 (2016): 185, https://doi.org/10.1177/0160597616643868.
80. Manne, *Down Girl*, 225–26.
81. Susan Faludi, *Backlash: The Undeclared War Against American Women* (New York: Crown, 1991).
82. Sarah Banet-Weiser, "Popular Feminism: Male Victimhood," *Los Angeles Review of Books*, February 22, 2019, https://lareviewofbooks.org/article/popular-feminism-male-victimhood/.
83. De Benedictis, Orgad, and Rottenberg, "#MeToo, Popular Feminism, and the News."
84. Gilmore, *Tainted Witness*, 1.
85. Srinivasan, *The Right to Sex*, 9.
86. Ashwini Tambe, "Reckoning with the Silences of #MeToo," *Feminist Studies* 44, no. 1 (2018): 199.

87. Kimberlé Crenshaw, "Demarginalizing the Intersection of Race and Sex: A Black Feminist Critique of Antidiscrimination Doctrine, Feminist Theory, and Antiracist Politics," *University of Chicago Legal Forum* 140 (1989): 149, emphasis in original, https://philarchive.org/rec/CREDTI.

88. Along similar lines, Michael Rothberg argues that we should go beyond the victim/perpetrator binary and develop analytical vocabularies sensitive enough to capture how varying intersections of privilege, power, and injustice allow for impure positions that cannot be conflated with either the victim or the perpetrator of an act. Rothberg proposes the position of the "implicated subject," a category of the self between the perpetrator and the bystander, and further nuances this position by analyzing the self not only as possibly complicit to an injustice but also as a beneficiary, a descendent, or a perpetuator of injustice. See Michael Rothberg, *The Implicated Subject: Beyond Victims and Perpetrators* (Stanford, CA: Stanford University Press, 2019).

89. Boltanski, *Distant Suffering*, 5, emphasis in original.

90. Ross qtd. in Daphne Chouliaraki Milner, "Calling In: Loretta J. Ross's Antidote to Cancel Culture," *Atmos*, August 2020, https://atmos.earth/calling-in-macarthur-fellow-loretta-j-ross-cancel-culture/.

91. Sonia Livingstone, "Children's Rights Apply in the Digital World!," *LSE Blog*, March 24, 2021, emphasis in original, https://webcache.googleusercontent.com/search?q=cache:eoMk9INZbsMJ:https://blogs.lse.ac.uk/parenting4digitalfuture/2021/03/24/general-comment-25/&cd=23&hl=el&ct=clnk&gl=uk.

92. Chouliaraki, *The Ironic Spectator*, 2.

93. Chouliaraki, *The Ironic Spectator*, 2.

94. Dannagal Goldthwaite Young, *Irony and Outrage: The Polarized Landscape of Rage, Fear, and Laughter in the United States* (Oxford: Oxford University Press, 2020), 207.

95. Young, *Irony and Outrage*, 190.

96. Young, *Irony and Outrage*, 210.

97. Ross quoted in Daphne Chouliaraki Milner, "Shades of Grey."

98. Deen Freelon, Charlton D. McIlwain, and Meredith Clark, "Beyond the Hashtags: #Ferguson, #Blacklivesmatter, and the Online Struggle for Offline Justice," Center for Media & Social Impact, School of Communication, American University, 2016, 45, 63, 62.

4. HOW CAN VICTIMHOOD BE RECLAIMED? ❧ 199

99. Matthew Smith, "Britons Tend to Oppose Planned RMT Rail Strikes This Winter," YouGov, November 29, 2022, https://yougov.co.uk/topics/politics/articles-reports/2022/11/29/britons-tend-oppose-planned-rmt-rail-strikes-winte. For the strike period of December 2022–January 2023, contrary to the misleading title of this article, Britons in the age groups of 18–49 years old supported the strike (18–24 years old: 51 percent in support, 32 percent opposed; 25–49 years old: 45 percent in support, 41 percent opposed), with older age groups either being split (20–65 years old: 43 percent in support, 49 percent opposed) or tipping the balance (older than 65: 27 percent in support, 65 percent opposed).

100. James Greig, "Why RMT Leader Mick Lynch Is the Hero We Need Right Now," *DAZED*, June 23, 2022, https://www.dazeddigital.com/politics/article/56394/1/rmt-leader-mick-lynch-internets-favourite-person-hero-union-go-off-king. See also Zoë Grünewald, "Mick Lynch Is Winning the Media War Over Rail Strikes," *New Statesman*, July 28, 2022, https://www.newstatesman.com/politics/uk-politics/2022/07/mick-lynch-rail-strikes-media-war.

101. Jayson Harsin, "Regimes of Posttruth, Postpolitics, and Attention Economies," *Communication, Culture, & Critique* 8, no. 2 (2015): 332.

102. Sheera Frenkel and Kate Conger, "Hate Speech's Rise on Twitter Is Unprecedented, Researchers Find," *New York Times*, December 2, 2022, https://www.nytimes.com/2022/12/02/technology/twitter-hate-speech.html.

103. Ergin Bulut, "Interview with Safiya Noble: Algorithms of Oppression, Gender, and Race," *Moment Dergi* 5, no. 2 (2018): 300, https://dergipark.org.tr/en/download/article-file/653368.

104. Anna Lauren Hoffmann and Anne Jonas, "Recasting Justice for Internet and Online Industry Research Ethics," in *Internet Research Ethics for the Social Age: New Cases and Challenges*, ed. Michael Zimmer and Katharina Kinder-Kuranda (Bern, Switzerland: Peter Lang, 2016), 3.

105. Ian Bogost, "The Age of Social Media Is Ending. It Never Should Have Begun," *Atlantic*, November 10, 2022, https://www.theatlantic.com/technology/archive/2022/11/twitter-facebook-social-media-decline/672074/.

106. Hannah Arendt, "Reflections on Violence," *Journal of International Affairs* 23, no. 1 (1969): 1–35, https://www.jstor.org/stable/95f4f82f-fc7d-3ce4-bebe-f5e0077edbfd.

BIBLIOGRAPHY

Agamben, Giorgio. *Where Are We Now? The Epidemic as Politics.* London: Rowman and Littlefield, 2021.

Ahmed, Sara. *The Cultural Politics of Emotion.* Edinburgh: Edinburgh University Press, 2004.

Alderman, Derek H., and G. Rebecca Dobbs. "Geographies of Slavery: Of Theory, Method, and Intervention." In "Geographies of Slavery," ed. Derek H. Alderman and G. Rebecca Dobbs. Special issue, *Historical Geography* 39 (2011): 29–40.

Alexander, Jeffrey C. "On the Social Construction of Moral Universals: The 'Holocaust' from War Crime to Trauma Drama." *European Journal of Social Theory* 5, no. 1 (2002): 5–85. https://doi.org/10.1177/1368431002005001001.

———. "Social Subjectivity: Psychotherapy as Central Institution." *Thesis Eleven* 96 (2009): 128–34.

Allen, Irving M. "Posttraumatic Stress Disorder Among Black Vietnam Veterans." *Psychiatric Services* 37, no. 1 (1986): 55–61.

Archer, Christon I. *World History of Warfare.* Lincoln: University of Nebraska Press, 2002.

Arditi, Benjamín. "Populism as a Spectre of Democracy: A Response to Canovan." *Political Studies* 52, no. 1 (2003): 135–43. https://doi.org/10.1111/j.1467-9248.2004.00468.x.

Arendt, Hannah. *On Revolution.* 1963. Reprint. New York: Penguin, 2006.

———. "Reflections on Violence." *Journal of International Affairs* 23, no. 1 (1969): 1–35. https://www.jstor.org/stable/95f4f82f-fc7d-3ce4-bebe-f5e0077edbfd.

———. "Truth and Politics." *The New Yorker*, February 17, 1967. https://www.newyorker.com/magazine/1967/02/25/truth-and-politics.

Arnett, Peter. *Live from the Battlefield: From Vietnam to Baghdad: 35 Years in the World's War Zones*. New York: Simon & Schuster, 1994.

Badalič, Vasja. *The War Against Civilians: Victims of the "War on Terror" in Afghanistan and Pakistan*. Cham, Switzerland: Springer International, 2019.

Baer, Hester. "Redoing Feminism: Digital Activism, Body Politics, and Neoliberalism." *Feminist Media Studies* 16, no. 1 (2016): 17–34. https://doi.org/10.1080/14680777.2015.1093070.

Baker, Michael, and Andrew Anglemyer. "Successful Elimination of COVID-19 Transmission in New Zealand." *New England Journal of Medicine* 383 (2020): e56. https://www.nejm.org/doi/full/10.1056/NEJMc2025203.

Baker, Michael, Nick Wilson, and Andrew Anglemyer. "Excess Mortality due to COVID-19 in Germany." *Journal of Infection* 81, no. 5 (2020): 797–801. https://www.nejm.org/doi/full/10.1056/NEJMc2025203.

Banet-Weiser, Sarah. *Empowered: Popular Feminism and Popular Misogyny*. Illus. ed. Durham, NC: Duke University Press, 2018.

———. "'Ruined' Lives: Mediated White Male Victimhood." *European Journal of Cultural Studies* 24, no. 1 (2021): 60–80. https://doi.org/10.1177/1367549420985840.

Banet-Weiser, Sarah, and Kathryn Clare Higgins. *Believability: Sexual Violence, Media, and the Politics of Doubt*. Cambridge: Polity, 2023.

———. "Television and the 'Honest' Woman: Mediating the Labor of Believability." *Television & New Media* 23, no. 2 (2022): 127–47. https://doi.org/10.1177/15274764211045742.

Barrett, Frank J. "The Organizational Construction of Hegemonic Masculinity: The Case of the US Navy." *Gender, Work, & Organization* 3, no. 3 (1996): 129–42. https://doi.org/10.1111/j.1468-0432.1996.tb00054.x.

Barrett, Michèle. *Casualty Figures: How Five Men Survived the First World War*. London: Verso, 2007.

Beard, Mary. *Women & Power: A Manifesto*. London: Profile, 2017.

Bektas, Yakup. "The Crimean War as a Technological Enterprise." *Notes and Records: Royal Society Journal of the History of Science* 71, no. 3 (2017): 233–62.

Ben-Ghiat, Ruth. *Strongmen: How They Rise, Why They Succeed, How They Fall.* London: Profile, 2000.

Benjamin, Walter. *The Storyteller: Tales out of Loneliness.* Brooklyn, NY: Verso, 2016.

Berlant, Lauren. *The Female Complaint: The Unfinished Business of Sentimentality in American Culture.* Durham, NC: Duke University Press, 2008.

Bermeo, Nancy, and Larry M. Bartels, eds. *Mass Politics in Tough Times: Opinions, Votes, and Protest in the Great Recession.* Illus. ed. Oxford: Oxford University Press, 2014.

Berridge, Anne Louise. "Off the Chart: The Crimean War in British Public Consciousness." *19: Interdisciplinary Studies in the Long Nineteenth Century* 20 (2015): 1–23. https://doi.org/10.16995/ntn.726.

Bjerre, Thomas Ærvold. "From Warrior Heroes to Vulnerable Boys: Debunking 'Soldierly Masculinity' in Tim Hetherington's Infidel Photos." In *Visualizing War: Emotions, Technologies, Communities,* ed. Anders Engberg-Pedersen and Kathrin Maurer, 146–64. London: Routledge, 2017.

Blanton, DeAnne, and Lauren Cook Wike. *They Fought Like Demons: Women Soldiers in the American Civil War.* Baton Rouge: Louisiana State University Press, 2002.

Blight, David W. "'For Something Beyond the Battlefield': Frederick Douglass and the Struggle for the Memory of the Civil War." *Journal of American History* 75, no. 4 (1989): 1156–78. https://doi.org/10.2307/1908634.

Boltanski, Luc. *Distant Suffering: Morality, Media, and Politics.* Trans. Graham D. Burchell. Cambridge: Cambridge University Press, 1999.

Bonner, Eric. "From Modernity to Bigotry." In *Critical Theory and Authoritarian Populism,* ed. Jeremiah Morelock, 85–105. London: University of Westminster Press, 2018.

Boudreau, Tyler. "The Morally Injured." *Massachusetts Review* 52, nos. 3–4 (2011): 746–54. https://www.jstor.org/stable/23210143.

Bourke, Joanna. "Effeminacy, Ethnicity, and the End of Trauma: The Sufferings of 'Shell-Shocked' Men in Great Britain and Ireland, 1914–39." *Journal of Contemporary History* 35, no. 1 (2000): 57–69. https://www.jstor.org/stable/261181.

———. "Fear and Anxiety: Writing About Emotion in Modern History." *History Workshop Journal* 55 (February 2003): 111–33. https://doi.org/10.1093/hwj/55.1.111.

Bratich, Jack. "'Give Me Liberty or Give Me COVID!': Anti-lockdown Protests as Necropopulist Downsurgency." *Cultural Studies* 35, nos. 2–3 (2021): 257–65. https://doi.org/10.1080/09502386.2021.1898016.

Braudy, Leo. *From Chivalry to Terrorism: War and the Changing Nature of Masculinity*. New York: Knopf, 2003.

Brock, Rita, and Gabriella Litini. *Soul Repair: Recovering from Moral Injury After War*. Boston, MA: Beacon, 2013.

Brown, Alexander. "What Is Hate Speech? Part 1: The Myth of Hate." *Law and Philosophy* 36 (August 2017): 419–68. https://doi.org/10.1007/s10982-017-9297-1.

Brown, Wendy. *States of Injury: Power and Freedom in Late Modernity*. Princeton, NJ: Princeton University Press, 1995.

———. "Wounded Attachments: Late Modern Oppositional Political Formations." *Political Theory* 21, no. 3 (1993): 390–410.

Brubaker, Rogers. "Paradoxes of Populism During the Pandemic." *Thesis Eleven* 164, no. 1 (2021): 73–87. https://doi.org/10.1177/0725513620970804.

Bulut, Ergin. "Interview with Safiya Noble: Algorithms of Oppression, Gender, and Race." *Moment Dergi* 5, no. 2 (2018): 294–301. https://dergipark.org.tr/en/download/article-file/653368.

Burke, Roland. "Emotional Diplomacy and Human Rights at the United Nations." *Human Rights Quarterly* 39 (May 2017): 273–95.

Butler, Judith. *Precarious Life. The Powers of Mourning and Violence*. London: Verso, 2004.

Butler, Judith, Zeynep Gambetti, and Leticia Sabsay, eds. *Vulnerability in Resistance*. Durham, NC: Duke University Press, 2016.

Buxton, Hilary. "Imperial Amnesia: Race, Trauma, and Indian Troops in the First World War." *Past & Present* 241, no. 1 (2018): 221–58. https://doi.org/10.1093/pastj/gty023.

Campbell, Bradley, and Jason Manning. *The Rise of Victimhood Culture: Microaggressions, Safe Spaces, and the New Culture Wars*. New York: Palgrave Macmillan, 2018.

Cammaerts, Bart. "The Abnormalisation of Social Justice: The 'Anti-woke Culture War' Discourse in the UK." *Discourse & Society* 33, no. 6 (2022): 730–43.

Canovan, Margaret. "Trust the People! Populism and the Two Faces of Democracy." *Political Studies* 47, no. 1 (1999): 2–16. https://doi.org/10.1111/1467-9248.00184.

Carden-Coyne, Ana. "Masculinity and the Wounds of the First World War: A Centenary Reflection." *Revue française de civilisation britannique*, online publication, May 1, 2015. https://doi.org/10.4000/rfcb.305.

Carney, Nikita. "All Lives Matter, but so Does Race: Black Lives Matter and the Evolving Role of Social Media." *Humanity & Society* 40, no. 2 (2016): 180–99. https://doi.org/10.1177/0160597616643868.

Carreira da Silva, Filipe, and Mónica Brito Vieira. "Populism and the Politics of Redemption." *Thesis Eleven* 149, no. 1 (2018): 10–30. https://doi.org/10.1177/0725513618813374.

Carreira da Silva, Kumarini. "COVID-19 and the Mundane Practices of Privilege." *Cultural Studies* 35, nos. 2–3 (2021): 238–47. https://doi.org/10.1080/09502386.2021.1898034.

Caruth, Cathy. *Unclaimed Experience: Trauma, Narrative, and History*. Baltimore, MD: Johns Hopkins University Press, 2016.

Césaire, Aimé. *Discourse on Colonialism*. New York: New York University Press, 2001.

Chouliaraki, Lilie. *The Ironic Spectator: Solidarity in the Age of Posthumanitarianism*. New York: Wiley, 2013.

———. *The Spectatorship of Suffering*. London: Sage, 2006.

Chouliaraki, Lilie, and Myria Georgiou. *The Digital Border: Migration, Technology, Power*. New York: New York University Press, 2022.

Chouliaraki, Lilie, and Anne Vestergaard, eds. *Routledge Handbook of Humanitarian Communication*. London: Routledge, 2022.

Cohen, Susan A. "Abortion and Women of Color: The Bigger Picture." *Policy Review* 11, no. 3 (2008): 2–12. https://www.guttmacher.org/sites/default/files/article_files/gpr110302.pdf.

Coker, Christopher. *Humane Warfare*. London: Routledge, 2001.

Cole, Alyson M. *The Cult of True Victimhood: From the War on Welfare to the War on Terror*. Stanford, CA: Stanford University Press, 2007.

Cole, Alyson, and Sumru Atuk. "What's in a Hashtag? Feminist Terms for Tweeting in Alliance." *philoSOPHIA: A Journal of Continental Feminism* 9, no. 1 (2019): 26–52.

Coleman, Mathew. "Immigration Geopolitics Beyond the Mexico–US Border." *Antipode* 39, no. 1 (2007): 54–76. https://doi.org/10.1111/j.1467-8330.2007.00506.x.

Cook, Tim, Emira Kursumovic, and Simon Lennane. "Exclusive: Deaths of NHS Staff from COVID-19 Analysed." *HSJ: Health Services Journal*,

April 22, 2020. https://www.hsj.co.uk/exclusive-deaths-of-nhs-staff-from-covid-19-analysed/7027471.article.

"COVID-19—Break the Cycle of Inequality." Editorial. *Lancet*, February 1, 2021. https://www.thelancet.com/journals/lanpub/article/PIIS2468-2667(21)00011-6/fulltext.

"The COVID-19 Infodemic." Collective editorial. *Lancet: Infectious Diseases* 20, no. 8 (2020): 875. https://www.thelancet.com/journals/laninf/article/PIIS1473-3099(20)30565-X/fulltext.

Cox, David. "Pandemic Reflections." *International Journal of Community and Social Development* 2, no. 3 (2020): 349–54. https://doi.org/10.1177/2516602620959506.

Craps, Stef. *Postcolonial Witnessing: Trauma out of Bounds*. New York: Palgrave Macmillan, 2013.

Crenshaw, Kimberlé. "Demarginalizing the Intersection of Race and Sex: A Black Feminist Critique of Antidiscrimination Doctrine, Feminist Theory, and Antiracist Politics." *University of Chicago Legal Forum* 140 (1989): 139–67. https://philarchive.org/rec/CREDTI.

Crossland, James. *War, Law, and Humanity: The Campaign to Control Warfare, 1853–1914*. London: Bloomsbury, 2018.

Crouthamel, Jason. "Male Sexuality and Psychological Trauma: Soldiers and Sexual Disorder in World War I and Weimar Germany." *Journal of the History of Sexuality* 17 (February 2008): 60–84. https://doi.org/10.1353/sex.2008.0006.

Dada, Sara, Henry Charles Ashworth, Marlene Joannie Bewa, and Roopa Dhatt. "Words Matter: Political and Gender Analysis of Speeches Made by Heads of Government During the COVID-19 Pandemic." *BMJ Global Health* 6, no. 1 (2021): e003910. https://doi.org/10.1136/bmjgh-2020-003910.

Dahlgren, Peter. "Media, Knowledge, and Trust: The Deepening Epistemic Crisis of Democracy." *Javnost—the Public* 25, nos. 1–2 (2018): 20–27. https://doi.org/10.1080/13183222.2018.1418819.

Danielsen, Ann Caroline, Marion Boulicault, Annika Gompers, Tamara Rushovich, Katherine M. N. Lee, and Sarah S. Richardson. "How Cumulative Statistics Can Mislead: The Temporal Dynamism of Sex Disparities in COVID-19 Mortality in New York State." *International Journal of Environmental Research and Public Health* 19, no. 21 (2022): article 14066. https://doi.org/10.3390/ijerph192114066.

Das, Santanu. "Colors of the Past: Archive, Art, and Amnesia in a Digital Age." *American Historical Review* 124, no. 5 (2019): 1771–81. https://doi.org/10.1093/ahr/rhz1021.

———. "The Indian Sepoy in the First World War." British Library Archive, February 6, 2014. https://www.bl.uk/world-war-one/articles/the-indian-sepoy-in-the-first-world-war.

———, ed. *Race, Empire, and First World War Writing*. Cambridge: Cambridge University Press, 2011.

Davies, William. *The Limits of Neoliberalism: Authority, Sovereignty, and the Logic of Competition*. London: Sage, 2016.

Dean, Carolyn J. *The Moral Witness: Trials and Testimony After Genocide*. Ithaca, NY: Cornell University Press, 2019.

De Benedictis, Sara, Shani Orgad, and Catherine Rottenberg. "#MeToo, Popular Feminism, and the News: A Content Analysis of UK Newspaper Coverage." *European Journal of Cultural Studies* 22, nos. 5–6 (2019): 718–38. https://doi.org/10.1177/1367549419856831.

Delanty, Gerard. "Six Political Philosophies in Search of a Virus: Critical Perspectives on the Coronavirus Pandemic." *LEQS Paper* 156 (2020): 5–24. https://www.lse.ac.uk/european-institute/Assets/Documents/LEQS-Discussion-Papers/LEQSPaper156.pdf.

Demertzis, Nicolas. "Emotions and Populism." In *Emotion, Politics, and Society*, ed. Paul Hoggett, Simon Clarke, and Simon Thompson, 103–22. London: Palgrave Macmillan, 2006.

———. *The Political Sociology of Emotions: Essays on Trauma and Ressentiment*. London: Routledge, 2020.

Demertzis, Nicolas, and Ron Eyerman. "COVID-19 as Cultural Trauma." *American Journal of Cultural Sociology* 8, no. 3 (2020): 428–50. https://doi.org/10.1057/s41290-020-00112-z.

Devakumar, Delan, Geordan Shannon, Sunil Bhopal, and Ibrahim Abdukar. "Racism and Discrimination in COVID-19 Responses." *Lancet*, April 11, 2020. https://www.thelancet.com/journals/lancet/article/PIIS0140-6736(20)30792-3/fulltext.

Dodman, Trevor. "'Belated Impress': River George and the African American Shell Shock Narrative." *African American Review* 44 (January 2011): 149–66. https://doi.org/10.1353/afa.2011.0023.

Douglass, Frederick. "The Claims of the Negro Ethnologically Considered" (1854). In *The Speeches of Frederick Douglass: A Critical Edition*, ed. John R.

McKivigan, Julie Husband, and Heather L. Kaufman, 116–50. New Haven, CT: Yale University Press, 2018.

Dragiewicz, Molly, Jean Burgess, Ariadna Matamoros-Fernández, Michael Salter, Nicolas P. Suzor, Delanie Woodlock, and Bridget Harris. "Technology Facilitated Coercive Control: Domestic Violence and the Competing Roles of Digital Media Platforms." *Feminist Media Studies* 18, no. 4 (2018): 609–25. https://doi.org/10.1080/14680777.2018.1447341.

Du Bois, W. E. B. *Black Reconstruction in America: Toward a History of the Part Which Black Folk Played in the Attempt to Reconstruct Democracy in America, 1860–1880.* 1935. Reprint. London: Routledge, 2012.

———. *On Sociology and the Black Community.* Ed. Dan Green and Edwin Driver. Chicago: University of Chicago Press, 1978.

———. *Worlds of Color.* 1925. Reprint. Edinburgh: Mainstream/Random House, 1961.

Enns, Diane. *The Violence of Victimhood.* University Park: Pennsylvania State University Press, 2012.

Evanega, Sarah, Mark Lynas, Jordan Adams, and Karinne Smolenyak. "Coronavirus Misinformation: Quantifying Sources and Themes in the COVID-19 'Infodemic.'" *Journal of Medical Internet Research*, preprint publication, October 19, 2020. https://doi.org/10.2196/preprints.25143.

Evans, Brad, and Julian Reid. "Exhausted by *Resilience*: Response to the Commentaries." *Resilience* 3, no. 2 (2015): 154–59. https://doi.org/10.1080/21693293.2015.1022991.

Eyerman, Ron. *Memory, Trauma, and Identity.* London: Palgrave Macmillan, 2019.

Faludi, Susan. *Backlash: The Undeclared War Against American Women.* New York: Crown, 1991.

Fanon, Frantz. *The Wretched of the Earth.* Trans. Constance Farrington. New York: Grove, 1963.

Farias, Debora Barros Leal, Guilherme Casarões, and David Magalhães. "Radical Right Populism and the Politics of Cruelty: The Case of COVID-19 in Brazil Under President Bolsonaro." *Global Studies Quarterly* 2, no. 2 (2022): 1–13. HYPERLINK "https://doi.org/10.1093/isagsq/ksabo48" https://doi.org/10.1093/isagsq/ksabo48.

Farris, Samantha G., Mindy M. Kibbey, Erick J. Fedorenko, and Angelo M. DiBello. "A Qualitative Study of COVID-19 Distress in University

Students." *Emerging Adulthood* 9, no. 5 (2021): 462–78. https://doi.org/10.1177/21676968211025128.

Farris, Sara, Nira Yuval-Davis, and Catherine Rottenberg. "The Frontline as Performative Frame: An Analysis of the UK COVID Crisis." *State Crime Journal* 10, no. 2 (2021): 284–303.

Fassin, Didier, and Richard Rechtman. *The Empire of Trauma: An Inquiry Into the Condition of Victimhood*. Trans. Rachel Gomme. Princeton, NJ: Princeton University Press, 2009.

Faust, Drew Gilpin. *This Republic of Suffering*. New York: Knopf Doubleday, 2008.

Fell, Alison S., and Christine E. Hallett. *First World War Nursing: New Perspectives*. London: Routledge, 2013.

Felman, Shoshana. "Theaters of Justice: Arendt in Jerusalem, the Eichmann Trial, and the Redefinition of Legal Meaning in the Wake of the Holocaust." *Critical Inquiry* 27, no. 2 (2001): 201–38. https://www.jstor.org/stable/1344248.

Felman, Shoshana, and Dori Laub. *Testimony: Crises of Witnessing in Literature, Psychoanalysis, and History*. New York: Routledge, 1992.

Figes, Orlando. *Crimea*. London: Penguin, 2011.

Figley, Charles R. *Stress Disorders Among Vietnam Veterans: Theory, Research*. London: Routledge, 2014.

Forster, Timon, and Mirko Heinzel. "Reacting, Fast and Slow: How World Leaders Shaped Government Responses to the COVID-19 Pandemic." *Journal of European Public Policy* 28, no. 8 (2021): 1299–320. https://doi.org/10.1080/13501763.2021.1942157.

Foster, Gaines M. *Ghosts of the Confederacy: Defeat, the Lost Cause, and the Emergence of the New South, 1865–1913*. 1985. Reprint. New York: Oxford University Press, 1987.

Foucault, Michel. *The Government of Self and Others: Lectures at the Collège de France, 1982–1983*. Ed. Frédéric Gros. Trans. Graham Burchell. London: Picador, 2010.

Franke, Katherine M. "Becoming a Citizen: Reconstruction Era Regulation of African American Marriages." *Yale Journal of Law & the Humanities* 11 (1991): 251–309.

Freelon, Deen, Charlton D. McIlwain, and Meredith Clark. "Beyond the Hashtags: #Ferguson, #Blacklivesmatter, and the Online Struggle for

Offline Justice." Center for Media & Social Impact Publication, School of Communication, American University, 2016.

Frosh, Paul, and Amit Pinchevski. "Introduction: Why Witnessing? Why Now?" In *Media Witnessing: Testimony in the Age of Mass Communication*, ed. Paul Frosh and Amit Pinchevski, 1–22. London: Palgrave Macmillan, 2009.

Furedi, Frank. *Therapy Culture: Cultivating Vulnerability in an Uncertain Age*. London: Routledge, 2003.

Fussell, Paul. *The Great War and Modern Memory*. London: Sterling, 2009.

Galona, Yevgen. "From Ritual to Metaphor: The Semantic Shift in the Concept of 'Victim' and Medieval Christian Piety." *International Review of Victimology* 24, no. 1 (2018): 83–98. https://doi.org/10.1177/0269758017732923.

García-Favaro, Laura, and Rosalind Gill. "'Emasculation Nation Has Arrived': Sexism Rearticulated in Online Responses to Lose the Lads' Mags Campaign." *Feminist Media Studies* 16 (November 2015): 379–97. https://doi.org/10.1080/14680777.2015.1105840.

Garland, Ruth, and Darren Lilleker. "From Consensus to Dissensus: The UK's Management of a Pandemic in a Divided Nation." In *Political Communication in the Time of Coronavirus*, ed. Peter Van Aelst and Jay G. Blumler, 17–32. New York: Routledge, 2021.

Garrett, Laurie. "COVID-19: The Medium Is the Message." *Lancet* 395, no. 10228 (2020): 942–43. https://www.thelancet.com/journals/lancet/article/PIIS0140-6736(20)30600-0/fulltext.

Gerbaudo, Paolo. "The Pandemic Crowd: Protest in the Time of COVID-19." *Journal of International Affairs* 73, no. 2 (2020): 61–76. https://www.jstor.org/stable/26939966.

Gerodimos, Roman. "Greece's Ongoing Tragedy." *Political Insight* 6, no. 3 (2015): 26–27. https://doi.org/10.1111/2041-9066.12111.

———. "Humiliation, Shame, and Violence: Honor, Trauma, and Political Extremism Before and After the 2009 Crisis in Greece." *International Forum of Psychoanalysis* 31, no. 1 (2022): 34–45.

Al-Ghazzi, Omar. "We Will Be Great Again: Historical Victimhood in Populist Discourse." *European Journal of Cultural Studies* 24, no. 1 (2021): 45–59.

Gilbert, Jonas. *Freedom's Sword: The NAACP and the Struggle Against Racism in America, 1909–1969*. New York: Routledge, 2006.

Gill, Rosalind, and Shani Orgad. "Confidence Culture and the Remaking of Feminism." *New Formations* 91 (April 2017): 16–34. https://doi.org/10.3898/NEWF:91.01.2017.

———. "The Shifting Terrain of Sex and Power: From the 'Sexualization of Culture' to #MeToo." *Sexualities* 21, no. 8 (2018): 1313–24. https://doi.org/10.1177/1363460718794647.

Gilligan, Carol. "Moral Injury and the Ethic of Care: Reframing the Conversation About Differences." *Journal of Social Philosophy* 45, no. 1 (2014): 89–106. https://doi.org/10.1111/josp.12050.

Gilmore, Leigh. "Policing Truth: Confession, Gender, and Autobiographical Authority." In *Autobiography and Postmodernism*, ed. Gerald Peters, Kathleen Ashley, and Leigh Gilmore, 54–78. Boston: University of Massachusetts Press, 1994.

———. *Tainted Witness: Why We Doubt What Women Say About Their Lives*. New York: Columbia University Press, 2017.

Giroux, Henry A. "The Culture of Cruelty in Trump's America." Truthout, 2017. https://truthout.org/articles/the-culture-of-cruelty-in-trump-s-america/.

Gravelle, Timothy, Joseph Phillips, Jason Reifler, and Thomas J. Scotto. "Estimating the size of 'Anti-vax' and Vaccine Hesitant Populations in the US, UK, and Canada: Comparative Latent Class Modeling of Vaccine Attitudes." *Human Vaccines and Immunotherapeutics* 18, no. 1 (2022). https://doi.org/10.1080/21645515.2021.2008214.

Grogan, Suzie. *Shell Shocked Britain: The First World War's Legacy for Britain's Mental Health*. Illus. ed. Barnsley, U.K.: Pen & Sword, 2014.

Grossberg, Lawrence. *Under the Cover of Chaos: Trump and the Battle for the American Right*. London: Pluto, 2018.

Grossman, Daniel, Sarah Baum, Liza Fuentes, Kari White, Kristine Hopkins, Amanda Stevenson, and Joseph E. Potter. "Change in Abortion Services After Implementation of a Restrictive Law in Texas." *Contraception* 90, no. 5 (2014): 496–501. https://doi.org/10.1016/j.contraception.2014.07.006.

Grove, Kevin, Lauren Rickards, Ben Anderson, and Matthew Kearnes. "The Uneven Distribution of Futurity: Slow Emergencies and the Event of COVID-19." *Geographical Research* 60, no. 1 (2022): 6–17. https://doi.org/10.1111/1745-5871.12501.

Hall, Stuart. "On Postmodernism and Articulation: An Interview with Stuart Hall." Ed. Lawrence Grossberg. *Journal of Communication Inquiry* 10, no. 2 (1986): 45–60.

Hallin, Daniel. *The Uncensored War: The Media and Vietnam*. Berkeley: University of California Press, 1989.

Halttunen, Karen. "Humanitarianism and the Pornography of Pain in Anglo-American Culture." *American Historical Review* 100, no. 2 (1995): 303–34. https://doi.org/10.2307/2169001.

Hamad, Ruby. *White Tears / Brown Scars: How White Feminism Betrays Women of Color*. Melbourne: Melbourne University Press, 2019.

Hao, Karen. "How Facebook and Google Fund Global Misinformation." *MIT Technology Review*, November 11, 2021. https://www.technologyreview.com/2021/11/20/1039076/facebook-google-disinformation-clickbait/.

Harari, Yuval Noah. *Renaissance Military Memoirs: War, History, and Identity, 1450–1600*. Suffolk, U.K.: Boydell and Brewer, 2004.

Harding, Meghan. "Representation of Women in the Armed Forces." U.K. House of Commons Library, 2021. https://commonslibrary.parliament.uk/representation-of-women-in-the-armed-forces/.

Harman, Sophie, Parsa Erfani, Tinashe Goronga, Jason Hickel, Michelle Morse, and Eugene T. Richardson. "Global Vaccine Equity Demands Reparative Justice—Not Charity." *BMJ Global Health* 6 (2021): e006504. https://gh.bmj.com/content/bmjgh/6/6/e006504.full.pdf.

Harsin, Jayson. "Regimes of Posttruth, Postpolitics, and Attention Economies." *Communication, Culture, & Critique* 8, no. 2 (2015): 327–33.

——. "Toxic White Masculinity, Post-truth Politics, and the COVID-19 Infodemic." *European Journal of Cultural Studies* 23, no. 6 (2020): 1060–68. https://doi.org/10.1177/1367549420944934.

Hemmings, Robert. "'The Blameless Physician': Narrative and Pain, Sassoon and Rivers." *Literature and Medicine* 24, no. 1 (2005): 109–26. https://doi.org/10.1353/lm.2005.0026.

Henry, Nicola, and Anastasia Powell. "Embodied Harms: Gender, Shame, and Technology-Facilitated Sexual Violence." *Violence Against Women* 21, no. 6 (2015): 758–79. https://doi.org/10.1177/1077801215576581.

Hensman, Savitri. "Whose Views, and Lives, Truly Count? The Meaning of Co-production Against a Background of Worsening Inequalities."

In *COVID-19 and Co-production in Health and Social Care Research, Policy, and Practice*, vol. 1: *The Challenges and Necessity of Co-production*, ed. Peter Beresford, Michelle Farr, Gary Hickey, Meerat Kaur, Josephine Ocloo, Doreen Tembo, and Oli Williams, 19–27. Cambridge: Policy, 2021.

Herman, Judith L. *Trauma and Recovery: The Aftermath of Violence—from Domestic Abuse to Political Terror.* New York: Basic, 1992.

Higgins, Kathryn Claire. "Realness, Wrongness, Justice: Exploring Criminalization as a Mediated Politics of Vulnerability." PhD diss., London School of Economics and Political Science, 2022.

Hines, Sally. "The Feminist Frontier: On Trans and Feminism." *Journal of Gender Studies* 28, no. 2 (2019): 145–57.

——. "Sex Wars and (Trans) Gender Panics: Identity and Body Politics in Contemporary UK Feminism." *Sociological Review* 6, no. 4 (2020): 699–717. https://doi.org/10.1177/0038026120934684.

Hobsbawm, Eric. *Age of Extremes: A History of the World, 1914–1991.* 1994. Reprint. London: Abacus, 1995.

Hochschild, Arlie Russell. *Strangers in Their Own Land: Anger and Mourning on the American Right.* Illus. ed. New York: New Press, 2016.

Hoffmann, Anna Lauren, and Anne Jonas. "Recasting Justice for Internet and Online Industry Research Ethics." In *Internet Research Ethics for the Social Age: New Cases and Challenges*, ed. Michael Zimmer and Katharina Kinder-Kuranda, 3–15. Bern, Switzerland: Peter Lang, 2016.

Hood, Caroline, and Alice Butler-Warke. "Living on the Edge: Spatial Exclusion Rendered Visible by the COVID-19 Pandemic." *Discover Society*, April 28, 2020. https://archive.discoversociety.org/2020/04/28/living-on-the-edge-spatial-exclusion-rendered-visible-by-the-covid-19-pandemic/.

Hornsey, Matthew J., Matthew Finlayson, Gabrielle Chatwood, and Christopher T. Begeny. "Donald Trump and Vaccination: The Effect of Political Identity, Conspiracist Ideation, and Presidential Tweets on Vaccine Hesitancy." *Journal of Experimental Social Psychology* 88 (May 2020): article 103947. https://doi.org/10.1016/j.jesp.2019.103947.

Horwitz, Robert. "Politics as Victimhood, Victimhood as Politics." *Journal of Policy History* 30 (July 2018): 552–74. https://doi.org/10.1017/S0898030 618000209.

Hoskins, Andrew. "Digital War." In *Routledge Handbook of Humanitarian Communication*, ed. Lilie Chouliaraki and Anne Vestergaard, 66–86. London: Routledge, 2022.

Howard, Stephen. "The Vietnam Warrior: His Experience, and Implications for Psychotherapy." *American Journal of Psychotherapy* 30, no. 1 (1976): 121–35.

Hubner, Austin. "How Did We Get Here? A Framing and Source Analysis of Early COVID-19 Media Coverage." *Communication Research Reports* 38, no. 2 (2021): 112–20. https://doi.org/10.1080/08824096.2021.1894112.

Humphreys, Cathy, and Stephen Joseph. "Domestic Violence and the Politics of Trauma." *Women's Studies International Forum* 27 (2004): 559–70. https://doi.org/10.1016/j.wsif.2004.09.010.

Humphreys, Margaret. *Intensely Human: The Health of the Black Soldier in the American Civil War*. Illus. ed. Baltimore, MD: Johns Hopkins University Press, 2008.

Hunter, Anna. "The Holocaust as the Ultimate Trauma Narrative." In *Trauma and Literature*, ed. J. Roger Kurtz, 66–82. Cambridge: Cambridge University Press, 2018.

Huszár, Ferenc, Sofia Ira Ktena, Conor O'Brien, Luca Belli, Andrew Schlaikjer, and Moritz Hardt. "Algorithmic Amplification of Politics on Twitter." *Proceedings of the National Academy of Sciences* 119 (January 2022) : 1–6. https://doi.org/10.1073/pnas.2025334119.

Hutchings, Kimberly. "Making Sense of Masculinity and War." *Men and Masculinities* 10, no. 4 (2008): 389–404. https://doi.org/10.1177/1097184X07306740.

Hutchison, Emma. *Affective Communities in World Politics*. Cambridge: Cambridge University Press, 2016.

Hynes, Samuel. *The Soldiers' Tale: Bearing Witness to Modern War*. New York: Allen Lane, 1997.

Illouz, Eva. *Cold Intimacies: The Making of Emotional Capitalism*. Cambridge: Polity, 2007.

———. "The Culture of Management: Self-Interest, Empathy, and Emotional Control." In *An Introduction to Social Entrepreneurship: Voices, Preconditions, Contexts*, ed. Rafael Ziegler, 107–32. Cheltenham, U.K.: Edward Elgar, 2009.

———. *Oprah Winfrey and the Glamour of Misery: An Essay on Popular Culture.* New York: Columbia University Press, 2003.

———. *Saving the Modern Soul: Therapy, Emotions, and the Culture of Self-Help.* Berkeley: University of California Press, 2008.

———. "'That Shadowy Realm of the Interior': Oprah Winfrey and Hamlet's Glass." *International Journal of Cultural Studies* 2, no. 1 (1999): 109–31. https://doi.org/10.1177/136787799900200106.

Islam, Nazrul, Vladimir M. Shkolnikov, Rolando J. Acosta, Ilya Klimkin, Ichiro Kawachi, Rafael A. Irizarry, Gianfranco Alicandro, et al. "Excess Deaths Associated with COVID-19 Pandemic in 2020: Age and Sex Disaggregated Time Series Analysis in 29 High Income Countries." *British Medical Journal* 373, no. 1137 (2021). https://www.bmj.com/content/373/bmj.n1137.

Jackson, Peter. *They Shall Not Grow Old.* Documentary. WingNut Films, 2018.

Jacoby, Tami Amanda. "A Theory of Victimhood: Politics, Conflict, and the Construction of Victim-Based Identity." *Millennium* 43, no. 2 (2015): 511–30. https://doi.org/10.1177/0305829814550258.

Jarvis, Christina Sharon. *The Male Body at War: American Masculinity and Embodiment During World War II.* University Park: Pennsylvania State University Press, 2000.

Jeffords, Susan. "Debriding Vietnam: The Resurrection of the White American Male." *Feminist Studies* 14, no. 3 (1988): 525–43.

Jenkinson, Jacqueline. "'All in the Same Uniform?' The Participation of Black Colonial Residents in the British Armed Forces in the First World War." *Journal of Imperial and Commonwealth History* 40, no. 2 (2012): 207–30. https://doi.org/10.1080/03086534.2012.697611.

Jerman, Jenna, Rachel K. Jones, and Tsuyoshi Onda. "Characteristics of U.S. Abortion Patients in 2014 and Changes Since 2008." Working Paper no. 29, Guttmacher Institute, New York, 2016. https://www.guttmacher.org/report/characteristics-us-abortion-patients-2014?utm_source=flin%20flon%20reminder&utm_campaign=flin%20flon%20reminder%3A%20outbound&utm_medium=referral.

Johnson, Carol, and Blair Williams. "Gender and Political Leadership in a Time of COVID." *Politics & Gender* 16, no. 4 (2020): 943–50. https://doi.org/10.1017/S1743923X2000029X.

Johnson, Paul Elliott. "The Art of Masculine Victimhood: Donald Trump's Demagoguery." *Women's Studies in Communication* 40, no. 3 (2017): 229–50. https://doi.org/10.1080/07491409.2017.1346533.

Jones, Edgar. "The Psychology of Killing: The Combat Experience of British Soldiers During the First World War." *Journal of Contemporary History* 41, no. 2 (2006): 229–46. https://www.jstor.org/stable/30036384.

Jones, Edgar, and Simon Wessely. "A Paradigm Shift in the Conceptualization of Psychological Trauma in the 20th Century." *Journal of Anxiety Disorders* 21, no. 2 (2007): 164–75. https://doi.org/10.1016/j.janxdis.2006.09.009.

Kaiser, David E. *American Tragedy: Kennedy, Johnson, and the Origins of the Vietnam War.* Cambridge, MA: Harvard University Press, 2000.

Kalpokas, Ignas. "On Guilt and Post-truth Escapism: Developing a Theory." *Philosophy & Social Criticism* 44, no. 10 (2018): 1127–47. https://doi.org/10.1177/0191453718794752.

Kalyvas, Stathis, and Matthew Adam Kocher. "The Dynamics of Violence in Vietnam: An Analysis of the Hamlet Evaluation System (HES)." *Journal of Peace Research* 46, no. 3 (2009): 335–55. https://www.jstor.org/stable/25654409.

Kazin, Michael. *The Populist Persuasion: An American History.* Ithaca, NY: Cornell University Press, 1995.

Kellison, Rosemary. *Expanding Responsibility for the Just War: A Feminist Critique.* Cambridge: Cambridge University Press, 2018.

Kemp, Simon. "Digital 2021 October Global Statshot Report." *DataReportal—Global Digital Insights*, October 2021. https://datareportal.com/reports/digital-2021-october-global-statshot.

Kennedy, David. "Modern War and Modern Law." *International Legal Theory* 12, no. 55 (2006): 471–94. https://heinonline.org/HOL/Page?handle=hein.journals/intltr12&id=61&div=&collection=.

King, Martin Luther, Jr. "The World House." In *Where Do We Go from Here: Chaos or Community?* (1967), introduction by Vincent Harding, foreword by Coretta Scott King, 177–201. Boston, MA: Beacon, 2010.

Kinnvall, Catarina. "Populism, Ontological Insecurity, and Hindutva: Modi and the Masculinization of Indian Politics." *Cambridge Review of International Affairs* 32, no. 3 (2019): 283–302.

Kissas, Angelos. "Performative and Ideological Populism: The Case of Charismatic Leaders on Twitter." *Discourse & Society* 31, no. 3 (2020): 268–84. https://doi.org/10.1177/0957926519889127.

Klinenberg, Eric, and Melina Sherman. "Face Mask Face-Offs: Culture and Conflict in the COVID-19 Pandemic." *Public Culture* 33, no. 3 (2021): 441–66. https://doi.org/10.1215/08992363-9262919.

Krasner, David. "Book Review: *Oprah Winfrey and the Glamour of Misery: An Essay on Popular Culture* by Eva Illouz." *African American Review* 38, no. 3 (2004): 539–41.

Kryder, Daniel. *Divided Arsenal: Race and the American State During World War II*. Cambridge: Cambridge University Press, 2001.

Krzyzanowski, Michal, and Ruth Wodak. "Right-Wing Populism in Europe & USA: Contesting Politics & Discourse Beyond 'Orbanism' and 'Trumpism.'" *Journal of Language and Politics* 16 (October 2017): 471–84. https://doi.org/10.1075/jlp.17042.krz.

LaCapra, Dominick. *Writing History, Writing Trauma*. Baltimore, MD: Johns Hopkins University Press, 2014.

Laclau, Ernesto. "Populism: What's in a Name?" In *Populism and the Mirror of Democracy*, ed. Francisco Panizza, 103–14. London: Verso, 2005.

Lacquer, Thomas. "Memory and Naming in the Great War." In *Commemorations: The Politics of National Identity*, ed. John R. Gillis, 150–67. 1994. Reprint. Princeton, NJ: Princeton University Press, 1996.

Leask, Julie, Claire Hooker, and Catherine King. "Media Coverage of Health Issues and How to Work More Effectively with Journalists: A Qualitative Study." *BMC Public Health* 10, no. 1 (2010): 1–7.

Leed, Eric. "Fateful Memories: Industrialized War and Traumatic Neuroses." *Journal of Contemporary History* 35, no. 1 (2000): 85–100. https://doi.org/10.1177/002200940003500108.

——. *No Man's Land: Combat and Identity in World War 1*. Cambridge: Cambridge University Press, 1979.

Levitsky, Steven, and Daniel Ziblatt. *How Democracies Die*. New York: Crown, 2018.

Levy, Daniel, and Natan Sznaider. "The Politics of Commemoration: The Holocaust, Memory, and Trauma." In *Handbook of Contemporary European Social Theory*, ed. Gerard Delanty, 289–97. London: Routledge, 2006.

Leys, Ruth. "Traumatic Cures: Shell Shock, Janet, and the Question of Memory." In *Tense Past: Cultural Essays in Trauma and Memory*, ed. Paul Antze and Michael Lambek, 103–48. London: Routledge, 1996.

Lilleker, Darren G., and Thomas Stoeckle. "The Challenges of Providing Certainty in the Face of Wicked Problems: Analysing the UK Government's Handling of the COVID-19 Pandemic." *Journal of Public Affairs* 2733 (2021): 1–10. https://www.ncbi.nlm.nih.gov/pmc/articles/PMC8420585/#pa2733-note-0003.

Lim, Merlyna. "Clicks, Cabs, and Coffee Houses: Social Media and Oppositional Movements in Egypt, 2004–2011." *Journal of Communication* 62, no. 2 (2012): 231–48. https://doi.org/10.1111/j.1460-2466.2012.01628.x.

Lipiński, Artur, and Gabriella Szabo. "Heroisation and Victimisation: Populism, Commemorative Narratives, and National Days in Hungary and Poland." *Journal of Contemporary European Studies* 32, no. 1 (2023): 345–62.

Littler, Jo. *Against Meritocracy: Culture, Power, and Myths of Mobility*. London: Routledge, 2017.

Livingstone, Sonia. "Developing Social Media Literacy: How Children Learn to Interpret Risky Opportunities on Social Network Sites." *Communications* 39 (September 2014): 283–303. https://doi.org/10.1515/commun-2014-0113.

Livingstone, Sonia, and Peter K. Smith. "Annual Research Review: Harms Experienced by Child Users of Online and Mobile Technologies: The Nature, Prevalence and Management of Sexual and Aggressive Risks in the Digital Age." *Journal of Child Psychology and Psychiatry* 55, no. 6 (2014): 635–54. https://doi.org/10.1111/jcpp.12197.

Livingstone, Sonia, and Amanda Third. "Children and Young People's Rights in the Digital Age: An Emerging Agenda." *New Media & Society* 19, no. 5 (2017): 657–70. https://doi.org/10.1177/1461444816686318.

Luckhurst, Roger. *The Trauma Question*. London: Routledge, 2008.

Lucks, Daniel. "African American Soldiers and the Vietnam War: No More Vietnams." *The Sixties* 10, no. 2 (2017): 196–220. https://doi.org/10.1080/17541328.2017.1303111.

Lupton, Deborah, and Ben Williamson. "The Datafied Child: The Dataveillance of Children and Implications for Their Rights." *New*

Media & Society 19, no. 5 (2017): 780–94. https://doi.org/10.1177/1461444 816686328.

Lyotard, Jean-François. *The Postmodern Condition: A Report on Knowledge.* Manchester: Manchester University Press, 1984.

MacCurdy, John T. *The Psychology of War.* 1918. Reprint. Minneapolis, MN: Franklin Classics, 2018.

MacLeish, Kenneth. "On 'Moral Injury': Psychic Fringes and War Violence." *History of the Human Sciences* 31, no. 2 (2018): 128–46. https://doi.org/10 .1177/0952695117750342.

Magelinski, Thomas, and Kathleen M. Carley. "Detecting Coordinated Behavior in the Twitter Campaign to Reopen America." Paper presented at the Center for Informed Democracy & Social-Cybersecurity Annual Conference, Carnegie Mellon University, Pittsburgh, PA, 2020. https://www.cmu.edu/ideas-social-cybersecurity /events/conference-archive/2020papers/magelinski_ideas_abstract _reopen.pdf.

Mandelbaum, Michael. "Vietnam: The Television War." *Daedalus* 111, no. 4 (1982): 157–69.

Manne, Kate. *Down Girl: The Logic of Misogyny.* Oxford: Oxford University Press, 2017.

———. *Entitled: How Male Privilege Hurts Women.* New York: Crown, 2020.

Marlier, Grant, and Neta Crawford. "Incomplete and Imperfect Institutionalisation of Empathy and Altruism in the 'Responsibility to Protect' Doctrine." *Global Responsibility to Protect* 5 (January 2013): 397–422. https://doi.org/10.1163/1875984X-00504003.

Marshall, David. "Adam Smith and the Theatricality of Moral Sentiments." *Critical Inquiry* 10, no. 4 (1984): 592–613. https://www.jstor.org/stable /1343313.

Marwick, Alice, and Robyn Caplan. "Drinking Male Tears: Language, the Manosphere, and Networked Harassment." *Feminist Media Studies* 18, no. 4 (2018): 543–59.

Mascheroni, Giovanna, and Donell Holloway. *The Internet of Toys: Practices, Affordances, and the Political Economy of Children's Smart Play.* London: Palgrave Macmillan, 2019.

Mbembe, Achille. "Necropolitics." *Public Culture* 15, no. 1 (2003): 11–40. https://doi.org/10.1215/08992363-15-1-11.

McCormick, Lisa. "Marking Time in Lockdown: Heroization and Ritualization in the UK During the Coronavirus Pandemic." *American Journal of Cultural Sociology* 8, no. 3 (2020): 324–51. https://doi.org/10.1057/s41290-020-00117-8.

McGill, Harold W. *Medicine and Duty: The World War I Memoir of Captain Harold W. McGill, Medical Officer, 31st Battalion, C.E.F.* Ed. Marjorie Barron Norris. Calgary, Canada: University of Calgary Press, 2007.

McMillan Cottom, Tressie. "Where Platform Capitalism and Racial Capitalism Meet: The Sociology of Race and Racism in the Digital Society." *Sociology of Race and Ethnicity* 6, no. 4 (2020): 441–49. https://doi.org/10.1177/2332649220949473.

McNay, Lois. "Suffering, Silence, and Social Weightlessness: Honneth and Bourdieu on Embodiment and Power." In *Embodied Selves*, ed. Stella Gonzalez-Arnal, Gill Jagger, and Kathleen Lennon, 230–48. London: Palgrave Macmillan, 2012.

McQueen, Fiona. "Male Emotionality: 'Boys Don't Cry' Versus 'It's Good to Talk.'" *NORMA* 12, nos. 3–4 (2017): 205–19. https://doi.org/10.1080/18902138.2017.1336877.

Meranze, Michael. "Distant Suffering: Morality, Media, and Politics." *History Workshop Journal* 53, no. 1 (2002): 252–58. https://doi.org/10.1093/hwj/53.1.252.

Meron, Theodor. *The Humanization of International Law*. Leiden, Netherlands: Martinus Nijhoff, 2006.

Meyer, Jessica. "Separating the Men from the Boys: Masculinity and Maturity in Understandings of Shell Shock in Britain." *Twentieth Century British History* 20, no. 1 (2009): 1–22. https://doi.org/10.1093/tcbh/hwn028.

Micale, Mark. *Approaching Hysteria: Disease and Its Interpretations*. Princeton, NJ: Princeton University Press, 1995.

Mill, John Stuart. "Civilization." In *Essays on Politics and Culture*, ed. Gertrude Himmelfarb, 45–76. New York: Basic, 1963.

Mills, Charles. "White Ignorance." In *Race and Epistemologies of Ignorance*, ed. Shannon Sullivan and Nancy Tuana, 11–38. Albany: State University of New York Press, 2007.

Mitchell, Juliet. "Trauma, Recognition, and the Place of Language." *Diacritics* 28, no. 4 (1998): 121–33. https://doi.org/10.1353/dia.1998.0035.

Mkono, Muchazondida. "'Troll Alert!' Provocation and Harassment in Tourism and Hospitality Social Media." *Current Issues in Tourism* 21, no. 7 (2015): 791–804. https://doi.org/10.1080/13683500.2015.1106447.

Moffitt, Benjamin, and Simon Tormey. "Rethinking Populism: Politics, Mediatisation, and Political Style." *Political Studies* 62, no. 2 (2014): 381–97. https://doi.org/10.1111/1467-9248.12032.

Mondon, Aurelien, and Aaron Winter. *Reactionary Democracy: How Racism and the Populist Far Right Became Mainstream*. London: Verso, 2020.

Moore, Suzanne. "On Talk Shows the Democracy of Pain Reigns Supreme." *New Statesman* 128, no. 4432 (1996): 17.

Mosse, George Lachmann. *The Image of Man: The Creation of Modern Masculinity*. Oxford: Oxford University Press, 1998.

———. *Nationalism and Sexuality: Respectability and Abnormal Sexuality in Modern Europe*. Madison: University of Wisconsin Press, 1985.

Moyn, Samuel. *The Last Utopia: Human Rights in History*. Cambridge, MA: Harvard University Press, 2010.

———. *Not Enough: Human Rights in an Unequal World*. Cambridge, MA: Belknap Press of Harvard University Press, 2018.

Naples, Nancy. "To Interpret the World and to Change It: An Interview with Nancy Fraser." *Signs: Journal of Women in Culture and Society* 29, no. 4 (2004): 1103–24. https://www.journals.uchicago.edu/doi/full/10.1086/382631.

Nash, Kate. "The Cultural Politics of Human Rights and Neoliberalism." *Journal of Human Rights* 18, no. 5 (2019): 490–505.

Neer, Robert M. *Napalm*. Cambridge, MA: Harvard University Press, 2013.

Negra, Diane, and Julia Leyda. "Querying 'Karen': The Rise of the Angry White Woman." *European Journal of Cultural Studies* 24, no. 1 (2021): 350–57. https://doi.org/10.1177/1367549420947777.

Nerlich, Brigitte, and Rusi Jaspal. "Social Representations of 'Social Distancing' in Response to COVID-19 in the UK Media." *Current Sociology* 69, no. 4 (2021): 566–83. https://doi.org/10.1177/0011392121990030.

Newsom, Kimmery, and Karen Myers-Bowman. "'I Am Not a Victim. I Am a Survivor': Resilience as a Journey for Female Survivors of Child Sexual Abuse." *Journal of Child Sexual Abuse* 26, no. 8 (2017): 927–47.

Norris, Pippa. "Varieties of Populist Parties." *Philosophy & Social Criticism* 45, nos. 9–10 (2019): 981–1012. https://doi.org/10.1177/0191453719872279.

Norris, Pippa, and Ronald Inglehart. *Cultural Backlash: Trump, Brexit, and Authoritarian Populism*. Cambridge: Cambridge University Press, 2019.

Nye, Robert A. "Western Masculinities in War and Peace." *American Historical Review* 112, no. 2 (2007): 417–38. https://www.jstor.org/stable/4136608.

Oakeshott, Michael. *The Politics of Faith and the Politics of Scepticism*. Ed. Timothy Fuller. New Haven, CT: Yale University Press, 1996.

O'Connor, Alison. "Coming Home to the Arts: Theatre as Reconnection." Paper presented at the Culture, Health, and Wellbeing International Conference, June 20–22, 2017, Bristol, U.K. https://pure.southwales.ac.uk/en/publications/coming-home-to-the-arts-theatre-as-reconnection.

O'Connor, Rory C., Karen Wetherall, Seonaid Cleare, Heather McClelland, Ambrose J. Melson, Claire L. Niedzwiedz, Ronan E. O'Carroll, et al. "Mental Health and Well-Being During the COVID-19 Pandemic: Longitudinal Analyses of Adults in the UK COVID-19 Mental Health & Wellbeing Study." *British Journal of Psychiatry: The Journal of Mental Science* 218, no. 6 (2021): 326–33. https://doi.org/10.1192/bjp.2020.212.

Olza, Inés, Veronika Koller, Iraide Ibarretxe-Antuñano, Paula Pérez-Sobrino, and Elena Semino. "The #ReframeCOVID Initiative: From Twitter to Society Via Metaphor." *Metaphor and the Social World* 11 (September 2021): 98–120. https://doi.org/10.1075/msw.00013.olz.

Orgad, Shani. "The Survivor in Contemporary Culture and Public Discourse: A Genealogy." *Communication Review* 12, no. 2 (2009): 132–61. https://doi.org/10.1080/10714420902921168.

Orgad, Shani, and Rosalind Gill. *Confidence Culture*. Durham, NC: Duke University Press, 2021.

Orgad, Shani, and Radha Sarma Hegde. "Crisis-Ready Responsible Selves: National Productions of the Pandemic." *International Journal of Cultural Studies* 25, nos. 3–4 (2022): 287–308. https://doi.org/10.1177/13678779211066328.

Ouditt, Sharon. *Fighting Forces, Women Writing: Identity and Ideology in the First World War*. London: Routledge, 2020.

Pain, Rachel. "Intimate War." *Political Geography* 44 (January 2015): 64–73. https://doi.org/10.1016/j.polgeo.2014.09.011.

Paltrow, Lynn M., and Jeanne Flavin. "Arrests of and Forced Interventions on Pregnant Women in the United States, 1973–2005: Implications for Women's Legal Status and Public Health." *Journal of Health Politics, Policy, and Law* 38, no. 2 (2013): 299–343. https://doi.org/10.1215/03616878-1966324.

Panizza, Francisco. Introduction to *Populism and the Mirror of Democracy*, ed. Francisco Panizza, 1–31. London: Verso, 2005.

Pantti, Mervi, and Karin Wahl-Jorgensen. "On the Political Possibilities of Therapy News: Social Responsibility and the Limits of Objectivity in Disaster Coverage." *Communication Studies* 1, no. 1 (2007): 3–25.

Pascual-Ferrá, Paola, Niel Alperstein, Daniel Barnett, and Rajiv Rimal. "Toxicity and Verbal Aggression on Social Media: Polarized Discourse on Wearing Face Masks During the COVID-19 Pandemic." *Big Data & Society*, Online First, June 10, 2021. https://doi.org/10.1177/20539517211023533.

Phelan, Sean. "Neoliberalism, the Far Right, and the Disparaging of 'Social Justice Warriors.'" *Communication, Culture, & Critique* 12, no. 4 (2019): 455–75.

Phipps, Alison. "White Tears, White Rage: Victimhood and (as) Violence in Mainstream Feminism." *European Journal of Cultural Studies* 24, no. 1 (2021): 81–93. https://doi.org/10.1177/1367549420985852.

Piketty, Thomas. "Capital in the Twenty-First Century: A Multidimensional Approach to the History of Capital and Social Classes." *British Journal of Sociology* 65, no. 4 (2014): 736–47.

Pinchevski, Amit. *Transmitted Wounds: Media and the Mediation of Trauma*. Oxford: Oxford University Press, 2019.

Regehr, Kaitlyn, and Jessica Ringrose. "Celebrity Victims and Wimpy Snowflakes: Using Personal Narratives to Challenge Digitally Mediated Rape Culture." In *Mediating Misogyny: Gender, Technology, and Harassment*, ed. Jacqueline Ryan Vickery and Tracy Everbach, 353-64. Cham, Switzerland: Springer, 2018.

Reid, Fiona. *Broken Men: Shell Shock, Treatment, and Recovery in Britain, 1914–1930*. Illus. ed. London: Continuum, 2010.

Retzepi, Andriani, Angelos Nastoulis, and Panayis Panagiotopoulos. "The 'Deserved' Victimhood of Far-Left Terrorism: Shame, Guilt, and Status Reversal." In *Interdisciplinary Applications of Shame/Violence Theory*, ed. Roman Gerodimos, 177–89. London: Palgrave Macmillan, 2022.

Rho, Hye Jin, Hayley Brown, and Shawn Fremstad. "A Basic Demographic Profile of Workers in Frontline Industries." U.S. Center for Economic and Policy Research, April 7, 2020. https://cepr.net/a-basic-demographic-profile-of-workers-in-frontline-industries/.

Ringrose, Jessica, and Emma Renold. "Slut-Shaming, Girl Power, and 'Sexualisation': Thinking Through the Politics of the International SlutWalks with Teen Girls." *Gender and Education* 24, no. 3 (2012): 333–43.

Ristovska, Sandra. "Witnessing and the Failure of Communication." *Communication Review* 17, no. 2 (2014): 143–58. https://doi.org/10.1080/10714421.2014.901062.

Robinson, Lori, and Michael O'Hanlon. "Women Warriors: The Ongoing Story of Integrating and Diversifying the American Armed Forces." Brookings Institute Report, 2020. https://www.brookings.edu/essay/women-warriors-the-ongoing-story-of-integrating-and-diversifying-the-armed-forces/.

Roper, Michael. "Between Manliness and Masculinity: The 'War Generation' and the Psychology of Fear in Britain, 1914–1950." *Journal of British Studies* 4, no. 2 (2005): 343–62.

——. "Between the Psyche and the Social: Masculinity, Subjectivity, and the First World War Veteran." *Journal of Men's Studies* 15, no. 3 (2008): 251–70.

Rose, Nikolas. *Powers of Freedom: Reframing Political Thought*. Cambridge: Cambridge University Press, 1999.

——. "Still 'Like Birds on the Wire'? Freedom After Neoliberalism." *Economy and Society* 46, nos. 3–4 (2017): 303–23. https://doi.org/10.1080/03085147.2017.1377947.

Rosenberg, Jonathan. *How Far the Promised Land? World Affairs and the American Civil Rights Movement from the First World War to Vietnam*. Princeton, NJ: Princeton University Press, 2006.

Rothberg, Michael. *The Implicated Subject: Beyond Victims and Perpetrators.* Stanford, CA: Stanford University Press, 2019.

———. *Multidirectional Memory: Remembering the Holocaust in the Age of Decolonization.* Stanford, CA: Stanford University Press, 2009.

Rothschild, Emma. "The Theory of Moral Sentiments and the Inner Life." *Adam Smith Review* 5 (2010): 2425–36.

Rottenberg, Catherine. "Neoliberal Feminism and the Future of Human Capital." *Signs: Journal of Women in Culture and Society* 42, no. 2 (2017): 329–48. https://doi.org/10.1086/688182.

Roy, Arundhati. "Noam Chomsky, Neoliberalism, and the New War on Iraq." *Contemporary Justice Review* 6, no. 4 (2003): 321–27. HYPERLINK "https://doi.org/10.1080/1028258032000144767" https://doi.org/10.1080/1028258032000144767.

———. *War Talk.* Boston, MA: South End Press, 2003.

Rudwick, Elliott. "The Niagara Movement." *Journal of Negro History* 42, no. 3 (1957): 177–200.

Safari, Beata A. "Intangible Privacy Rights: How Europe's GDPR Will Set a New Global Standard for Personal Data Protection." *Seton Hall Law Review* 47 (2016): 809–48.

Said, Edward W. *Orientalism.* New York: Pantheon, 1978.

———. "Orientalism." *Counterpunch*, August 5, 2003. https://www.counterpunch.org/2003/08/05/orientalism/.

Sanders, Rebecca. "Human Rights Abuses at the Limits of the Law: Legal Instabilities and Vulnerabilities in the 'Global War on Terror.'" *Review of International Studies* 44, no. 1 (2018): 2–23.

Saull, Richard. "Racism and Far Right Imaginaries Within Neo-liberal Political Economy." *New Political Economy* 23, no. 5 (2018): 558–608.

Savage, Mike. *The Return of Inequality: Social Change and the Weight of the Past.* Cambridge, MA: Harvard University Press, 2021.

Scarry, Elaine. *The Body in Pain: The Making and Unmaking of the World.* Oxford: Oxford University Press, 1987.

Schaffer, Neal. *The Age of Influence: The Power of Influencers to Elevate Your Brand.* New York: HarperCollins Leadership, 2020.

Schneider, Shari Kessel, Lydia O'Donnell, Ann Stueve, and Robert W. S. Coulter. "Cyberbullying, School Bullying, and Psychological Distress: A Regional Census of High School Students." *American Journal of Public*

Health 102, no. 1 (2012): 171–77. https://www.academia.edu/11327868/Cyberbullying_School_Bullying_and_Psychological_Distress_A_Regional_Census_of_High_School_Students.

Schradie, Jen. "'Give Me Liberty or Give Me COVID-19': Anti-lockdown Protesters Were Never Trump Puppets." *Communication and the Public* 5, nos. 3–4 (2020): 126–28. https://doi.org/10.1177/2057047320969433.

Schwarz, Elke. "Prescription Drones: On the Techno-biopolitical Regimes of Contemporary 'Ethical Killing.'" *Security Dialogue* 47, no. 1 (2016): 59–75. https://www.jstor.org/stable/26293585.

Semino, Elena. "'Not Soldiers but Fire-Fighters'—Metaphors and COVID-19." *Health Communication* 36, no. 1 (2021): 50–58. https://doi.org/10.1080/10410236.2020.1844989.

Sharafutdinova, Gulnaz. *The Red Mirror: Putin's Leadership and Russia's Insecure Identity*. Oxford: Oxford University Press, 2020.

Sharma, Amalesh, and Sourav Bikash Borah. "COVID-19 and Domestic Violence: An Indirect Path to Social and Economic Crisis." *Journal of Family Violence* 37, no. 5 (2022): 759–65. https://doi.org/10.1007/s10896-020-00188-8.

Shelton, Taylor. "A Post-truth Pandemic?" *Big Data & Society* 7, no. 2 (2020): 1–6.

Showalter, Elaine. "Hysteria, Feminism, and Gender." In Sander Gilman, Helen King, Roy Porter, G. S. Rousseau, and Elaine Showalter, *Hysteria Beyond Freud*, 286–344. Berkeley: University of California Press, 1993.

Smicker, Josh. "COVID-19 and 'Crisis as Ordinary': Pathological Whiteness, Popular Pessimism, and Pre-apocalyptic Cultural Studies." *Cultural Studies* 35, nos. 2–3 (2021): 291–305. https://doi.org/10.1080/09502386.2021.1898038.

Smiley, Calvin John, and David Fakunle. "From 'Brute' to 'Thug': The Demonization and Criminalization of Unarmed Black Male Victims in America." *Journal of Human Behavior in the Social Environment* 26 (January 2016): 1–17. https://doi.org/10.1080/10911359.2015.1129256.

Smith, Adam. *The Theory of Moral Sentiments*. 1759. Reprint. Oxford: Oxford University Press, 1976.

Smith, S. G., X. Zhang, K. C. Basile, M. T. Merrick, J. Wang, M. Kresnow, and J. Chen. *The National Intimate Partner and Sexual Violence*

Survey (NISVS): 2015 Data Brief—Updated Release. Atlanta, GA: National Center for Injury Prevention and Control, Centers for Disease Control and Prevention, 2018. https://www.nsvrc.org/sites/default/files/2021-04/2015data-brief508.pdf.

Snyder, Timothy. *On Tyranny: Twenty Lessons from the Twentieth Century*. New York: Crown/Random House, 2017.

——. *The Road to Unfreedom*. New York: Crown/Random House, 2018.

Sonnevend, Julia. "A Virus as an Icon: The 2020 Pandemic in Images." *American Journal of Cultural Sociology* 8 (2020): 451–61.

Spelman, Elizabeth. *Fruits of Sorrow: Framing Our Attention to Suffering*. Boston, MA: Beacon, 2001.

Spivak, Gayatri Chakravorty. "Three Women's Texts and a Critique of Imperialism." *Critical Inquiry* 12, no. 1 (1985): 243–61. https://www.jstor.org/stable/1343469.

Srinivasan, Amia. *The Right to Sex: Feminism in the Twenty-First Century*. New York: Farrar, Straus and Giroux, 2021.

Stammers, Neil. *Human Rights and Social Movements*. London: Pluto, 2009.

Standifer, Leon C. *Not in Vain: A Rifleman Remembers World War II*. Baton Rouge: Louisiana State University, 1992.

Stanley, Jason. *How Fascism Works: The Politics of Us and Them*. Illus. ed. New York: Random House, 2018.

Stavrakakis, Yannis. "Jacques Lacan: Negotiating the Psychosocial in and Beyond Language." In *The Routledge Handbook of Language and Politics*, ed. Ruth Wodak and Bernhard Forchtner, 82–95. London: Routledge, 2017.

Stavrakakis, Yannis, and Giorgos Katsambekis. "Left-Wing Populism in the European Periphery: The Case of SYRIZA." *Journal of Political Ideologies* 19, no. 2 (2014): 119–42.

Stavrakakis, Yannis, Giorgos Katsambekis, Alexandros Kioupkiolis, Nikos Nikisianis, and Thomas Siomos. "Populism, Anti-populism, and Crisis." *Contemporary Political Theory* 17 (2018): 4–27.

Steel, Zachary, Catherine R. Bateman Steel, and Derrick Silove. "Human Rights and the Trauma Model: Genuine Partners or Uneasy Allies?" *Journal of Traumatic Stress* 22, no. 5 (2009): 358–65. https://doi.org/10.1002/jts.20449.

Steele, Brent J. "'The Cruelty of Righteous People': Niebuhr on the Urgency of Cruelty." *Journal of International Political Theory* 17, no. 2 (2021): 203–20. https://doi.org/10.1177/1755088221989745.

Stein, Arlene. "Feminism, Therapeutic Culture, and the Holocaust in the United States: The Second-Generation Phenomenon." *Jewish Social Studies* 16, no. 1 (2009): 27–53. https://doi.org/10.2979/jss.2009.16.1.27.

Stiglitz, Joseph E. "COVID Has Made Global Inequality Much Worse." *Scientific American*, March 1, 2022. https://www.scientificamerican.com/article/covid-has-made-global-inequality-much-worse/.

Stith, Richard. "Abortion Is More Than a Murder: Nietzsche vs Christ." *New Oxford Review* 72 (November 2005). https://www.newoxfordreview.org/documents/abortion-is-more-than-murder/.

Stovall, Mady, Lissi Hansen, and Michelle van Ryn. "A Critical Review: Moral Injury in Nurses in the Aftermath of a Patient Safety Incident." *Journal of Nursing Scholarship* 52, no. 3 (2020): 320–28.

Strachan, Hew. *The Direction of War: Contemporary Strategy in Historical Perspective*. Cambridge: Cambridge University Press, 2013.

Summers, Jennifer, Hao-Yuan Cheng, Hsien-Ho Lind, Lucy Telfar Barnardf, Amanda Kvalsvig, Nick Wilson, and Michael G. Baker. "Potential Lessons from the Taiwan and New Zealand Health Responses to the COVID-19 Pandemic." *Lancet Regional Health* 4 (November 2020). https://www.sciencedirect.com/science/article/pii/S2666606520300444.

Sweet, Paige L. "The Sociology of Gaslighting." *American Sociological Review* 84, no. 5 (2019): 851–75.

Syvertsen, Trine, and Gunn Enli. "Digital Detox: Media Resistance and the Promise of Authenticity." *Convergence* 26, nos. 5–6 (2020): 1269–83. https://doi.org/10.1177/1354856519847325.

Sznaider, Natan. "The Sociology of Compassion: A Study in the Sociology of Morals." *Journal for Cultural Research* 2, no. 1 (1998): 117–39.

Tambe, Ashwini. "Reckoning with the Silences of #MeToo." *Feminist Studies* 44, no. 1 (2018): 197–203.

Thomsen, Carly, Zach Levitt, Christopher Gernon, and Penelope Spencer. "Presence and Absence: Crisis Pregnancy Centers and Abortion Facilities in the Contemporary Reproductive Justice Landscape." *Human Geography* 16, no. 1 (2023): 64–74. https://doi.org/10.1177/19427786221109959.

Traverso, Enzo. *The New Faces of Fascism: Populism and the Far Right*. London: Verso, 2019.

Tripodi, Francesca Bolla. *The Propagandists' Playbook: How Conservative Elites Manipulate Search and Threaten Democracy*. New Haven, CT: Yale University Press, 2022.

Trott, Verity. "Networked Feminism: Counterpublics and the Intersectional Issues of #MeToo." *Feminist Media Studies* 21, no. 7 (2021): 1125–42. https://doi.org/10.1080/14680777.2020.1718176.

Tuerkheimer, Deborah. "Incredible Women: Sexual Violence and the Credibility Discount." *University of Pennsylvania Law Review* 166, no. 1 (2017): 1–56.

Turner, Bryan. *Vulnerability and Human Rights*. University Park: Pennsylvania State University Press, 2006.

Uchida, Carina M. "Constraints on Rape as a Weapon of War: A Feminist and Post-colonial Revision." *E-International Relations*, November 20, 2018. https://www.e-ir.info/2018/11/20/constraints-on-rape-as-a-weapon-of-war-a-feminist-and-post-colonial-revision/.

U.K. House of Commons Science and Technology Committee and Health and Social Care Committee. "Coronavirus: Lessons Learned to Date." 2021. https://committees.parliament.uk/publications/7496/documents/78687/default/.

Urbinati, Nadia. *Me the People: How Populism Transforms Democracy*. Cambridge, MA: Harvard University Press, 2019.

Van Dijck, José. *The Culture of Connectivity: A Critical History of Social Media*. Oxford: Oxford University Press, 2013.

Van Dijk, Jan. "Free the Victim: A Critique of the Western Conception of Victimhood." *International Review of Victimology* 16, no. 1 (2009): 1–33.

Welland, Julia. "Compassionate Soldiering and Comfort." In *Emotions, Politics, and War*, ed. Linda Åhäll and Thomas Gregory, 115–27. London: Routledge, 2015.

Westheider, James E. *Fighting on Two Fronts: African Americans and the Vietnam War*. New York: New York University Press, 1997.

Wieviorka, Annette. *The Era of the Witness*. Ithaca, NY: Cornell University Press, 2006.

Wilkerson, Isabel. *Caste: The Origins of Our Discontents*. New York: Random House, 2020.

Williams, Chad. "World War I in the Historical Imagination of WEB Du Bois." *Modern American History* 1, no. 1 (2018): 3–22.

Williams, Raymond. *Keywords: A Vocabulary of Culture and Society*. Oxford: Oxford University Press, 2014.

Winter, Jay. "Foreword: Historical Remembrance in the Twenty-First Century." In "Historical Remembrance in the Twenty-First Century," ed. Jay Winter. Special issue, *Annals of the American Academy of Political and Social Science* 617, no. 1 (2015): 6–13. https://doi.org/10.1177/0002716207312761.

——. *Remembering War: The Great War Between Memory and History in the 20th Century*. Annotated ed. New Haven, CT: Yale University Press, 2006.

——. *Sites of Memory, Sites of Mourning: The Great War in European Cultural History*. Cambridge: Cambridge University Press, 1998.

Wodak, Ruth. "Crisis Communication and Crisis Management During COVID-19." *Global Discourse* 11, no. 3 (2021): 329–53.

——. *The Politics of Fear: The Shameless Normalization of Far-Right Discourse*. 2nd ed. Los Angeles: Sage, 2020.

——. *The Politics of Fear: What Right-Wing Populist Discourses Mean*. Los Angeles: Sage, 2015.

Wood, Helen, and Beverley Skeggs. "Clap for Carers? From Care Gratitude to Care Justice." *European Journal of Cultural Studies* 23, no. 4 (2020): 641–47. https://doi.org/10.1177/1367549420928362.

Woolf, Steven, Derek Chapman, and Roy Sabo. "Excess Deaths from COVID-19 and Other Causes." *JAMA* 324, no. 15 (2020): 1562–64. https://jamanetwork.com/journals/jama/fullarticle/2771761.

World Health Organization. COVID-19 *Vaccine Delivery Partnership (2022): Situation Report*. Geneva: World Health Organization, October 2022. file:///C:/Users/Health%20Policy/Downloads/CoVDP-SitRep_Issue-8_October.pdf.

Yancy, Clyde. "COVID-19 and African Americans." *JAMA* 323, no. 19 (April 15, 2020): 1891–92. https://jamanetwork.com/journals/jama/fullarticle/2764789.

Young, Dannagal Goldthwaite. *Irony and Outrage: The Polarized Landscape of Rage, Fear, and Laughter in the United States*. Oxford: Oxford University Press, 2020.

Zelizer, Barbie. *Remembering to Forget: Holocaust Memory Through the Camera's Eye.* Chicago: University of Chicago Press, 1998.

Zuboff, Shoshana. "Big Other: Surveillance Capitalism and the Prospects of an Information Civilization." *Journal of Information Technology* 30, no. 1 (2015): 75–89. https://doi.org/10.1057/jit.2015.5.

Zucman, Gabriel. "Global Wealth Inequality." *Annual Review of Economics*, no. 11 (2019): 109–38.

INDEX

abortion: patient inequality in, 102; pro-women critique of, 105; reverse victimhood in legal cases, 102–3; right to, 101, 107; violence, 102. *See also Roe v. Wade*
abortion-vulnerable, 103–4
abuse, 3–4, 31, 33, 144–45n17; domestic, 86, 123; sexual, 29, 37, 47, 124, 128. *See also specific topics*
activism, 25, 31. *See also specific movements*
affective centering, 118–19
Afghanistan War, 66, 69, 73
age of catastrophe, 39, 70, 77, 155n121
age of social media, 138
#All rhetoric, 124–25
American Civil War (1861–1865), 51–55, 59
American women, sexual assault for, 4, 143n14
antilockdown movement, 82, 95, 99, 106, 177–78n27, 186n85
antislavery movement, 23

antivaccine movement, 82, 94, 96, 185n78, 188n91
antivictimism, 110, 112, 114, 122
assault, sexual, 1, 4, 102–3, 143n14. *See also* Blasey Ford, Christine
authoritarian populism, 97, 99, 104, 106; antivictimist agenda of, 110; cruelty in, 114; during pandemic, 77–82, 95; variations in, 172n9
authority, institutional, 4, 8

believability, 129, 145n17, 154n115
#BelieveWomen, 2, 129
Black Americans, 53–55, 111, 125
Black criminality, as racist narrative, 119
Black liberation, human rights and, 64, 166–67n93
Black Lives Matter movement, 124, 135–36
Black pain, 54, 136
Black soldiers, 53, 55, 59
Black veterans, 63

Black women, suffering of, 38, 92
Blasey Ford, Christine, 1–4, 7, 10, 29, 118. *See also* Kavanaugh–Blasey Ford
bodily fragility, 52
bodily suffering, psychological suffering and, 71
border security, narratives of, 124
branding, of human rights, 134

campaign, "clap for our carers," 90, 183n60
capital, voice as, 37
capital accumulation, 37
capitalism. *See* emotional capitalism
catastrophe. *See* age of catastrophe
centering, affective, 118–19
Centers for Disease Control, U.S., 93
children, rights of, 132–33
civil rights, 23, 108, 133; leaders of, 64; movement for, 63–65, 110; violations of, 71, 81
Civil Rights Movement, 63–65, 110
civilians, in war zones, 47, 49
claim: condition of suffering compared to, 6, 36; hybrid, 29; to pain, 6–7, 28–29, 32–33, 35–36, 38, 40, 85, 126; to victimhood, 107
"clap for our carers" campaign, 90, 183n60
Cold War, 62, 70
collectivism, religious, 12
collectivist narratives, 50, 133, 134–35, 139

colonial dynamics, of Western armies, 159n20
colonial experience, of victimhood, 15
colonial suffering and violence, 15
colonialism, Holocaust and, 15
combat violence, 52
communication: experience and, 104; of pain, 27; politics of, 106; populist strategies of, 39; strategies for, 81–88, 90, 92–95; of victimhood, 33, 72, 74, 131, 139
compassion, suppression of, 97, 109
compassion fatigue, 48
compassionate conservatism, 112
compassionate soldier, 69
condition: of suffering, 6, 36, 126, 133; of vulnerability, 107
construction, of heroes, 90
contemporary styles, of humanitarian communication, 134
conversational therapy, 18, 21–22, 24
COVID-19, 39, 75–76, 85; inequality during, 112, 188n90; racism and, 183–84n67
Crimean War (1853–1856), 160n29
crisis, migration as, 124, 197n77
critical interrogation, of victimhood, 109, 125–26
critique, on victimhood and politics of pain, 116–17, 137
cruelty: in authoritarian populism, 114; culture of, 115; dual politics of pain and, 100, 109; in emotional capitalism, 113,

115–16; politics of, 114; of resilience, 123; tropes of, 117–18, 125–26
cultural narratives, of war victimhood, 70
culture: of cruelty, 115; of sympathy, 20, 24, 48, 127; therapy, 19, 20, 65; of victimhood, 6, 144n17; Western, 4

das Opfer (offering and sufferer), 12
dataveillance, 34
de-emotionalization, of pain, 88
dehumanizing hierarchy, in U.K., 182n56
Depp, Johnny, 120
digital rights, 34, 153–54n109
digital violence, 33–34
disidentification, semantic, 121–22
domestic abuse, 86, 123
domestic violence, 46–47, 120
Du Bois, W. E. B., 23, 54, 166–67n93
dual politics, of pain and cruelty, 100, 109
duality: of populism, 173–74n16; of victimhood, 13

education: civil, 21; sentimental, 48, 108
Eichmann trial, 14, 63, 167n94
emotion, performance of, 72
emotional capitalism, 16–17, 19, 34, 97, 99, 138; communication of victimhood in, 72; cruelty in, 113, 115–16; inner self expression in, 51; languages of pain in, 30; legacy of, 139; masculinity and racialization of, 39–40, 49, 73; populism and, 176–77n26; power dynamics of, 43–44; racism in, 49; in twenty-first century, 106
emo-truths, 94, 114, 137
empowerment, vocabulary of, 123
enmity, in victimhood, 79, 91
essential workers demographics, 104, 183–84n67
euphemism, 122–23
excess death, during pandemic, 84
exclusion, history of, 73–74, 104, 139
experience, of pain, 15, 104

fake victims, real victims compared to, 36
far Right, 9, 40, 110; communities of reverse victimhood within, 114; narratives of hate from, 10; rhetoric of, 115
fatigue, compassion, 48
female believability, 129
female bodies, 45
female hysteria, 46
female suffering, domestic violence as form of, 46
female victim: labor of believability of, 120; motives, 30, 128; normative view of, 119; Trump empathy reversal on, 10
female voice, male compared to, 4, 17
feminism, 23, 32, 47
Feminists for Life, 101, 105

feminization, of men, 46
fetus, as victim, 101, 103, 105, 110, 127
first wave, of pandemic, 75, 80, 97, 172n10
First World War. *See* World War I
foundational trauma, as Holocaust, 19
freedom, libertarian discourse of, 96
frontline workers, in U.K., 122

gaslighting, 98
gendered hierarchies, of victimhood, 120
gendered politics, of believability, 5, 145n17
gendered trauma, 33
"General Comment 25 on Children's Rights in Relation to the Digital Environment," (United Nations), 132
genocidal violence, 14
global South, victimhood in, 143n10
grief, suppression of, 87–89

harassment, sexual, 22, 118, 143–44nn14–15
Health and Science Parliamentary Committee, U.K., 84
Heard, Amber, 120
hegemonic masculinity, 157n8
hegemonic victimhood, 17
herd immunity, 84, 178–79n32
heroes, 90, 122
heuristic method, 127

heuristics, of victimhood, 126, 128, 130–32
hierarchies: gendered, 120; neocolonial, 73; racial, 48, 60, 70; of suffering, 126, 130
himpathy, 118–20
history: of exclusion, 73–74, 104, 139; of human rights, 132; of victim, 39; of Western modernity, 116
Holocaust: colonialism and, 15; Eichman trial on, 14, 63, 167n94; foundational trauma as, 19; narrative templates of, 15; survivor, 13, 47, 167n94; visual templates of, 149n51; as white-on-white violence, 148n50
House of Commons Science and Technology Committee, U.K., 76
human rights, 18, 27, 166–67n93; branding of, 134; history of, 132; language of, 22–25, 64, 98; movement for, 24; political-legal framework of, 63; suppression of, 105
humanitarian communication, contemporary styles of, 134
humanitarian wars, 51, 68, 69, 168n100
humanity, moral hierarchy of, 60
hysteria, female, 46

#IBelieveHer, 2, 21
idealization, 119
identity, of victim, 29, 35, 37, 58

immunity, herd, 178–79n32
Imperial War Graves Commission (U.K.), 59–60
Indian soldiers, 164–65n72
indignation, narratives of, 25–26
individualism, secular, 12
individualistic narratives, 50, 133
industrial war, 41, 51–52, 56
inequality, 145n21; in abortion patients, 104; battlefield, 53; during COVID-19, 91, 112, 188n90; social, 8, 111; structures of power and, 11; in suffering, 139
infodemic, 93–94
injured self, 18, 22, 26
injury: moral, 42, 47, 67, 158n19; trauma or, 153n107
institutional racism, 135
interrogation, critical, 109, 125–26
intersectionality: of pain, 128–29; of vulnerability, 131–32
"intimate publics," 108
Iraq War, 42, 66, 69
irony, in liberal discourse, 134–36

Jewish trauma, 13
Johnny Depp–Amber Heard trial, 120
Johnson, Boris, 39, 187–88n88. *See also* pandemic response, of U.K. and U.S.
judgment, 131, 137
junctures, in vulnerability, 129
justice: narratives of, 40, 109, 131–35, 137, 139; politics of, 5

Karen, trope of, 118–19
Kavanaugh, Brett, 1–4, 7, 29, 118, 127
Kavanaugh–Blasey Ford, 36–37, 142n7
King, Martin Luther, Jr., 64

language: as healing tool, 20; human rights, 22–25, 64, 98; of PTSD, 71; of trauma and rights, 14, 19, 58, 60, 67, 79; victimhood as war, 62
language of pain: digital violence changing, 34; emotional capitalism using, 30, 43; inequalities within, 104, 112–13; within narratives of justice, 136; during pandemic, 80, 88, 98; twentieth-century use of, 11–13, 16; victimhood using, 28, 108; war and, 42, 50, 64–67
legacy: of emotional capitalism, 139; victimhood as, 101, 103–4, 106
legal discourse, of victimhood, 14
legal subjecthood, of victim, 14
liberal discourse, 133–36
libertarian discourse, of freedom, 96
linguistic reversal, 120–21
linguistics, of victim and victimhood, 12, 103
lockdown, violence due to, 86

macho performance, 89, 111
male suffering, 44–45, 48
male voice, 4, 17

manosphere, 31–32
marketization, neoliberal, 26–27, 30
masculine self, 44–45, 49, 51–52, 72
masculinity: hegemonic, 157n8; modern, 159n23; racialization of emotional capitalism and, 73; toxic, 89, 96, 111; twentieth-century, 159–60n23
mass gaslighting, 98
mass suffering, 41, 75, 78
mass violence, twentieth-century, 43
#MeToo movement, 2–3, 21–22, 109, 124, 144n15; testimonies of, 128–29
media industry, 17; during pandemic, 94, 99; social, 2, 31–32, 114, 120, 135
memory: collective, 6, 16, 39, 55; postbellum project on, 53; public, 39, 45, 55, 104; traumatic, 63; universal, 25; of war, 43, 48
men, feminization of, 46
mental health campaigns, for veterans, 170n121
microaggressions, 144n17
migration, as crisis, 124, 197n77
militarization, of communicating pain, 81–82, 86–88, 90–92
minorities, racialized, 26, 81, 86–87, 98, 144n17
misogynistic activism, 31
moral injury, 42, 47, 67, 68, 158n19
movement: antilockdown, 82, 95, 99, 106, 177–78n27, 180n41, 186n85; antislavery, 23;

antivaccine, 82, 94, 96, 185n78, 188n91; Black Lives Matter, 124, 135–36; human rights, 24; Me Too, 2–3, 21–22, 109, 124, 128–29, 144n15
mutability, of pain, 107

narrative templates, of Holocaust, 15
narratives: antivictimism, 112; border security, 124; collectivist compared to individualistic, 50; of hate, from far Right, 10; of indignation, 25–26; of justice, 40, 109, 131–33, 136–37; psyche compared to social inequality, 23; racist, 119; of redemption, 91, 95, 111, 116; of reformation, 24–26, 108; of revolution, 23–26, 108; uneven, 16
National Health Service (NHS), 81, 90, 92
necropopulism, 95, 111
neocolonial hierarchy, 73
neoliberal marketization, 26–27, 30
neoliberalism, 9–11, 17, 66, 114, 123, 146–47n30; flipped dynamics in, 128
neurosis, war, 56, 58, 163n57
NHS. *See* National Health Service
Niagara Movement, 166–67n93
nonwhite soldiers, 43, 49, 59
normalization, of communicating pain, 81–86
North Atlantic Treaty Organization, 66

obfuscation, of communicating pain, 81, 83, 92–95
OECD. *See* Organization for Economic Cooperation and Development
offering and sufferer (*das Opfer*), 12
offerings, sacrificial, 11
Organization for Economic Cooperation and Development (OECD), 176n25
overturning of *Roe v. Wade*, 40, 101, 103, 107, 127

PAC. *See* Public Accounts Committee
pain, 5; Black, 54, 136; claims to, 6–7, 28–29, 32–33, 35–36, 38, 40, 85, 126; communication of, 27, 81–83; de-emotionalization of, 88; dual politics of cruelty and, 100, 109; emotionality of, 18; erasure of, 82; experiences of, 15; of humanitarian wars, 68; intersectionality of, 128–29; liberal discourse on, 133; mutability of, 107; platformization of, 30–35; postcolonial, 16; soldierly, 67; weaponization of, 9, 81. *See also* politics of pain
pain, language of: digital violence changing, 34; emotional capitalism using, 30, 43; inequalities within, 104, 112–13; within narratives of justice, 136; during pandemic, 80, 88, 98; in twentieth-century, 11–13, 16; victimhood using, 28, 108; war and, 42, 50, 64–67
pan-Africanism, 166–67n93
pandemic: effects of, 8; excess death during, 84; first wave of, 75, 80, 97, 172n10; inequality in mortality rates of, 91; re-emotionalization of, 90; social media during, 94, 99; suffering other in, 113; suicides during, 180n39; in U.K. and U.S., 76–77, 83, 113, 186–87nn86–87; war as, 87. *See also* COVID-19
pandemic response, of U.K. and U.S., 76; authoritarian populism during, 78–79; inquiry of, 76–77, 171n6; weaponizing pain during, 81
paradox of protection, 80, 99
patriarchy, oppression from, 11
performance: of emotion, 72; macho, 89, 111; of modern identity, 17; of victimhood, 29, 77; of vulnerability, 30
performativity, of populism, 175–76n23
perpetrator, victim and, 121, 198n88
perpetrator-victim, soldier as, 61–62, 65
platformization of pain, 30–35, 137
platforms: digital, 31–32, 132; social media, 11, 30–31, 33, 94, 99, 114, 137–38; talk therapy, 22
policing of pregnant bodies, 103, 105, 107

politicization of PTSD, 63
politics: of believability, 154n115; of communication, 106; of cruelty, 114; of justice, 5
politics of pain, 138; abortion rights and, 102, 105, 107; antivictimism, 115–17; authoritarian populism within, 77, 79, 80, 97, 99; critique on, 117; emotions of, 137; privilege within, 37, 44–45, 70, 72, 129; reorganizing, 31, 38; victimhood as, 26–28; war and, 48–49, 51
populism, 173n15; duality of, 173–74n16; emotional capitalism and, 176–77n26; performativity of, 175–76n23. *See also* authoritarian populism
populist strategies, of communication, 39
populist victimhood, strategies of, 82, 96–98
postcolonial pain, 16
postfascism, 115, 117
postfeminist vocabulary, 102
postindustrial war, industrial and, 41
postlockdown strategy, Johnson on, 187–88n88
post-traumatic stress disorder (PTSD), 42, 47, 62, 67, 167n95; language of, 71; moral injury contrasted with, 68; politicization of, 63; vocabulary of, 64–65
power, 78; balance of, 7; reconstruction of, 38; significance of, 36; structures of inequality and, 11; symbolic, 38; victimhood and, 4, 6
pragmatism, 174–75n22
presidential authority, weaponization of, 93
private sphere, public and, 20
privilege: gendered, 120, 125; of grievances, 5, 176–77n26; of pain, 18, 42, 112–13, 118, 127, 129–30; power and, 6, 36–37; racialized, 10, 55, 81, 119; systemic, 110; of voice, 5–6, 9, 130
profit: for big tech, 138; in liberal politics, 134; logic of, 8; of migration, 10; during pandemic, 90, 94; using pain to, 17, 22, 31–32, 99
projection, temporal, 123–24
pro-life rhetoric, 102
protection: of civilians, 47; paradox of, 80, 99
pro-vaccine support, 188n91
psyche: human, 71; social inequality compared to narratives of, 23; soldier, 61
psychic trauma, 21, 46
psychic wound, 57
psychological suffering, 71
psychology, role of, 20
psychosocial victimhood, 45
PTSD. *See* post-traumatic stress disorder
Public Accounts Committee (PAC), 184n69

public figure, sufferer as, 21–22
public inquiry, of U.K. pandemic response, 76–77, 171n6
public sphere, private *versus*, 20

racial hierarchy, 48, 60, 70
racial segregation, in U.S. army, 165n74
racialized minorities, 26, 81, 86–87, 98, 144n17
racialized suffering, 49
racism: COVID-19 and, 183–84n67; within emotional capitalism, 49; institutional, 135; in U.K. army, 169–70n117
racist narrative, Black criminality as, 119
rail workers, trade union strike of, 136, 199n99
rape violence, 102, 129
real victims, fake victims compared to, 36
realms of suffering, 31, 33, 35
Red Cross, 160n29
redemption, narratives of, 91, 95, 111, 116
re-emotionalization, of pandemic, 90
reformation, narratives of, 24–26, 108
religious collectivism, 12
remasculinization, 45, 157n9
resentful victimhood, 10, 146n26
resentment, in political spectrum, 9
resilience, cruelty of, 123
reverse victimhood, 30, 32, 81, 96, 98; in abortion cases, 102–3; far Right communities of, 114; in Rittenhouse case, 121
revolution, narratives of, 23–26, 108
rhetoric: #All rhetoric, 124–25; far Right, 115; pro-life, 102
rights: abortion, 101, 107; of children, 132–33; Civil Rights Movement, 63–65, 110; digital, 34, 153–54n109; trauma and, 14, 19, 58, 60, 67, 79; of working people, 136. *See also* civil rights; human rights
Rittenhouse, Kyle, 121
Roe v. Wade, 40, 101, 103, 107, 127
role: of platforms, 138; of psychology, 20

sacrificial offerings, 11
sacrificial victimhood, 12
Scientific Advisory Group of Emergencies, U.K., 84
Second World War. *See* World War II
secular individualism, 12
securitized nationalism, 66
self: injured, 18, 22, 26; masculine, 44–45, 49, 51–52; soldierly, 50, 67, 72; suffering, 56, 106; technologies of, 64, 71; traumatized, 18, 20, 22; vulnerable, 28, 43; Western, 44; white compared with nonwhite male, 49
self-sacrificing soldier, 163n59
semantic disidentification, 121–22
Senate Judiciary Committee, U.S., 1

sentimental education, 48, 108
sentimental novels, 108
sexual abuse, 29, 37, 47, 124, 128
sexual assault, 1, 4, 102–3, 143n14.
    See also Blasey Ford, Christine
sexual harassment, 22,
    143–44nn14–15; false, 118
shame, 1, 4, 14, 33–34, 61
shell shock, 56–59, 71, 162–63n55
silence, 15, 19, 36, 126; of voices and
    suffering, 33, 39, 50, 54, 69, 106,
    129, 137, 139
social inequality, 8; in U.S. and
    U.K., 111
social media, 2, 31–32, 114, 120, 135;
    age of, 138; during pandemic,
    94, 99; platformization of pain
    and, 137
social significance of violence, 63
social struggles of twentieth-
    century, 122
society, power relations in, 154n112
soldierly pain, 67–68
soldierly self, 50, 67, 72
soldierly suffering, 44, 50, 53–60,
    68, 70
soldierly trauma, 13
soldierly victimhood, 159n20
soldiers: Black, 53, 55, 59;
    compassionate, 69; Indian,
    164–65n72; nonwhite, 43, 49, 59;
    perpetrator-victim as, 61–62, 65;
    psyche of, 61; self-sacrificing,
    163n59; women, 156n7
stoic sufferer, 52, 57
stoicism, 72

strategies: communication, 81–88,
    90, 92–95; populist, 39; of
    populist victimhood, 82, 96–98;
    postlockdown, 187–88n88
structural injustice: of global
    capitalism, 24; injured self and,
    22–23, 25–26; of justice system,
    120; racial, 136; in society, 9, 40,
    116, 133–34, 198n88
structures of violence, 130, 133,
    144n17
struggle, victimhood as, 101, 106
sufferer: as public figure, 21–22;
    stoic, 52, 57
suffering, 19; of Black women, 38,
    92; colonial, 15; condition of, 6,
    36, 126, 133; emotional, 41;
    female, 46; hierarchies of, 126,
    130; inequality in, 139; male,
    44–45, 48; mass, 41, 75, 78; other
    in pandemic, 113; power
    dynamics of, 105; racialized, 49;
    realms of, 31, 33, 35; self, 56, 106;
    soldierly, 44, 50, 53–60, 68, 70;
    as spectacle, 27; tactical
    compared to systemic, 35, 37, 40
suicides, during pandemic, 180n39
suppression: of compassion, 97, 109;
    of grief, 87–89; of human rights,
    105
Supreme Court, U.S., 1, 101
survivor: of abuse, 3, 47; Holocaust,
    13, 47, 167n94. *See also* Blasey
    Ford, Christine
symbolic power, 38
symbolic violence, 117, 129

sympathy, culture of, 20, 24, 48, 127
symptoms, of trauma, 47
systemic destruction, of Black Americans, 125
systemic suffering, 35, 37, 40, 82
systemic vulnerability, 5, 7, 9, 112–13, 130

tactical suffering, 35, 37, 40, 82
tactical victimhood, 125, 128, 130
technologies of self, 64, 71
televising, of Vietnam War, 61, 165n77
temporal projection, 123–24
temporality of judgment, 131
testimonies: Me Too movement, 128–29; of PTSD from Vietnam, 63; of trauma, 13
therapy, conversational, 18, 21–22, 24
therapy culture, 19, 20, 65
toxic masculinity, 89, 96, 111
trade union strike, of rail workers, 136, 199n99
transexclusionary radical feminists, 124, 190n11
transitions, in masculine self, 72
trauma, 19; of abuse, 3–4; gendered, 33; injury or, 153n107; language of rights and, 14, 19, 58, 60, 67, 79; psychic, 21, 46; rights and, 14, 19, 58, 60, 67, 79; soldierly and Jewish, 13; symptoms of, 47; testimonies of, 13; Vietnam War, 62; of war, 56; weaponization of, 86
traumatized self, 18, 20, 22

trench warfare, 41, 55, 56, 57
trope: of cruelty, 117–18, 125–26; of Karen, 118–19
Trump, Donald, 2, 10, 39, 127. *See also* pandemic response, of U.K. and U.S.
truth, 5, 18, 75; lies compared to, 77
twentieth-century: masculinity, 159–60n23; mass violence, 43; social struggles of, 122; victim of, 41; victimhood in, 11
twenty-first century: emotional capitalism in, 106; mass suffering in, 75, 78; victimhood in, 6–7; wars during, 60; wealth gap of, 112

U.K. *See* United Kingdom
Unborn Victims of Violence Act (2004), 110
uneven narratives, of victimhood, 16
United Kingdom (U.K.): dehumanizing hierarchy in, 182n56; frontline workers in, 122; government of, 92; Health and Science Parliamentary Committee, 84; House of Commons Science and Technology Committee, 76; pandemic in, 76–77, 83, 113, 186–87nn86–87; racism in army of, 169–70n117; Scientific Advisory Group of Emergencies, 84; social inequality in, 111. *See also* pandemic response, of U.K. and U.S.

United Nations, "General Comment 25 on Children's Rights in Relation to the Digital Environment," 132
United States (U.S.), 54; Centers for Disease Control, 93; pandemic in, 76–77; racial segregation in army of, 165n74; Senate Judiciary Committee of, 1; social inequality in, 111; Supreme Court, 1, 101. *See also* pandemic response, of U.K. and U.S.
universalization, 124–25, 128
U.S. *See* United States
us vs. them, 9, 78, 87, 113
uses of victimhood, 5

vaccines, 112; pro-vaccine support, 188n91. *See also* antivaccine movement
veterans, 63, 69, 170n121. *See also* post-traumatic stress disorder; *specific wars*
victim, 28; female, 10, 30, 119–20, 128; fetus as, 101, 103, 105, 110, 127; history of, 39; identity of, 29, 35, 37, 58; legal subjecthood of, 14; linguistics of, 12; perpetrator and, 121, 198n88; real compared to fake, 36; twentieth-century, 41; war, 39, 50; as white male, 49–50, 77
victimhood. *See specific topics*
Vietnam War (1965–1973), 60–62, 64–65, 68, 165n77; testimonies of PTSD from, 63

violations, civil rights, 71, 81
violence, 116; colonial, 15; combat, 52; digital, 33–34; domestic, 46–47, 120; genocidal, 14; lockdown creating, 86; physical and symbolic, 129; rape, 102, 129; social significance of, 63; structures of, 130, 133, 144n17; symbolic, 117, 129; war, 42
visual templates, of Holocaust, 149n51
vocabulary: of empowerment, 123; of heroes, 122; of moral injury, 68; post-feminist, 102; of PTSD, 64–65; of victimhood, 27, 35, 51, 58, 70, 73, 85, 97, 117, 138–39
voice: as capital, 37; privilege of, 5–6, 130; silenced, 33, 39, 50, 54, 69, 106, 129, 137, 139
vulnerability: conditions of, 107; individual, 16; intersections of, 131–32; junctures in, 129; performance of, 30; reclamation of, 139; systemic, 5, 7, 9, 112–13, 130; white male privilege of, 73
vulnerable communities, 138
vulnerable self, 28, 43

war: humanitarian, 51, 69, 168n100; industrial, 51–52, 56; neurosis from, 163n57; pandemic as, 87; postindustrial and industrial, 41; racial hierarchies of victimhood in, 70; trauma of, 56; twenty-first century, 60; victim of, 39, 50; victimhood as

language of, 62; violence of, 42; wounds from, 48
warfare, trench, 41, 55–57
wealth gap, of twenty-first century, 112
weaponization: of pain, 9, 81; of presidential authority, 93; of trauma, 86; of victimhood, 110
Weinstein scandal, 144n15
Western armies, 60, 159n20
Western cultures, victimhood in, 4
Western modernity, history of, 116
Western self, 44
white male: leaders, 88; pain of, 50, 73; reverse victimhood of, 30, 39; transformation of, 49, 106; victim as, 49–50, 77
white supremacy, 54, 98
"white victimcould," 123
WHO. *See* World Health Organization
#WhyIDidntReport, 2
World Health Organization (WHO), 75, 93
World War I (1914–1918), 41–42, 46, 55, 57–58, 60–61; soldierly suffering during, 53–60, 68
World War II (1939–1945), 61
wound: psychic, 57; Vietnam, 62; war, 48

Printed and bound by CPI Group (UK) Ltd, Croydon, CR0 4YY
01/05/2024

14496473-0001